CHINA IN AFRICA

The JAMESTOWN
F O U N D A T I O N

A Compendium of Articles from
The Jamestown Foundation's *China Brief*

Edited By
Dr. Arthur Waldron

Jamestown's Mission

The Jamestown Foundation's mission is to inform and educate policy makers and the broader policy community about events and trends in those societies which are strategically or tactically important to the United States and which frequently restrict access to such information. Utilizing indigenous and primary sources, Jamestown's material is delivered without political bias, filter or agenda. It is often the only source of information which should be, but is not always, available through official or intelligence channels, especially in regard to Eurasia and terrorism.

Origins

Launched in 1984 after Jamestown's late president and founder William Geimer's work with Arkady Shevchenko, the highest-ranking Soviet official ever to defect when he left his position as undersecretary general of the United Nations, The Jamestown Foundation rapidly became the leading source of information about the inner workings of closed totalitarian societies.

Over the past two decades, Jamestown has developed an extensive global network of experts – from the Black Sea to Siberia, from the Persian Gulf to the Pacific. This core of intellectual talent includes former high-ranking government officials and military officers, political scientists, journalists, scholars and economists. Their insight contributes significantly to policymakers engaged in addressing today's new and emerging global threats, including that from international terrorists.

THE JAMESTOWN FOUNDATION

Published in the United States by
The Jamestown Foundation
1111 16th St. N.W.
Suite 320
Washington, DC 20036
http://www.jamestown.org

For more information on this book or The Jamestown Foundation, email pubs@jamestown.org.

ISBN 978-0-9816905-0-6

Cover photo by Getty Images/AFP

TABLE OF CONTENTS

ABBREVIATIONS

ADB	African Development Bank
AGIP	Azienda Generale Italiana Petroli
AGOA	African Growth and Opportunity Act
AMIS	United Nations Mission in the Sudan
ANC	African National Congress
ASEAN	Association of Southeast Asian Nations
AU	African Union
BOCOG	Beijing Organizing Committee for the Games of the XXIX Olympiad
BPD	Barrels Per Day
BPI	Brimax Petroleum, Limited
CADF	China Africa Development Fund
CASS	Chinese Academy of Social Sciences
CATIC	China National Aero-Technology Import and Export Corporation
CCP	Chinese Communist Party
CCTV	China Central Television
CICIR	China Institutes of Contemporary International Relations
CIOG	China International Oil and Gas Group
CMC	Central Military Commission
CNOOC	China National Offshore Oil Corporation
CNPC	China National Petroleum Corporation
CNUC	China National Uranium Corporation
COSL	China Oilfield Services, Limited
CPA	Comprehensive Peace Agreement
CWE	China International Water and Electric Corporation
CWHEC	China National Water Resources and Hydropower Engineering Corporation
DDRRR	Disarmament, Demobilization, Repatriation, Resettlement, and Reintegration
DINDIR	Dindir Petroleum International
DRC	Democratic Republic of the Congo
ETAP	Entreprise Tunisienne d'Activités Pétrolières
FADM	Armadas de Defense de Mozambique
FDI	Foreign Direct Investment
FNLA	National Front for the Liberation of Angola
FOCAC	Forum on China-Africa Cooperation
FTA	Free Trade Agreement
FTZ	Free Trade Zone
GDP	Gross Domestic Product
GEPetrol	National Oil Company of the Republic of Equatorial Guinea
GNPOC	Greater Nile Petroleum Operating Company
HIPC	Heavily Indebted Poor Countries
HTP	High-Tech Petroleum Group

ICBC	Industrial and Commercial Bank of China
IMF	International Monetary Fund
JEM	Justice and Equality Movement
LPEB	Liaohe Pertroleum Exploration Bureau
MEIL	Madagascar Energy International Limited
MEND	Movement for the Emancipation of the Niger Delta
MINURSO	United Nations Mission for the Referendum in Western Sahara
MNJ	Le Mouvement des Nigerien pour la Justice
MOL	Madagascar Oil, Limited
MONUC	UN Mission in the Democratic Republic of the Congo
MPIL	Madagascar Petroleum International
MPLA	Popular Movement for the Liberation of Angola
NAASP	New Asian-Africa Strategic Partnership
NAM	Non-Aligned Movement
NEPAD	New Partnership for Africa's Development
NGO	Non-governmental Organization
NNPC	Nigerian National Petroleum Corporation
NOC	National Oil Company
NORINCO	China North Industries Corporation
NPT	Nuclear Non-Proliferation Treaty
NWFZ	Nuclear Weapons Free Zone
ONLF	Ogaden National Liberation Front
ONGC	Oil and Natural Gas Corporation Limited
OPEC	Organization of Petroleum Exporting Countries
PBC	People's Bank of China
PDOC	Petrodar Operating Company
Petronas	Petroliam Nasional Berhad
PLA	People's Liberation Army
PLAN	People's Liberation Army Navy
PRC	People's Republic of China
RIEPA	Rwanda Investment and Export Promotion Agency
ROC	Republic of China (Taiwan)
SCO	Shanghai Cooperation Organization
Sinopec	China Petroleum and Chemical Corporation
Sino-Uranium	China Nuclear International Uranium Corporation
SLM	Sudan Liberation Movement
SME	Small and Medium-sized Enterprise
SSI	Sonangol-Sinopec Consortium
Sudapet	Sudan National Petroleum Corporation
SUNPEC	Sino Union Petroleum and Chemical International Limited
TICAD	Tokyo International Conference on African Development
UN	United Nations

UNCTAD	United Nations Conference on Trade and Development
UNESCO	United Nations Education, Scientific, and Cultural Organization
UNITA	National Union for the Total Independence of Angola
UNMEE	United Nations Mission in Ethiopia and Eritrea
UNMIL	United Nations Mission in Liberia
UNMIS	United Nations Mission in the Sudan
UNOCI	United Nations Operation in Cote d'Ivoire
UNPKO	United Nations Peacekeeping Operations
UNROCA	United Nations Register on Conventional Arms
UNSC	United Nations Security Council
USAFRICOM	United States Africa Command
WTO	World Trade Organization
YBP	Yetebaberut Beherawi Petroleum
ZANLA	Zimbabwe African National Liberation Army
ZPEB	Zhongyuan Petroleum Exploration Bureau
ZTE	Zhong Xing Telecommunication Equipment Company Limited

CHINA IN AFRICA: A CHRONOLOGY

1415

The first instance of Sino-African contact occurs on one of Ming Dynasty (1368-1644 AD) Admiral Zheng He's seven voyages. Known as the "Admiral of the Western Sea," Zheng He visits more than 30 countries, including what is today Kenya and manages to collect treasures and tributes for the Ming Emperor. A painting by Shen Tu documents the extent of Zheng's travels—the arrival in Beijing of an African giraffe presented to the Ming Emperor in October 1415, as a gift from the ruler of the Kingdom of Malindi in Kenya [1].

1421

Emperor Zhu Di invites a number of dignitaries from Africa for the inauguration of Beijing as the new capital of the Ming dynasty.

1949

October 1 – Chinese Communist Party (CCP), led by Mao Zedong, defeats Chiang Kai-shek and the Nationalists in the Chinese civil war and proclaims the founding of the People's Republic of China (PRC).

1955

April 18 - 24 – Representatives of 29 African and Asian nations meet in the first Bandung Summit, also known as the Asian-African Conference, in Bandung, Indonesia, in an effort to promote Afro-Asian economic and cultural cooperation and to oppose colonialism and neocolonialism. Chinese Premier Zhou Enlai distributes a statement and makes an off-cuff speech at the end of the conferences summarizing China's commitment to establishing healthy Asian-African relations: "there exists common ground among the Asian and African countries the basis of which is that the overwhelming Asian and African countries and their peoples have suffered and are still suffering from the calamities of colonialism" [2].

August – Egyptian Minister of Commerce and Industry, Mohammed Abu Nosseir visits China and signs a three year trade agreement [3].

1956

May 30 – Official diplomatic relations are established between China and the Arab Republic of Egypt, at the same time China offers an aid commitment of $4.7 million to Egypt.

September 17 – Chairman Mao Zedong visits with Egyptian Ambassador to China, Hassan Ragab, in China, and affirms that "the Chinese people (are) firmly behind Egypt in its struggle to resume sovereignty over the Suez Canal. China is willing to do its best to help Egypt without attaching any conditions and to offer what you need within our power" [4].

1958

November 1 – Official diplomatic relations are established between China and the Kingdom of Morocco.

December 20 – Official diplomatic relations are established between China and the People's Democratic Republic of Algeria.

1959

February 4 – Official diplomatic relations are established between China and the Republic of Sudan.

October 14 – Official diplomatic relations are established between China and the Republic of Guinea.

1960

China offers an interest free loan of $25 million to Guinea [5].

October 25 – Official diplomatic relations are established between China and Republic of Mali.

December 14 – Official diplomatic relations are established between China and the Somali Republic.

1962

October 18 – Official diplomatic relations are established between China and the Republic of Uganda.

1963

Emmerson M'nangagwa, the presumptive "heir apparent" to Robert Mugabe's regime in Zimbabwe, leads the first squad of recruits of the Zimbabwe African National Liberation Army (ZANLA) to China for guerrilla training [6]. He is also educated at the Beijing School of Ideology, run by the Chinese Communist Party (CCP) [7].

June – China offers interest free loans totaling $22 million to Somalia and $50 million to the People's Democratic Republic of Algeria in June and October, respectively [8].

December 14 – Official diplomatic relations are established between China and the Republic of Kenya. Chinese Foreign Minister and Vice Premier Chen Yi attends the independence ceremonies of Kenya.

December 5 - February 4, 1964 – Chinese Premier Zhou Enlai and Vice Premier Chen Yi make a seven-week tour of 10 African nations that have recognized China: Egypt, Algeria, Morocco, Tunisia, Ghana, Mali, Guinea, Sudan, Ethiopia and Somalia.

1964

China sends its first international medical team upon receiving the invitation of the Algerian government.

January 10 – Official diplomatic relations are established between China and the Tunisian Republic.

February 22 – Official diplomatic relations are established between China and the Republic of Congo.

September 29 – Official diplomatic relations are established between China and the Central African Republic.

October 29 – Official diplomatic relations are established between China and the Republic of Zambia.

November 26 – Official diplomatic relations are established between China and the United Republic of Tanzania.

1965

March - April – Chinese Premier Zhou Enlai visits Egypt and Algeria.

April 21 – China grants $1 million and provides a $4 million interest-free loan to Uganda [9].

June – Chinese Premier Zhou Enlai visits Tanzania and Egypt.

July 19 – Official diplomatic relations are established between China and the Islamic Republic of Mauritania.

1966

January – Colonel Jean-Bédel Bokassa's government in the Central African Republic suspends diplomatic ties with China.

1967

June 30 – A new government in Kenya declares the Chinese charge d'affaires *ad interim persona non grata*. As the Cultural Revolution in China begins to reach its peak the Chinese government recalls its ambassadors in every African country except for Egypt [10].

September – Government delegations from Tanzania and Zambia held talks with their Chinese counterparts in Beijing and formally sign the "Agreement of the Government of the People's Republic of China, the Government of the United Republic of Tanzania and the Government of the Republic of Zambia on the Construction of the Tanzania-Zambia Railway." The Tanzania-Zambia Railroad, also known as the Tazara Railroad, is one of the biggest projects that China has ever undertaken overseas. The 1860-kilometer long railroad starts from Dar-es-Salaam in the East, the capital of Tanzania, and ends in Kapri Mposhi in Zambia in the West [11].

1968

July 6 – In Tanzania, China inaugurates the completion of its largest textile mill in East Africa [12].

1970

China offers $41.6 million to Sudan to fund two road construction projects, a construction of a weaving and textile factory, a bridge and a conference center; $10 million in budget support is extended to Guinea and $20.3 million to Mali [13].

October 1970 - July 1976 – Engineers and workers from China, Tanzania and Zambia begin building the Tanzania-Zambia Railroad. Its total cost is estimated at $455 million and 64 of the thousands sent to work on it from China died during its construction [14].

October 15 – Official diplomatic relations are established between China and the Republic of Equatorial Guinea.

November 11 – Official diplomatic relations are established between China and the Federal Democratic Republic of Ethiopia.

1971

According to the African Union Liberation Committee, between 1971 and 1972, 75 percent of the military aid given to the African Union from outside Africa comes from China [15].

China and Ethiopia sign the agreement on Economic and Technical Cooperation. As part of the agreement China offers an interest free loan of $85.5 million in return for goods or hard currency [16].

February 10 – Official diplomatic relations are established between China and the Federal Republic of Nigeria.

March 26 – Official diplomatic relations are established between China and the Republic of Cameroon.

July 29 – Official diplomatic relations are established between China and the Republic of Sierra Leone.

October 13 – Official diplomatic relations are established between China and Republic of Burundi.

October 25 – UN Resolution 2758 is passed by the UN General Assembly, withdrawing recognition of the Republic of China (ROC) as the legitimate government of China, and recognizing the People's Republic of China (PRC) as the sole legitimate government of

China. African countries play a significant role in restoring China's seat – 26 of the 76 votes for the PRC are from African countries.

November 12 – Official diplomatic relations are established between China and the Republic of Rwanda.

1972

Official diplomatic relations between China and the Republic of Guinea are restored.

China offers aid for the first time to Burundi, Benin, Madagascar, Mauritius, Nigeria, Rwanda, Togo, and Tunisia in the form of Economic and Technical Agreements. Each nation received about $30 million [17].

April 15 – Official diplomatic relations are established between China and the Republic of Mauritius.

September 19 – Official diplomatic relations are established between China and the Togolese Republic.

November 6 – Official diplomatic relations are established between China and Republic of Madagascar.

November 24 – Official diplomatic relations are established between China and the Democratic Republic of the Congo.

December 12 – Official diplomatic relations between China and the Republic of Benin are restored.

1973

January – China extends an interest free loan of $100 million to the Democratic Republic of the Congo for the development of agriculture. The terms of the loan stipulate that it is repayable over a period of twenty years following a ten year grace period [18].

1974

January – China extends a loan worth $74.5 million to Tanzania to fund the mining of coal and iron ore, as well as for the construction of a rail line to connect the Tanzania-Zambia Railroad to the region of Tanzania where the coal and iron ore deposits are located [19].

February 22 – Chairman Mao Zedong put forward his view on differentiating the "three worlds" in a talk with Zambian President Kenneth David Kaunda. He said, "I hope the Third World unites. In Asia, all countries except for Japan belong to the Third World. The whole of Africa belongs to the Third World, and Latin America also belongs to the Third World."

April 20 – Official diplomatic relations are established between China and the Gabonese Republic.

1975

China and Gabon sign the Economic and Technical Cooperation Agreement [20] in which China extends a loan of $25.6 million to fund agricultural development.

January 6 – Official diplomatic relations are established between China and the Republic of Botswana.

July 25 – Official diplomatic relations are established between China and the Republic of Mozambique.

November 13 – Official diplomatic relations are established between China and the Union of Comoros.

1976

China donates 1,000 tons of maize and 10,000 blankets to aid drought victims in Ethiopia [21].

China offers a loan of $31.7 million to Morocco in order to fund the construction of a dam for water control and irrigation [22].

April 25 – Official diplomatic relations are established between China and the Republic of Cape Verde.

June 30 – Official diplomatic relations are established between China and the Republic of Seychelles.

July – China completes the 1,860 km long Tanzania- Zambia Railroad [23].

1978

August 9 – Official diplomatic relations are established between China and the Great Socialist People's Libyan Arab Jamahiriya.

1979

August 8 – Official diplomatic relations are established between China and the Republic of Djibouti.

1980

April – Official diplomatic relations are established between China and the Republic of Zimbabwe.

1982

December 21 - January 17, 1983 – Premier Zhao Ziyang visits 11 African countries: Egypt, Algeria, Morocco, Guinea, Gabon, the Democratic Republic of the Congo, the Republic of Congo, Zambia, Zimbabwe, Tanzania and Kenya.

1983

January 12 – Official diplomatic relations are established between China and the Republic of Angola.

March 2 – Official diplomatic relations are established between China and the Republic of Cote d'Ivoire.

1985

China formally joins the African Development Bank (ADB).

1986

March 14-21 – President Li Xiannian and his wife visit Egypt. President Li holds a talk with Egyptian President Hosni Mubarak and meets Prime Minister Ali Lotfy, Speaker of the People's Assembly El-Mahgob, chairman of the Shura Council. President Li lays the foundation stone for the Cairo International Conference Center.

1989

March 23 – Chairman Deng Xiaoping of the Central Military Commission (CMC) meets with Ugandan President Yoweri Museveni.

1990

March 22 – Official diplomatic relations are established between China and the Republic of Namibia.

1993

May 24 – Official diplomatic relations are established between China and the State of Eritrea.

1994

January 12 – Official diplomatic relations are established between China and the Kingdom of Lesotho.

1995

A Chinese ship carrying 152 tons of ammunition and light weapons meant for the army of Burundi is refused permission to dock in Tanzania [24].

October 5-6 – First Tokyo International Conference on African Development (TICAD) is held. Subsequent conferences occur in 1998 and 2003 and are all Pan-African in their coverage.

1996

China Foreign Affairs University hosts the first "Understanding China Symposium," designed specifically for young African diplomats [25]. The event was held annually from 1996 to 2004. Over the course of the nine years the conference was held, 161 young African diplomats visited China.

May – President Jiang Zemin visits Kenya, Ethiopia, Mali, Namibia, and Zimbabwe. In which President Jiang proposed five principles concerning the development of a long-term, stable, and all-round cooperative relationship between China and the African countries oriented toward the 21st century: 1) Being sincere, friendly, and mutually reliable and becoming all-weather friends; 2) Equality, mutual respect for each other's sovereignty, and non-interference in each other's internal affairs; 3) Seeking common development and mutual benefits; 4) Strengthening consultations and forming close cooperation in international affairs; 5) Looking toward the future and creating a more beautiful world.

December – China National Petroleum Corporation (CNPC), a state-owned corporation, invests in Sudanese oil for the first time as part of the Greater Nile Petroleum Operating Company (GNPOC).

1997

Laurent Kabila, the dictator of the Democratic Republic of the Congo sends his son, Joseph Kabila to China for military training. Joseph returns and becomes the army chief of staff before inheriting the presidency in 2001 [26].

1998

China breaks diplomatic relations with the Republic of Chad.

1999

April – When Egyptian President Hosni Mubarak is visiting China, he and President Jiang Zemin sign the Joint Communiqué on Establishing Strategic Cooperative Relationship Between the People's Republic of China and Arab Republic of Egypt.

October 18 - November 3 – President Jiang Zemin makes a six-country trip to Europe and Northern Africa that includes Algeria and Morocco. During his visit to Algeria, President Jiang proposes four principles for the development of the 21st century-oriented China-

Algeria relations. They included: 1) to expand common ground and promote an all-round stable development of the bilateral relations in a strategic and long-term perspective; 2) to upgrade economic ties, and scientific and technical cooperation to the benefit of common development by tapping the potentials and carrying forward an innovative spirit; 3) to enhance consultation and coordination in order to defend the rights and interests of developing countries and maintain world peace; and 4) to lay a solid foundation for the development of the bilateral relations in the new century through increased exchanges at various levels and enhanced mutual understanding [27].

2000

Two-way trade between China and Africa reaches $10.6 billion [28].

April 17 – President Jiang Zemin meets Egyptian President Hosni Mubarak in Alexandria, Egypt.

July – Rear Admiral Huan Jiang leads People's Liberation Army Navy (PLAN) ship visit to Africa stopping in Tanzania and South Africa. The visit was composed of the *Shenzhen*, a Luhai-class guided missile destroyer, and the *Nancang* supply ship [29].

October – President Jiang Zemin spoke at the opening ceremony of the FOCAC—Ministerial Conference Beijing 2000. He said that China and Africa should make concerted efforts to establish a new international political and economic order through strengthening solidarity and actively promote South-South cooperation; enhancing dialogue and improve North-South relations; taking part in international affairs on the basis of equality and in an enterprising spirit; looking forward into the future and establish a new long-term stable partnership of equality and mutual benefit [30].

October 10-12 – At the first ministerial conference of the "Forum on China-Africa Co-Operation" (FOCAC), the ministers in charge of foreign affairs, foreign trade and international co-operation, economic and social affairs from both China and African countries, meet in Beijing. This is the first gathering of its kind in the history of China-Africa relations and is hailed as a landmark event.

2001

China joins the World Trade Organization (WTO).

2002

January 23-26 – Egyptian President Hosni Mubarak visits China.

April 19-23 – Chinese Premier Zhu Rongji visits Egypt.

June – China signs debt exemption protocols with 31 African states, canceling 156 African debts with a total value of 10.5 billion *Renminbi* [31].

June – A naval visit composed of the *Qingdao*, a guided missile destroyer, and the *Taicang*, a supply ship, stop in Egypt [32].

September 10 – The Chinese Ministry of Health conducts a two-part international training program teaching techniques to prevent and treat malaria and other tropical diseases. Thirty students from 17 African nations attended [33].

2003

China deploys a total 860 medical professionals in 35 teams to 34 African countries [34].

April – China sends its first team of peacekeeping personnel to Africa to participate in the United Nations peacekeeping operations in the Democratic Republic of the Congo. The team is made up of 175 engineers and 43 medical technicians [35].

April – South Africa and China initiate the Meeting of the Sino-South African Defense Committee.

June – During talks with the visiting Comoro Union President Azali Assoumani, President Hu Jintao points out that consolidating and strengthening unity and cooperation with all African countries is a vital part of China's independent foreign policy of peace. He said that China would abide by the basic principles of "sincere friendship, equal treatment, unity and cooperation, common progress and looking forward into the future" in dealing with Africa and be dedicated to the long-term stable new partnership based on equality and mutual benefit [36].

October – Liberia and China resume diplomatic relations.

October 14-21 – Beijing hosts the "Sino-African Seminar on Economic Reform and Development Strategies," with 22 participants from different economic and financial units of 16 African countries together with seven officials from the African Development Bank. The seminar includes not only visits to popular sights such as the Great Wall and the Forbidden City, but also field visits to poverty alleviation projects and Pudong Economic Development Zone [37].

December – China deploys 90 peacekeepers to Liberia, just two months after that nation switched its recognition from Taiwan (ROC) to the PRC [38].

December 15-16 – Second Ministerial FOCAC Conference is held in Addis Ababa, Ethiopia, which marks the first time that the meeting is held in Africa. The conference focuses on the task of implementing the two documents passed during the first FOCAC conference. The Addis Ababa Action Plan, which demonstrates a consensus of the China-Africa views on political and international issues of common concern, is passed. A parallel Sino-African business conference is also held with representatives from over 100 Chinese enterprises meeting with their African counterparts and signing various international contracts on the spot [39].

December 23 – Chinese Export-Import Bank (Exim Bank) signs three agreements to fund the controversial Sudanese Merowe Dam Project on the Nile River, lending a total of nearly $520 million [40] to the project that is budgeted to reach $1.2 billion [41]. Additionally a consortium of two Chinese hydropower companies—the China International Water and Electric Corporation (CWE) and the China National Water Resources and Hydropower Engineering Corporation (CWHEC)—signs contracts to build the body of the dam. By the time the contracts are signed, the Merowe Dam is the largest international project that Chinese companies have ever participated in.

December 24 – Representatives from the China National Petroleum Corporation (CNPC) and Algerian state-owned hydrocarbons company Sonatrach sign the first oil and natural gas contract between China and Algeria [42].

2004

January 26 - February 7 – President Hu Jintao makes a four-nation tour visiting Egypt, Algeria, Gabon and France.

March – Angola accepts China's Exim Bank offer of a $2 billion oil-backed loan to Angola on very favorable terms, at the same time turning down an offer from the IMF to help reduce debt through a Staff Monitored Program that would have brought transparency and foreign aid to one of Africa's most corrupt governments [43]. The $2 billion line of credit to Angola is being used to rebuild Angola's infrastructure; however, a large portion of the contracts are going to Chinese firms. For example, the Benguela Railroad is being refurbished for $300 to $500 million by the China International Fund, Limited, Chinese firms have also won contracts to refurbish two other rail lines, government buildings and a new airport in Luanda [44]. China adds another $1 billion to its oil-backed loan in March 2006.

April 27 - May 31 – "Meet in Beijing," a month-long international art festival with African culture as the main theme, is held in Beijing [45].

June – Zimbabwe's state-run press reports the purchase of military equipment from China, including 12 FC-1 fighter planes and 100 military vehicles, worth an estimated $240 million. This order, which has been kept secret, circumvents the state procurement board tasked with appropriating Zimbabwe's $136 million defense budget [46].

July – The "Voyage of Chinese Culture to Africa," a traveling exhibition that features Chinese troupes of singers and dancers, acrobats and martial arts masters and performs in 11 African countries, is crowned as complete success by Chinese media [47].

August 22-31 – "China-Africa Youth Carnival" is held in Beijing. The event includes an inauguration ceremony, China-Africa youth cooperation forum and a grand youth festival. A China-Africa Youth Beijing Declaration is adopted during the event [48].

September 20-27 – Sponsored by the Secretariat of the Chinese Follow-up Committee of FOCAC, the first Annual Workshop for African Journalists is held in Beijing, hosting 20 journalists from 19 African countries. In the latest Journalist Workshop in 2006, over 40 journalists from 23 African countries participate in classes; take trips to Xinhua News Agency, China Central Television (CCTV) and Beijing Organizing Committee for the Games of the XXIX Olympiad (BOCOG); and pay visits to the cities of Hefei and Qingdao [49].

November 28 – Air Zimbabwe concludes its first flight from Harare to Beijing. Among the first group of passengers were senior Zimbabwean officials and business leaders as well as Chinese Ambassador to Zimbabwe, H.E. Zhang Xianyi [50].

2005

Bilateral Trade between China and South Africa reaches $6.3 Billion [51].

March – UN Mission to Sudan (UNMIS) is established. China contributes over 446 out of the 8,766 soldiers, 9 of the 662 police, and 14 of the 599 military observers [52].

April – Egyptian Defense Minister Muhammed Hussein Tantawi makes an official visit to Beijing were he meets with his Chinese counterpart Cao Gangchuan [53].

April 22-24 – The second Bandung Summit is held in Indonesia with an attendance of leaders and representatives from about 50 countries, as well as chiefs from nearly 23 international organizations, including UN Secretary-General Kofi Annan. The conference, titled "Reinvigorating the Bandung Spirit: Working Toward a New Asian-African Strategic Partnership," witnesses the signing of the New Asian-African Strategic Partnership (NAASP) and a joint statement on tsunamis, earthquakes and other national disasters. Chinese President Hu Jintao makes a three-point proposal in a speech at the official dinner reception of the Asian-African Business Summit 2005 in Jakarta. Hu proposed three main actions that Asia and Africa must work together on: 1) respond to opportunities and challenges posed by deepening economic globalization; 2) carry out mutually beneficial cooperation in all fields on an equal footing; and 3) work together to create an international development environment featuring win-win cooperation [54].

May 31 – Kenya Airways to start flights to Shanghai in August [55].

July 27 – Chairman Wu Bangguo of the Standing Committee of the National People's Congress (NPC) meets with Zimbabwean President Robert Mugabe in the Great Hall of the People. Wu said that "over the 25 years since the establishment of diplomatic ties between China and Zimbabwe the bilateral relations have been progressing healthily and smoothly" [56].

September 27 – The Chinese Ministries of Education, Foreign Affairs and Commerce co-sponsor the "Sino-African Education Minister Forum" in Beijing. Ministers of education from Benin, Egypt, the Republic of the Congo, Kenya, South Africa, Nigeria, Mali, Guinea,

Mauritius, Sudan, Ethiopia, Rwanda, Algeria, Mozambique, Tanzania, Djibouti, Mauritania, Senegal and Cameroon as well as officials from the Chinese ministries of education, foreign affairs, finance, and commerce and UNESCO are all in attendance. Chinese Education Minister Zhou Ji claims that China provides about 1,200 government scholarships to African students every year and that, by the end of 2004, a total of 17,860 scholarships had been granted to students from 50 African countries [57].

November 29 – Senegal and China resume diplomatic relations.

December 10 – The first Confucius Institute in Africa is launched at the University of Nairobi, specializing in Chinese language and culture education. By 2007 there are three Confucius Institutes established or under construction in Africa: one in Nairobi, a second in Stellenbosch University in South Africa and a third in Rwanda [58].

2006

In the first eleven months of this year Sino-Sudanese trade reached $2.9 billion [59].

January 11-19 – Chinese Foreign Minister Li Zhaoxing kicks off a tour of six African countries: Cape Verde, Senegal, Mali, Liberia, Nigeria and Libya.

January 12 – Beijing issues its first policy paper on African grand strategy that delineates fortifying across-the-board cooperation with Africa [60].

April 24-29 – Chinese President Hu Jintao makes a three-country trip to Africa visiting Morocco, Nigeria and Kenya. At the National Assembly in Abuja, Nigeria, Hu presents a proposal to establish "a new type of China-Africa Strategic partnership" [61].

May 9 – The Chinese government announces plans to invest $267 million in the establishment of the initial phase of the Lekki Free Trade Zone (FTZ) in Lagos [62].

May 12 – Sinopec, one of China's three leading oil companies, strikes a $2.2 billion deal with Sonangol, Angola's state-owned oil company, to develop two new blocks with estimated reserves of 4.5 billion barrels. As China's number one supplier of crude oil in 2006, Angola should supply the PRC with up to 2 million bpd by 2008 [63].

June 17-24 – Chinese Premier Wen Jiabao tours Egypt, Ghana, the Republic of the Congo, Angola, South Africa, Tanzania and Uganda. A total of 71 agreements are signed between China and the seven countries covering such topics as politics, economy, trade, infrastructure, culture, education and science and technology [64].

August – Though the resolution passes, China abstains from voting on UN Resolution 1706, which calls for UN peacekeepers to replace the ineffective African Union force in Darfur, condemning the resolution as "illegal" and having been passed without "consulting the Sudanese government" [65].

August – China resumes diplomatic relations with Chad

October 20 – Chinese Defense Minister Cao Gangchuan meets with Chadian Defense Minister Bichara Issa Djadallah to discuss the relationship between the two nation's armed forces which Cao said "constitutes an important part in overall bilateral relations [66].

November – Egyptian President Hosni Mubarak visits Beijing and Moscow. One of the most important issues discussed during the talks was the possibility of Egypt receiving assistance in the development of a nuclear energy program [67].

November 3-5 – The Third FOCAC Summit: Chinese President Hu Jintao announced eight measures to consolidate a "new type of strategic partnership" between China and Africa. These included further opening China's markets to Africa's least developed countries. The measures also included building three to five trade and economic cooperation zones in Africa in the next three years, providing three billion U.S. dollars in preferential loans and two billion U.S. dollars in preferential buyer credits to African countries. It would also include training 15,000 African professionals [68].

December 31 – China's Southern Airlines lands at the international airport of Lagos, Nigeria's commercial capital, marking the successful launch of the first regular flights offered by a Chinese airline between China and Africa [69].

December 31 - January 7, 2007 – Chinese Foreign Minister Li Zhaoxing pays official visits to Benin, Equatorial Guinea, Guinea Bissau, Chad, the Central African Republic, Eritrea and Botswana.

2007

January 30 - February 10 – President Hu Jintao makes an eight-nation tour of Africa, visiting Cameroon, Liberia, Sudan, Zambia, Namibia, South Africa, Mozambique and Seychelles. The trip's goal is to show China's efforts to carry out the "eight steps" unveiled during the third FOCAC. The "eight steps" include China's pledge to double its assistance to Africa by 2009. China will provide $3 billion of preferential loans and $2 billion of preferential buyer's credits to Africa. China will also establish a development fund of $5 billion to encourage Chinese firms to invest in Africa. Debt cancellation is among other major steps. During the trip more than 50 cooperation agreements were signed, most of them involving ways of implementing the outcome of the FOCAC [70].

April 24 – Armed guerillas attack a Chinese-operated oil field in Ethiopia leaving 77 dead. Shortly after the attacks, the Ogaden National Liberation Front (ONLF) claimed responsibility for the attacks. According to the *New York Times* the group circulated an email message that said, "We will not allow the mineral resources of our people to be exploited by this regime or any firm that it enters into an illegal contract" [71].

May 16-17 – The annual board meeting of the African Development Bank is held in Shanghai on May 16 and 17, sending a powerful message to the world that Africa and China are strengthening their "partnership of mutual benefit and cooperation" [72]. This marks the first time the meeting is held in Asia and the second time it is held out of Africa. The People's Bank of China (PBC) president Zhou Xiaochuan chairs the meeting, which is attended by finance ministers and governors of the central banks of member states, as well as representatives of the World Bank, the International Monetary Fund and other regional development finance organizations and non-governmental organizations. The meeting focuses on infrastructure construction in Africa, regional integrity and poverty relief.

May 21 – The World Bank and the China Exim Bank sign a memorandum of understanding to collaborate on projects that would focus primarily on infrastructure lending, namely in the transportation and energy sectors, and that their efforts would initially be concentrated on "sustained-growth" performers such as Ghana, Uganda and Mozambique [73].

June 26 – China launches a $1 billion fund to finance trade and investment by Chinese companies in Africa as part of efforts to nurture commercial ties [74].

July 3 – The Chinese government pledged to donate $600,000 to the African Union (AU)

September 18 – China donates goods valued at over $1.5 million to the Mozambican Defense Armed Forces Armadas de Defensa de Mocambique (FADM). Among the goods were seven new vehicles, 31 computers as well as new uniforms [75].

November 16 – Senior members of the Chinese government announce that Sino-African trade is likely to hit $100 billion by 2010 [76].

November 28 – Brazil and China said they will give Africa free satellite imaging of its landmass to help the continent respond to threats like deforestation, desertification and drought [77].

December – China's Sinosteel Corporation acquired a 67 percent stake in Zimbabwe's top ferrochrome company, Zimasco Holdings [78].

December 28 – China and the Republic of Malawi establish diplomatic relations.

2008

January 17 – The China Africa Development Fund (CADFund) signed a first batch of investment deals worth more than $90 million. The funds are to be invested in Sinosteel and three other Chinese companies with projects in Africa, with a total cost of $4 billion. Projects include a glass plant in Ethiopia with an annual production of 40,000 tons, a 200,000 kilowatt gas-fired power plant in Ghana, a chromite project in Zimbabwe, and a building material project [79].

February 28 – Nigerian President Umaru Yar'Adua met with Chinese President Hu Jintao at the Great Hall of the People in Beijing as part of a four-day trip. Trade between Nigeria and China reached $3.13 billion dollars in 2006, up from $1.1 billion dollars in 2001, according to the latest data from China's commerce ministry [80].

March 4 – Industrial and Commercial Bank of China (ICBC) finalizes $4.75 billion investment in South Africa's Standard Bank, giving ICBC a 20 percent stake in the South African bank [81].

April 23 – South Africa denies port access to a Chinese cargo ship (the *An Yuejiang*) carrying 77 tons of arms destined for Zimbabwe. The ship is reported to have been transporting three million rounds of AK-47 ammunition, 1,500 rocket-propelled grenades and 3,000 mortar rounds and mortar tubes. The South African government prohibited the ship from unloading under pressure from Western governments that fear the arms may be used to oppress civilians. Mozambique, Namibia and Angola also bar the ship from unloading at their ports [82].

May 12 – Zimbabwean Deputy Information Minister Bright Matonga announces that the arms shipment aboard the *An Yuejiang* had arrived in Zimbabwe. When questioned, a Chinese government official denied that the weapons had arrived in Zimbabwe, claiming that such reports were "utterly groundless" [83].

June 5 – The China National Petroleum Corporation (CNPC) signs a $5 billion dollar contract with Niger. The deal included provision for exploration, drilling and the construction of additional oil processing infrastructure [84].

Notes

1. *Eastern Perspectives and the Mapping of Africa* (Cape Town, South Africa: Parliamentary Millennium Programme, 2008), Poster, http://www.pmpsa.gov.za/PDFS/Eastern%20perspectives.pdf.zip.
2. Xinhua, "The Bandung Conference of 1955," *ChinaView.cn,* April 19, 2005, http://news.xinhuanet.com/english/2005-04/19/content_2849411.htm/.
3. Sithara Fernando, "Chronology of China Africa Relations" *China Report* 43, no. 3 (2007): 363-373.
4. He Wenping, "Moving Forward with the Time: The Evolution of China's Africa Policy," (*paper, China-Africa Relations: Engaging the International Discourse,* (November 2006, Hong Kong University of Science and Technology Center on China's Transnational Relations):4.
5. Fernando, *Chronology of China Africa Relations,* 363.
6. Mark Olden, "This Man has been called Zimbabwe's Che Guevara, Did Mugabe have him murdered?" *The New Statesman,* April 12, 2004, http://www.newstatesman.com/200404120020/.
7. "Profile: Emmerson Mnangagwa," *BBC.com,* March 30, 2007, http://news.bbc.co.uk/2/hi/africa/6506549.stm.
8. Fernando, *Chronology of China Africa Relations,* 364.
9. Library of Congress, "Foreign Military Assistance (Uganda)," Library of Congress Country Studies, December 1990.
10. *Washington Post,* "Kenya Orders Ouster Of Red China Envoy," Jun 30, 1967: A16.
11. Ministry of Foreign Affairs of the People's Republic of China, "China's Assistance in the Construction of the Tanzania-Zambia Railway," 2000, http://www.fmprc.gov.cn/eng/ziliao/3602/3604/t18009.htm.
12. Fernando, *Chronology of China Africa Relations,* 365.
13. Ibid.
14. Embassy of the People's Republic of China in India, "Tanzania-Zambia Railway symbolizes Sino-African friendship," 2006, http://www.chinaembassy.org.in/eng/zgbd/t259499.htm.
15. He Wenping, *Moving Forward with Time.*
16. Fernando, *Chronology of China Africa Relations,* 365.
17. Ibid., 366.

18. Ibid.

19. Ibid.

20. Ibid., 367.

21. Ibid., 368.

22. Ibid.

23. Ibid.

24. Ruchita Beri, "China's Rising Profile in Africa," *China Report* 43, no. 3 (2007): 297-308.

25. Li Anshan, "Transformation of China's Policy towards Africa"(working paper, Peking University, 2006).

26. "Profile: Joseph Kabila," *BBC.com*, December 6, 2006, http://news.bbc.co.uk/2/hi/africa/6209774.stm/.

27. Ministry of Foreign Affairs of the People's Republic of China, "Visit by President Jiang Zemin to Six Countries in Europe, Africa and Asia," 2000, http://www.mfa.gov.cn/eng/ziliao/3602/3604/t18049.htm.

28. Drew Thompson, "Economic Growth and Soft Power: China's Africa Strategy," *China Brief* 4, No. 24, (2004).

29. Susan Puska, "Resources, Security and Influence: The Role of the Military in China's Africa Strategy," *China Brief* 7 no.11 (2007).

30. Forum on China-Africa Cooperation, "China-Africa Relations Board the Ship of A New Century ," September 9, 2006, http://www.fmprc.gov.cn/zflt/eng/bjzl/t404145.htm.

31. Forum on China-Africa Cooperation, "The Implementation of the Follow-up Actions of the First Ministerial Conference of FOCAC," http://www.fmprc.gov.cn/zflt/eng/hxxd/jzgz/t157587.htm.

32. Susan Puska, *Resources, Security and Influence.*

33. Drew Thompson, "China's Soft Power in Africa: From the "Beijing Consensus" to Health Diplomacy," *China Brief* 5, no. 21 (2005).

34. Ibid.

35. Guo Nei, "Peace-keeping force sets out for Congo," *China Daily*, August 21 2004, http://www.chinadaily.com.cn/english/doc/2004-08/21/content_367465.htm/.

36. Embassy of the People's Republic of China in the Hellenic Republic, "President Hu Jintao Holds Talks with Comoros President," June 18, 2003, http://gr.china-embassy.org/eng/xwdt/xw2003/xw200306/t145622.htm.

37. Drew Thompson, *China's Soft Power in Africa.*

38. Li Anshan, *Transformation of China's Policy towards Africa.*

39. He Wenping, *Moving Forward with Time.*

40. Dams Implementation Unit, Merowe Dam Project, "Funding," http://www.merowedam.gov.sd/en/funding.html.

41. International Rivers, " Export Credit Agencies and Environmental Standards: An Invitation to Join the Dialogue," December 1, 2006, http://www.irn.org/programs/finance/index.php?id=061220exim.html.

42. Xinhua, "China, Algeria sign oil, natural gas contract," *China Daily*, December 24, 2003, http://www.chinadaily.com.cn/en/doc/2003-12/23/content_292766.htm/.

43. 50 years is enough, "Angola defies IMF as China enters the fray," August 18, 2005, http://www.50years.org/cms/updates/story/290.

44. Power and Interests News Report, "The Increasing Importance of African Oil," March 20 2006, http://www.pinr.com/report.php?ac=view_report&report_id=460.

45. Ministry of Foreign Affairs of the People's Republic of China, "Report on the Implementation of the Follow-up Actions of the 2nd Ministerial Conference of the Forum on China-Africa Cooperation (FOCAC)," 2004, http://www.fmprc.gov.cn/eng/topics/Second/t105886.htm.

46. Joshua Eisenman, "Zimbabwe: China's African Ally," *China Brief* 5, Issue 15 (2005).

47. Ministry of Foreign Affairs of the People's Republic of China, *Report on the Implementation of the Follow-up Actions.*

48. Ibid.

49. Forum on China-Africa Cooperation, "FOCAC to hold Workshop for African Journalists," September 19, 2004, http://www.fmprc.gov.cn/zflt/eng/zt/fzxwjzyxbpdefault.htm.

50. Embassy of the People's Republic of China in the Republic of Zimbabwe, "Air Zimbabwe Launches Flights to Beijing," November 28, 2004, http://www.chinaembassy.org.zw/eng/lsxx/t172317.htm.

51. Wenran Jiang, "Hu's Safari: China's Emerging Strategic Partnerships in Africa," China Brief 7, no. 4 (2007).

52. Susan Puska, *Resources, Security and Influence.*

53. Chris Zambelis, "Down the River Nile: China Gains Influence in Egypt," China Brief 5, no.22 (2005).

54. Hu Jintao, "Seize the Opportunity for All-round Cooperation and Common Development," (Speech, Official reception of the Asian-African Business Summit, Jakarta, Indonesia April 22, 2005), http://www.fmprc.gov.cn/zflt/eng/zt/yf/t192832.htm.

55. Forum on China-Africa Cooperation, "Kenya Airways to start flights to Shanghai in August," May, 31 2005, http://www.fmprc.gov.cn/zflt/eng/yhjl/t404098.htm.

56. Forum on China-Africa Cooperation, "Wu Bangguo Meets with Zimbabwean President Mugabe," July 27, 2005, http://www.fmprc.gov.cn/eng/wjb/zzjg/fzs/gjlb/3119/3121/t205424.htm.

57. "Respect, Cooperation Urged at Sino-Africa Forum," *China.org.cn*, November 28, 2005, http://www.china.org.cn/english/2005/Nov/150134.htm/.

58. Xinhua, "First Confucius Institute for Africa officially launched in Nairobi," *People's Daily*, December 20, 2005, http://english.people.com.cn/200512/20/eng20051220_229340.html/.

59. Wenran Jiang, *Hu's Safari.*

60. John C. K. Daly, "Feeding the Dragon: China's Quest for African Minerals," *China Brief* 8, no.3 (2008).

61. "A Chronology of China- Africa Relations," *Beijing Review*, November 2, 2006, http://www.bjreview.com/backgrounder/txt/2006-12/10/content_50421.htm.

62. Ian Taylor. "Sino-Nigerian Relations: FTZs, Textiles and Oil," *China Brief* 7, no.11 (2007)

63. Afrikenergy News, "Angola Bid Rounds," 1, no. 5 (2007).

64. Xinhua, "Chinese Premier's African tour 'fruitful': FM," *China Daily*, June 25, 2006, http://www.chinadaily.com.cn/china/2006-06/25/content_625316.htm/.

65. Xinhua, "Sudan Rejects UN Proposal After China Abstains," *China.org.cn*, September 1, 2006, http://www.china.org.cn/english/international/179887.htm/.

66. Forum on China-Africa Cooperation, "China, Chad vow to strengthen friendship between two armed forces," October 20, 2006, http://www.fmprc.gov.cn/zflt/eng/yhjl/t404112.htm.

67. Chris Zambelis, *Down the River Nile.*

68. Embassy of the People's Republic of China in Ireland, "Beijing Summit of the Forum on China-Africa Cooperation Adopts the Declaration and Beijing Action Plan," November 5, 2006, http://ie.china-embassy.org/eng/NewsPress/t279645.htm.

69. Forum on China-Africa Cooperation, "China's first regular flight to Africa arrives in Lagos," January 3, 2007, http://www.fmprc.gov.cn/zflt/eng/zxxx/t287007.htm.

70. Xinhua, "Chinese FM says President Hu's African tour successful," *China View*, February 22, 2007, http://news.xinhuanet.com/english/2007-02/11/content_5727009.htm/.

71. Jeffery Gettleman, "Ethiopian Rebels Kill 70 at Chinese-Run Oil Field," *New York Times*, April 24, 2007, http://english.people.com.cn/200512/20/eng20051220_229340.html/.

72. Xinhua, "African Development Bank to hold annual meeting in China," *People's Daily Online*, January 24, 2007, http://english.people.com.cn/200701/24/eng20070124_344428.html/.

73. Richard McGregor, "World Bank to work with Chinese in Africa." *Financial Times*, December 19, 2007, http://www.ft.com/cms/s/0/047cea58-add3-11dc-9386-0000779fd2ac.html?nclick_check=1/.

74. Associated Press, Joe McDonald, "China Launches $1B Africa Fund," *Global Policy Forum*, June 26, 2007, http://www.globalpolicy.org/socecon/trade/2007/0626chinafund.htm/.

75. "China donates $1.5 million to arm," *Mozambique News Agency*, September 18, 2007, http://www.poptel.org.uk/mozambique-news/newsletter/aim346.html#story9/.

76. Forum on China-Africa Cooperation, "Sino-African trade likely to hit $100 bln by 2010," January 16, 2007, http://www.fmprc.gov.cn/zflt/eng/hxxd/t381537.htm/.

77. Agence France-Presse,"China, Brazil give Africa free satellite land images," *Space Mart*, November 28, 2007, http://www.spacemart.com/reports/China_Brazil_give_Africa_free_satellite_land_images_999.html.

78. John C. K. Daly, *Feeding the Dragon*.

79. African Press Agency, "China sets up development fund to pump $90mn in Chinese projects in Africa," January 16 2008, http://www.apanews.net/apa.php?page=afric_item_eng&id_article=52111/.

80. Agence France-Presse, "Nigerian leader meets Hu as China continues Africa courtship," February 28, 2008, http://afp.google.com/article/ALeqM5iC0ayPzn2jwJ8r0JPHVW3JCN4Tow/.

81. Associated Press, "China's ICBC, South African partner launch US$1 billion investment fund for oil, minerals," *International Herald Tribune*, March 18, 2008, http://www.iht.com/articles/ap/2008/03/18/business/AS-FIN-COM-China-SAfrica-Banks.php.

82. Michael Sheridan, "Arms ship exposes Robert Mugabe's link to Chinese firm," *TimesOnline.com*, April 27, 2008, http://www.timesonline.co.uk/tol/news/world/africa/article3822568.ece/.

83. Levi Tillemann, "Blowback from Zimbabwe: China's Faltering Strategy on Arms Exports," *China Brief* 8, no. 13 (2008).

84. "CNPC strikes $5bn oil deal with Niger," *China Economic Review*, June 5, 2008, http://www.chinaeconomicreview.com/dailybriefing/2008_06_05/CNPC_strikes__5bn_oil_deal_with_Niger.html/.

ACKNOWLEDGEMENTS

The Jamestown Foundation is pleased to announce the publication of its first ever book on China—*China in Africa*. With the distribution of this book Jamestown is continuing to pursue its mission of providing the policymaking community with timely information and analysis based upon indigenous sources of the regions of the world that we monitor as part of our research and analysis on Eurasia. While this region represents only a portion of China's global activities, Beijing's involvement and strategic interaction with Africa is truly the one region of the world that creates a tremendous level of curiosity and interest in the China community and U.S. foreign policy circles.

In an effort to answer the larger strategic questions over where China's ties to Africa are leading, The Jamestown Foundation began preparing this book project over two years ago after policy experts in Washington began asking questions about what this means in terms of China's emerging global interests. With this in mind the staff of *China Brief* began soliciting articles from a wide range of authors in the field who have been analyzing Sino-African relations. Utilizing the analysis presented in *China Brief* we directed our team of analysts and experts to write about different aspects of Chinese involvement in the region that covered a wide array of Sino activities, ranging from military, energy, diplomatic and economic ties. Through this analysis we began to develop a strategic map of Africa identifying Chinese activities and interests that is now carefully outlined in this manuscript.

With the release of this book we feel that we have succeeded in developing a reasonably authoritative and detailed representation of Chinese activities that should enjoy a reasonable shelf life. One of our primary objectives in preparing this book was to provide analysts, researchers, and policymakers with a useful reference tool on Chinese involvement in Africa. Interestingly enough, when we first started putting this book together there were only two books in existence in English on China and Africa. Surprised by this finding, we pursued this project with even greater vigor in an effort to provide more diverse resources on the subject realizing that a major vacuum existed on the topic. Now two years later the number of books on this issue has grown significantly to nearly a dozen works and continues to increase in popularity in the China community. To answer this rise in interest Jamestown believes that *China in Africa* makes a worthy contribution to the growing number of works on this topic. We believe this book fills an important gap in western understanding on the region by using the insights of a diverse array of analysts and experts on China who offer an array of perspectives and thinking on Beijing's deepening involvement in Africa. Our chief goal is to provide students, researchers, and analysts with a unique reference tool that would be affordable and easily available to these diverse groups.

The list of persons who helped make this book possible is quite long. First, we owe a note of thanks to thanks to the writers and analysts who make *China Brief* one of the most widely read journals on China in the world. This core group of analysts stretches from Hong Kong to Nairobi and totals more than 100 analysts residing in over 200 countries around the globe who twice a month offer their insights and analysis of indigenous sourced material to provide Jamestown's readers with a diverse array of perspectives not found in the western media.

Second, a special note of thanks is due to the Jamestown staff who labored many hours to put this work together. Several persons played a major role in getting this project off the ground and seeing it through to its fruition. Our first round of thanks is to former *China Brief* Associate Editor Joseph Lin who conceived the idea for this project and helped get the book project off the ground by recruiting the authors and developing the valuable timeline on Chinese involvement in Africa. Filling his shoes was Russell Hsiao the new Associate Editor who took up where Joe left off by pushing this project through to fruition by laboring many hours editing the articles, compiling the invaluable index, overseeing the author recruitment for the various articles in this book, as well as conducting all the fact checking, cover page design, indexing and copy-editing of the book. His final push to the goal line and dedication to this organization deserve a special note of thanks. Another important contributor to this project is researcher Andrew Parker who proof read all the articles and assisted in compiling the timeline of Chinese involvement in Africa and created the wonderful charts detailing Chinese energy agreements and arms deals in Africa. Without the dedication of these individuals this book would have never materialized.

Third, we owe a great deal of gratitude to long-time Jamestown board member Dr. Arthur Waldron who spent many hours writing the excellent introduction to this book. Understanding the importance of this topic, Dr. Waldron eagerly accepted the offer to write the introduction and as a specialist on China for the past thirty years has long valued the importance of China's interaction with Eurasia. His insight on this issue has made the introduction even more timeless in terms of his own personal reflection on the strategic repercussions of Beijing's expanding ties to Africa which incorporates a long history of studying Chinese grand strategy.

Lastly, I would like to extend my gratitude to the Jamestown board, in particular its Chairman, James G. Gidwitz, for his guidance and direction in supporting our work. And lastly, a special note of thanks is owed to the readers of Jamestown's publications for their continuing financial support, feedback and encouragement. Without public support Jamestown would be unable to continue its broader mission of providing the policy community with timely fact-based information on conflict and instability in Eurasia.

Glen E. Howard
President

FOREWORD

This volume contains articles about China's relations with Africa that have appeared in the Jamestown Foundation publication *China Brief*. They speak for themselves as thoroughly documented analyses of important developments written by experts. Gathered into a single volume, they provide, we hope, a valuable reference. So what can a Foreword provide beyond stating those facts?

The answer is perhaps: some context and historical background. That is best gained by moving away from the present, to survey briefly the first, highly successful Chinese venture into African relations that filled the decade of the 1960s. The patterns are similar, both positive and negative. The difference this time, as will be argued below, is that Africa has changed in ways that will make achievement of Beijing's goals more difficult than was the case fifty years ago.

In 1969 Tanzanian President Julius Nyerere (1922-1999) observed: "We get along very well with the Chinese. One either gets along well with them or one doesn't get along at all" [1]. The comment is worth remembering today, as ties between Beijing and African states once again flower, for promising beginnings have been made in the past, notably in the 1960s, that have left results that are mixed at best.

Tanzania and China were very good friends indeed at the time that President Nyerere made his comment—to U.S. Ambassador John H. Burns (b. 1913). Symbolic of the friendship was China's undertaking, made two years earlier, to build a railway from the seaport of Dar-es-Salaam 1,115 miles to land-locked Zambia, the purpose being to end that country's dependence, for copper exports above all, on the (then) white controlled states of Rhodesia and South Africa. Completed in 1976 at a cost of $500 million to China, the railway has never made a profit. With the emergence of Zimbabwe and the end of white rule in South Africa, the railway lost its strategic significance. In 2005, Tanzania and Zambia agreed that it should be sold off and are now courting Chinese investors (*The Citizen* [Tanzania], March 7, 2008).

This unhappy story is worth bearing in mind almost forty years after "Mwalimu" ["teacher" in Swahili, referring to Nyerere] made his characteristically candid remarks to Ambassador Burns. For once again, after a period in which Beijing's economic and political attention was largely focused on the West, on Russia, and on Asia, Africa is once again being noticed in China—and China is again looming large in Africa. As the essays in this volume demonstrate, much has changed since the first Chinese-African engagement of the 1960s, but much still remains the same—above all the complex purposes and the high sensitivities of both sides.

To understand the Chinese activities in Africa that are discussed in this volume, three contexts are required. The first is Africa itself, which since the era of independence in the 1960s has offered to China opportunities, both economic and political, not found elsewhere. The second is the larger set of Chinese international activities of which her relations with Africa are a part. The third is the aggregate of the domestic setting within China of both these general international and specifically African operations. This volume supplies much about the African specifics. For that reason this introduction devotes primary attention to the domestic origins and general international setting of Beijing's newest Africa policy.

China and Africa: The Legacy

The story of Beijing's relations with Africa begins with the need to find a new approach to diplomacy after the Soviet Union abandoned China in the wake of the turbulent period known as the Great Leap Forward of 1958-1960, but before the Western powers were prepared to deal with the country, a development that would not come for a decade or more.

The Great Leap was an attempt by Mao Zedong (1893-1976) to make use of China's immense population to support a previously unknown form of industrialization that would be manpower, rather than capital, intensive. Instead of pouring scarce resources into vast steel kombinats of the Soviet style, for example, it would mobilize China's people to build small steel mills in their localities. Likewise, agriculture would be transformed not by new inputs such as fertilizers, but rather by reorganization of the population into communes, who would cultivate their fields with an intensity— by plowing deep and planting seedlings close together—that had never before been seen. The story ended in tragedy, however, with the deaths by starvation of tens of millions of people [2].

This catastrophe, which was well-concealed at the time but known in Moscow, was one of the factors, along with Mao's shelling in 1958 of the offshore island of Quemoy, held by Taiwan, that convinced the Soviet Union to break her hitherto close ties with China and withdraw all economic and military aid. In other words, after the Great Leap, Beijing could no longer count on diplomatic or other support from the then formidable Communist bloc led by Moscow.

The United States was also puzzled and worried by these developments in China. Since the 1950s a long-term policy had sought to establish relations of some sort with Beijing [3]. But the shelling of Quemoy (about which Beijing had not consulted Moscow) led to American assistance defending the island; a re-evaluation by Washington of the actual situation in China, which to some seemed dangerously chaotic; and a drop in diplomatic temperature that effectively froze possible diplomatic initiatives.

These developments in no way cooled Beijing's ambition to join the international community, however. All they did was create a situation in which China had no choice but to make that entry without the aid of either the Soviet bloc or the United States. Such were the circumstances that led China to turn to Africa and other non-aligned countries in her search for allies and friends.

In 1960 Premier Zhou Enlai (1898-1976) began travels that took him in April to Rangoon, New Delhi, and Kathmandu; in May to Phnom Penh and Hanoi, and then to Mongolia. In June 1961 President Sukarno (1901-1970) of Indonesia visited China and in the same year contracts for major agricultural sales were concluded with Australia and Canada. The war with India in 1962, a puzzling event that continues to this day to poison relations between New Delhi and Beijing, cast a brief pall over things, but that did not last long. April 1963 saw Chinese President Liu Shaoqi (1898-1969) return Sukarno's visit, accompanied by his glamorous American-educated fifth wife, Wang Guangmei (1921-2006), the first time that a Communist Chinese head of state visited a non-Communist country (Liu would perish in the Cultural Revolution). Zhou visited Albania in 1964, establishing a diplomatic foothold in Europe; Pakistan International Airlines landed its first flight to Shanghai in the same year. The Chinese even spoke to Moscow of discussing again the treaties of 1858 and 1860 that had created an enduring territorial dispute.

In classic fashion, then, China began in the 1960s to break her isolation from both the Soviet bloc and the West by paying systematic attention to countries those blocs tended to ignore. Nowhere was this clearer than in Africa [4].

The Sino-African People's Friendship Association had been founded in Beijing on April 12, 1960, and in the years that followed more and more of the new African states established relations with China. That Beijing's purpose was to create her own independent group of diplomatic friends and allies is made clear by her failure to take advantage of the many opportunities that embassies in African countries where the United States also had diplomatic representation created for communication with Washington. Thus, President John F. Kennedy (1917-1963) chose as his ambassador to Guinea a fairly high-profile figure, his old friend William Attwood (1918-1989) who was a star journalist for the now-defunct Look magazine. Kennedy's idea was that the charming Attwood would make informal contact with the large Chinese diplomatic contingent there. The foreign diplomats all used the same beach; they swam together every day, but nothing Attwood did elicited so much as an acknowledgement from the Chinese. It was as if the Americans simply did not exist [5].

Kennedy's hopes were frustrated. As for the USSR, by 1969 they would be at war on a small scale over the Damansky Island (*Zhenbaodao*) midstream in their Ussuri River border. China was playing an indirect game, however. She had no desire to break through to a new relationship, with the inequality and constraints inevitably associated, with either Moscow or Washington. Rather she sought to establish Beijing as the head of world revolution—it is important to remind one's self how the idea of "social revolution," now grown rather dusty particularly since the end of the Cold War, dominated political thought around the world in the decades of the 1960s and 1970s—and to do so bypassing the established powers, even the established "revolutionary" powers such as the USSR, by turning instead to the befriending of newly-emerged African states, and supporting armed insurgencies against South Africa and the Portuguese Empire. The diplomatic harvest was spectacular; in 1964 Chinese Premier Zhou Enlai and Foreign Minister Chen Yi visited Tunisia, Ghana, Mali, Guinea, Ethiopia, and Somalia, where they confirmed existing ties. Soon thereafter fourteen more African nations joined the Beijing camp, leaving only fifteen maintaining ties with the Republic of China (ROC) government in Taipei [6].

The full brilliance of this approach was manifest at the end of 1964, on December 17, when France, the European country having closest ties to Africa as well as the one most eager to avoid too close an embrace by either Washington or Moscow, announced that she would establish relations with Beijing. Charles De Gaulle (1890-1970) considered this a major strategic achievement, although he had not so much sought it as been maneuvered into it by the patient Chinese diplomatic work in Africa. France was bitterly disappointed when the Cultural Revolution, which began to gather less than a year later, turned China inward and xenophobic, so that nothing came of the French relationship—and when the storm passed, it was Washington that became Beijing's chief Western interlocutor [7].

During the 1970s China continued strong interest in Africa. African votes in the United Nations provided the majority that saw Beijing seated and Taipei expelled, with Tanzanian delegates dancing in the aisles, on October 25, 1971. But by the end of that decade it was clear that Beijing's priorities had changed. The great railway project in Tanzania, much resented by Chinese who had spent years working on it, was becoming a ruin. African students in China were resentful of the pervasive racism they felt and of the lack of any personal interest in them by the Chinese [8]. Most importantly, perhaps, the promise of socialism was placed in question by the catastrophe of Tanzania, while the revolutions that China had supported all succeeded—in Angola (1974), Mozambique (1975), Zimbabwe (1980) and (with a peaceful transfer of power) in South Africa (1994).

With these developments, the whole context of Chinese policies in Africa changed. No longer did the rulers of African countries so actively seek foreign assistance against domestic adversaries, though horrendous civil wars raged in all but South Africa. Nor were they any longer desperate seekers after foreign aid, though they remained poor. Like China herself after Mao Zedong's death, all of these countries discarded socialism and statism (several more completely than did China herself). As they took control of their natural resources they turned into something other than needy regimes in desperate economic straits.

Rather, Africa increasingly had something to offer, not just China but the world, in the form of markets, labor, resources, and political support. Not only that: Having experienced the advantages and disadvantages of association with China—summed up by Julius Nyerere at the beginning of this essay—and having viable alternatives, the Africans were no longer as willing as before to fall in with Beijing's agenda. Relationships with African countries still offered benefits to them and to China. But Beijing was a known and somewhat distrusted quantity.

These facts mean that although parallels exist today between China's current African policy and that she pursued some forty years ago, major differences have also come into being, as is evident in the essays in this volume. Below I will attempt to point out what some of these are, and how they should affect our evaluation of the relationship.

China and Africa: The Present:

Africa has once again become a major focus of Chinese policy. Officially the new relationship is based on "the three pillars of political, economic, and educational cooperation." Note that the political comes first: China promises to support the African states internationally and in the United Nations—although of course Africa is not homogenous in her interests—while expecting African support against China's own rivals. Second, in theory, China will absorb African exports, though the reality has been that Africa has become a market for Chinese exports, some of which have driven out of business textile factories that where built by China in the previous era of close relations. Third, educational cooperation means providing scholarships for Africans to attend institutions of higher learning in China [9].

The last few years have witnessed a striking acceleration in the pace of Chinese involvement with Africa. President Hu Jintao (b. 1942) visited Nigeria, Morocco and Kenya in April 2006; in June Premier Wen Jiabao (b. 1942) visited seven more African countries. The year ended with the largest-ever Chinese-African meeting, in November, attended by 48 out of 53 African leaders. In 2007 Hu Jintao visited Cameroon, Liberia, Zambia, Namibia, South Africa, Mozambique, Sudan and Seychelles (the last not strictly speaking "African"). In the first of these years, economic agreements were signed totaling $1.9 billion and loans of $1.5 billion promised. The following year saw an additional $3 billion promised in debt relief. This represents a level of political and economic activity not seen since the 1960s [10].

The usual explanation for this new level of interest is that China's growth has created an almost insatiable appetite for resources, of which Africa is potentially a major source. Official statistics indicate that China's economy has been growing with almost unprecedented speed since the early 1990s when, after the Tiananmen massacre, Deng Xiaoping (1904-1997) decided that economic development would be the key to stability [11].

China's trade with Africa is growing faster than with any area other than the Middle East. It increased ten-fold in the ten years up to 2008, and in 2006 reached $56 billion. China's share of Africa's trade with the world remains relatively small at ten percent but is expected to double by 2010. Direct investment has reached $6.6 billion [12].

Of commodities traded with Africa, petroleum is the most important. Beijing's planners have assumed that petroleum will provide the energy for a carbon-intensive economy similar to that of Europe or the United States, with highways and automobiles as the key component in the national transportation network. China has always been short of petroleum. Today, China is the second largest importer in the world, bringing in ninety million barrels per month, a quantity that is rising (even as prices at the pump are subsidized) (Manufacturing.net, January 22, 2008).

One third of China's oil imports come from Angola, Sudan, Congo, Equatorial Guinea, Chad, and Nigeria. Angola is now China's single largest provider of oil, bigger even than Saudi Arabia. This oil trade above all has made China the third largest trading partner of Africa, after the United States and France [13].

But as the Chinese saying has it, "far away water will not assuage immediate thirst" (*yuanshui jiebuliao jinke*)—a saying that applies very well to African oil. All African countries are very far away from China. Some of them are politically unstable. All of them have the choice of selling their oil to the highest bidder. Even direct Chinese ownership of African reserves such as blocs secured in Nigeria, Angola, and Sudan [14] cannot prevent such sales—for given the controls on fuel prices in China itself, even the big state-owned Chinese energy monopolies, such as Sinopec, already divert resources away from their own country to the international market, where prices are higher. The key here is not securing reserves, but rather pricing energy realistically, something that China (and India and others) are far from doing today.

To begin with, world petroleum resources are limited and are moving toward exhaustion within the not too distant future, Therefore it makes little sense for any country, and above all one that is building a new economy, to base it on automobiles and oil [15], as China has done. The diminishing resource of oil must be used ever more sparingly. But China wastes energy on a massive scale.

According to an important book authored by the editor of the officially-published China Petroleum News, the comparative energy intensiveness of production in China compared to other countries is as follows. One standard unit (defined as equivalent to a kilogram of coal) produces a value of $1.86 on average world-wide. Japan is one of the most efficient energy users, producing $5.58. France produces $3.24. South Korea produces $1.56, India $0.74 and China, $0.36 [16]. What these figures mean is that at a Japanese level of efficiency, China would use ninety three percent less energy to produce the same output value she does today. Even at India's far from dizzying heights of efficiency, China would halve her energy consumption per unit of output.

Increasing efficiency requires capital investments. With roughly a trillion dollars in foreign reserves, China could make a far more serious beginning toward efficient energy use than she has so far. Rather than try to save at home, however, Beijing has put most of her effort into acquiring oil from abroad. Much of China's investment in Africa (and Latin America and Central Asia and elsewhere) has been in oil.

This approach, however, has brought her into collision with international prices rising far more rapidly than anyone, Chinese included, expected even a few years ago. Rather than pass the price rise on to users, which sooner or later must spur attempts at conservation, however, Beijing has chosen to keep domestic energy prices artificially low even as international prices rise.

With world oil prices (June 2008) nearing one hundred forty dollars per barrel, Beijing has limited domestic prices to what they would be for sixty-dollar-per-barrel oil. Given consumption of perhaps seven million barrels per day (*China Daily*, September 15, 2005) that immense subsidy is unsustainable—but it is also built in, at the foundation, of China's new modernization—just as it is into the model of modernization, based on cheap oil, that the West has been following for a century.

China's policy is only slightly more irrational than that of the United States, which also relies on foreign oil, paid for with rapidly depreciating dollars (but which charges end users the market price) or even Europe's, where prices are higher owing to taxation. The point, however, is that although she appears to be planning to do so, China is simply not going to be able to follow the same trajectory to prosperity, propelled by cheap energy, that lifted the western industrial states. This fact is inescapable, no matter how much oil China secures in Africa or elsewhere.

Furthermore, oil fields abroad are an unreliable source of energy. Oil is transported worldwide in a fleet of a bit over four thousand tankers, ranging in size up to the immense Ultra Large Crude Carriers, of 550,000 deadweight tons [17]. These ships have small crews, between thirty and forty at most, including deck-hands and they are extremely vulnerable to attack, for example by anti-ship missiles or mines. Several hundred must be constantly at sea, shuttling back and forth from foreign sources to the United States, to carry our imports. That procession could easily be halted, by attack, or by blockade of the sources (much oil is loaded at multiple Saudi facilities in the Persian Gulf, which is easily closed. To the west, in the Red Sea, is a single set of Saudi loading facilities, but the

Red Sea, too, is easily blocked). China has invested a great deal in oil facilities in Sudan and in building new loading facilities north of Port Sudan in the Red Sea. A serious adversary, however—even a non-state actor—could sabotage this connection with little difficulty.

Furthermore, the path oil takes from Africa or the Middle East is an obstacle course of maritime choke points. The entrance to the Straits of Malacca is controlled by the Indian Andaman and Nicobar islands; the Straits themselves run between Malaysia and Indonesia, both Muslim countries deeply suspicious of their Chinese minorities. At the Philip Channel, the easternmost part of the Strait passing Singapore, through which north bound ships must pass, the waterway is a bit more than a mile wide in places, and piracy is rampant. Increasingly, crude carriers take the more distant Lombok Strait, between the island of that name and Bali in Indonesia. But however one navigates, sea lines of communication for energy are impossible to secure.

China and other states are also eagerly exploring for energy in Central Asia: Kazakhstan in particular. But pipelines are hostages to fortune: costly, difficult to build and maintain, and easily subjected to sabotage, for example, if the Muslim peoples of the area and within China itself should decide to do so.

The fact is that the petroleum-based economy is no longer sustainable and that India and China are making as much of a mistake by adopting it as their model as the West is by attempting to keep it alive.

Do those who make Chinese policy understand these facts? The answer is probably "only incompletely"—as would be true in Washington or New Delhi. But the fundamental economic irrationality of massive purchases of foreign resources—one could add Australian iron ore and many other items to the list—is so great as to render it doubtful as an explanation for China's behavior, even though at first glance it looks very much like resource hunting. The London Economist recently featured a cover photograph of a camel train in the desert, with the leader carrying a huge Chinese flag, with the headline: "The new colonialists: A 14-page special report on China's thirst for resources" (*The Economist*, March 15-28, 2008).

"New Colonialists" is, moreover, precisely how many Africans see the Chinese today. Large numbers of Chinese nationals are settling in Africa where, typically, they employ other Chinese and not Africans, purchase raw materials for processing elsewhere, and sell to foreign markets, in the classic fashion of European imperialists more than a century ago. A certain "blowback" effect, as Professor Harsh V. Pant of King's College, London, puts it, is beginning to be felt. Today's Africans are very different to those of the generation of Julius Nyerere and Zhou Enlai [18].

China recently supplied seventy-seven tons of weapons to the violently repressive regime of Robert Mugabe (b. 1924) in Zimbabwe as it was engaged in crushing popular and electoral opposition (Voice of America, May 18, 2008). Beijing's support for Sudan in its repressive policies has also come under incessant international criticism. Meanwhile China has provided a $13 million interest-free loan to build a presidential palace in that country and vetoed UN efforts to take effective measures to halt the killing there [19].

Such actions can only raise suspicions among Africans that Beijing's approach to the continent is guided only by a concept of expedient looting of resources, in service of which any regime or politician, however loathsome, will be supported—or dropped abruptly if circumstances change. This increasingly widespread conviction is making Africans into something far different from the rather eager, ideologically committed, and politically compliant partners of the 1960s. At the same time, the Chinese approach to Africa is undermining her often-reiterated positions of non-interference in foreign states, equal treatment, respect, and so forth—not only in Africa, but worldwide, where she is increasingly perceived as an unscrupulous player.

... the Chinese approach to Africa is undermining her often-reiterated positions of non-interference in foreign states, equal treatment, respect, and so forth—not only in Africa, but world-wide, where she is increasingly perceived as an unscrupulous player.

This is not to say that Africa and China cannot do beneficial trade. Rather it is to suggest that the way in which that trade is being carried out is creating obstacles for what would appear to be the deeper and broader purposes of China's new attention to Africa.

If Not Resources, Then What?

Although the informed consensus is very much that China's extraordinary external expansion of trade and investment is somehow of economic origin, yet as already suggested, this fact may be doubted. China has foreign reserves of roughly one trillion dollars U.S., and a sovereign wealth fund currently buying into blue chip foreign companies, totaling some $200 billion (UPI, June 4, 2008). Yet when a devastating earthquake struck Sichuan province in May 2008, China relied heavily on foreign donations for relief. Why her immense wealth is not invested inward is, to say the least, puzzling, for the infrastructure and development needs of China herself could easily absorb her foreign earnings for years.

My own inclination is to see a strategic purpose behind China's outward investment. Admittedly "strategic purpose" is very difficult to define. But briefly I would take is as meaning creating a China-centered community, mostly of small and medium-sized states, that could serve as a counterweight to the emerged or emerging powers of the West, Japan, India, and so forth. The Chinese Communist government is most interested not in the welfare of China's people, but in their own regime survival. The gradual disappearance of communism worries them deeply. So too does what one Japanese diplomat calls "bandwagoning with the United States." That may seem an odd phrase, given the ubiquitous anti-Americanism one finds abroad. But the diplomat is correct. Most countries today are more interested in being like the United States than China. Oddly, the Chinese model was more compelling in Maoist times than it is today. Then many people, in Africa not least, believed that only revolution could solve their problems. Now it is clear that growth is possible—and moreover, with the examples of Japan, Taiwan, India, and other states, it is clear that Chinese-style repression is not a necessary condition for growth. If anything it hampers genuine development [20].

Looked at this way, China's new interest in Africa would be part of an increasingly visible pattern of seeking to create her own set of economic and political friends. Chinese states have historically been uncomfortable with any but hierarchical foreign relations that they dominate. Today's China is not particularly happy with her truly advanced Asian neighbors, such as Japan, Korea and Taiwan, nor is she naturally congenial with India or Southeast Asia, which are less developed, or for that matter with Europe or the United States. In every case, purely economic considerations would suggest ever-closer cooperation, but as a single-party dictatorship in a world where Pakistan and South Africa and Russia hold elections, China worries about political contagion—not to mention the numerous territorial disputes that poison, for example, relations with India. Taking such considerations into mind, two areas of the world look attractive. One is Latin America, the other Africa. Particularly in the case of Africa, Beijing has the possibility of winning almost fifty friends (Africa has 49 states), many rich in resources, while facing little danger of liberal contagion, and not least being at least seemingly in command of the relationship by virtue of superior education, resources, and technology. All of these states vote in the United Nations. Many are deeply embedded and influential in international organizations. Furthermore, from Nigeria to Sudan to Tanzania, they offer what may seem to be strategic political and military positions, on the Atlantic, the Red Sea, and the Indian Ocean.

With a collection of such friends, China can create her own sphere of influence; secure her own resources, and develop military and political leverage without becoming overly entangled with the more problematical countries mentioned above. If China is following such a strategy now, it is not the first time.

We began with Nyerere. In the 1960s China used diplomacy in Africa with great effect to weaken western influence there, win diplomatic allies at a time when the United States and other major states still recognized Taipei as the government of China, and eventually leap the Mediterranean Sea to establish diplomatic relations with France. Now she would appear to be using trade and the export of capital to create what is sometimes called a "string of pearls"—a set of places around the world—harbors, airports, canals, countries—where by virtue of ownership and investment she gains a disproportionate influence. Not enough influence, to be sure, to make her the world leader, but enough to give her what strategists call a potentially "decisive weight" in a crisis—the classic approach taken by ambitious second-tier countries, such as Italy in the first half of the twentieth century.

Conclusion

As we suggested at the outset this seemingly well-conceived strategy of diplomacy and economic aid may not reap as good a harvest this time as it did a half century ago.

The relationship with the United States has proved steadily problematical. Combined with Japan, the United States accounts for forty percent of the world economy. For China to grow, she needs American money, American technology, and access to American markets. Too close connections with the United States, however, risk making China dependent—as indeed she is, to a large degree—on American demand for and willingness to accept imports. Such connections also jeopardized China's own ambitions for an independent world role and a paramount role in Asia, while bringing limited but still unwelcome prodding over human rights. Africa cannot fill this need.

Hence the vision of a multi-polar world as the lodestar of Chinese policy. Today's activities in Africa are consistent with that Chinese vision. The problem is that African states today are not what they were forty years ago. It is by no means clear that they share China's vision for themselves, or have no choice but to adopt it.

Other states, France most notably, are learning a similar lesson. Their long-successful attempts to maintain a franc zone in Africa and military presences in semi-client states are coming to an end, for solid objective reasons having to do with the waning of European power and the increasing ability of Africans to chart their own course.

There are, after all, reasons that the colonial powers left Africa, abruptly. China's apparent success in the past two decades, both economic and political, has been not least because certain basic problems have been neglected or concealed. China has believed her own propaganda and now sees her future as a seemingly preordained rise to world power—which, as the television series "The Rise of Great Powers" (*Daguo jueqi*), screened in 2006, misleadingly suggested, great power status depended upon the acquisition of colonial possessions and their exploitation, and not on internal development of the economy [21]. If China acts on that basis, she will encounter resistance everywhere. Remember that even the far more China-dominated Africa episode of the 1960s ended in tears.

Chinese relations with Africa will certainly continue to develop. Tanzania has long since cast aside its version of socialism, "Ujaama"—and done so more completely than China has abandoned collectivism and state control. Tanzania's experiment with the Chinese style collectivism, so bravely heralded by the Arusha declaration of 1967, brought impoverishment and ended with Nyerere's retirement in 1985. Once again Nyerere did not mince words. He said, of the whole Tanzanian socialist enterprise: "I failed. Let's admit it" [22].

That break, course, did not mean the end of officially cordial relations between Tanzania and Zambia, and China. This year Dar-es-Salaam will be the only African capital to host the Beijing Olympic torch relay (*People's Daily*, April 28, 2007). In Beijing, however, one can still hear official bitterness about this largest foreign aid project in Chinese history [23].

No imperative requires that we assume China has a single mind and a single policy, toward Africa or anywhere else. She most certainly does not. Although she is far more centralized than most states, she is also far larger and more populous, and getting the word from Beijing to, say, the deep south province of Guangdong is not easy. Perhaps the most convincing conclusion is that, as in so many other aspects of her policies, China is acting in Africa in an opportunistic manner, with the definition of opportunity varying from player to player. A state oil company may indeed seek petroleum reserves. But a small state-owned textile mill may open up operations in Africa chiefly as a way for its state administrators to get money out of China, and eventually into their own pockets. Foreign policy planners will see a bloc of pro-China votes at the United Nations as potentially useful to block unwelcome Russian or American or other initiatives. Military planners, dreaming of a blue-water navy, will see the string of ports ranging across South Asia and the coasts of Africa, as the support system for a fleet worthy of a great power. Not all of these goals are even compatible, let alone parallel. As the fine essays collected in this volume make clear, the Chinese-African relationship defies generalization and is best looked at from a wide range of viewpoints.

That said, this author would conclude by stating that in his opinion the issues of energy and waste of energy, along with the environmental price China is paying today for her growth, will probably be determinative factors in the years ahead—and not least, albeit indirectly, in her relations with Africa as with the rest of the world.

Arthur Waldron
Trustee, Jamestown Foundation and editor, *China Brief*

Notes

1. Quoted in: Central Intelligence Agency, "China's Presence in Africa," (Langley, VA: June 20, 1969), 8.
2. Jasper Becker, *Hungry Ghosts: Mao's Secret Famine* (New York: Henry Holt & Co., 1998).
3. See Arthur Waldron, "From Nonexistent to Almost Normal: U.S.-China Relations in the 1960s," in *The Diplomacy of the Crucial Decade: American Foreign Relations During the 1960s*, ed. Diane B. Kunz (New York: Columbia University Press, 1994), 218-250.
4. See Bruce D. Larkin, *China and Africa 1949-1970: The Foreign Policy of the People's Republic of China* (Berkeley: University of California Press, 1971); Alaba Ogunsanwo, *China's Policy in Africa 1958-1971* (Cambridge: Cambridge University Press, 1974), and George T. Yu, *China's African Policy: A Study of Tanzania* (New York: Praeger, 1975). Also Luo Jianbo, *Feizhou yitihua yu Zhong-Fei guanxi* (Beijing: China Academy of Social Sciences, 2006).
5. William Attwood, *The Reds and the Blacks: a Personal Adventure* (New York: Harper and Row, 1967), 96 and passim.
6. Gordon H. Chang, *Friends and Enemies: The United States, China, and the Soviet Union, 1948-1972* (Stanford: Stanford University Press, 1990).
7. The historical section above follows closely the relevant parts of my article, "From Nonexistent to Almost Normal" cited above.
8. Author's personal information from conversations in China.
9. See Luo Jianbo, 288 ff.

10. Harsh V. Pant, "China in Africa: The Push Continues But All's Not Well," *Defense & Security Analysis* 24.1 (March 2008), 36, 33.

11. Arthur Waldron, "The End of the Soviet Union and the Future of China: Literature Review and Analysis" (2006: manuscript prepared for U.S. government, to be published.)

12. Harsh.V. Pant, 35.

13. Harsh.V. Pant, 34.

14. Harsh.V. Pant, 36.

15. The rapid depletion of world oil supplies is well documented. See, for example, Kenneth S. Deffeyes, *Beyond Oil: The View From Hubbert's Peak* (Updated edition. New York: Hill and Wang, 2007).

16. See Li Xiangyang, *Shei lai wei 21 shiji Zhongguo* [Who will 'fill up" 21st century China?] (Beijing: Chinese Academy of Social Sciences, 2005), 278. Other Chinese-published sources on energy include Wu Lei, *China's Oil Security* [Zhongguo Shiyou Anquan] (Beijing: China Academy of Social Sciences, 2003); *International Energy* [Guoji Nengyuan (Shanghai: East China Normal University Press, 2005): According to the jacket this is a translation of Stanislav V. Zhiznin, *Fundamentals of Energy Diplomacy*, 2 v. published 2003, for which no further information is provided. Qian Xuewen, *Middle East, Offshore Oil Gas and China's Strategy for Energy Security* [Zhongdong, Lihai youqi yu Zhongguo nengyuan anquan zhanlue] (Beijing: Shishi chubanshe, 2007). See also Kang Wu and Fereidun, *Asia's Energy Future: Regional Dynamics and Global Implications* (Honolulu: East-West Center, 2007).

17. Office of Data and Economic Analysis (July 2006). "World Merchant Fleet 2001–2005" (PDF). 3, 5, 6 United States Maritime Administration. Retrieved on 2008-07-09

18. Harsh V. Pant, 33-43.

19. Harsh V. Pant, 40.

20. Author's personal conversation, Ministry of Foreign Affairs, Tokyo, December 2007.

21. "Control and Liberalization of the Chinese Media as Seen in the Suspension of the 'Bing Dian Zhou Kan' weekly magazine and 'Da Guo Jue Qi' (The Rise of Great Powers) TV documentary series," Bunken, http://www.nhk.or.jp/bunken/english/book/geppo_sum07030104.html

22. Maier, K. 1998, 'Into the House of the Ancestors', extract in The New York Times, February 1, 1998.

23. Author's personal information.

CHINESE SOFT & HARD POWER ON THE CONTINENT

ECONOMIC GROWTH AND SOFT POWER: CHINA'S AFRICA STRATEGY

By Drew Thompson

The UN Security Council's 2004 mid-November meeting in Nigeria highlighted China's growing interest in Africa since the end of the Cold War. The talks on November 18-19 were aimed at resolving the conflicts in Sudan by advancing the peace process between Khartoum and rebels in the South, and applying greater pressure on the government to stop the violence in Darfur. China's effort to dilute a September UN resolution against Sudan not only demonstrated Beijing's potentially more active role in the Security Council but also revealed its emerging interest in trade and energy in Africa. An increasingly influential player in Africa, China needs to be considered if the United States wants to achieve its goals of bringing democracy and economic development to the continent. Likewise, China has an opportunity to fulfill its aspirations as a "responsible power" through cooperating with the international community to help promote security and stability in the region.

China's Interests in African Cooperation

Chinese presence in Africa is illustrative of Beijing's efforts to create a paradigm of globalization that favors China. Beijing has long sought to portray itself as the leader of the Third World, and remains an attractive strategic partner to many African countries. By cultivating relations with African nations, providing aid, technical expertise and diplomatic support in multilateral institutions, China has attempted to better position itself in a multi-polar, post-cold war environment. Its history as a former colony of the European powers allows China to promote itself as sensitive to the dignity of Third World countries, in the hopes that African people will favorably relate to this invocation of a shared colonial past. Furthermore, China's professed respect for sovereignty and non-interference in internal affairs is appealing to many African leaders, some of whom face internal rebellions and ethnic unrest similar to China.

Chinese presence in Africa is illustrative of Beijing's efforts to create a paradigm of globalization that favors China. Beijing has long sought to portray itself as the leader of the Third World.

China's interests in Africa, however, have shifted over the past fifty years from a desire to be the leader of the Third World during the Cold War to expanding its spheres of influence and ensuring access to energy and raw materials through diplomacy, investment and trade.

Diplomacy, Aid and Trade

The Chinese government has invested heavily in Africa over the past four years to encourage trade relations, sponsoring the Forum on China-Africa Cooperation (FOCAC) to provide opportunities for governments and businesses to strengthen economic cooperation. The first FOCAC took place in Beijing in 2000. It established a mechanism for promoting diplomatic relations, trade and investment between China and African countries. That same year, two-way trade between China and Africa surpassed $10 billion for the first time in history, reaching $10.6 billion—this number increased to $18.545 billion in 2003. By 2004, 674 Chinese companies were operating in Africa. A forum held in Addis Ababa in December 2003, and attended by Chinese Premier Wen Jiabao, UN Secretary General Kofi Annan, 250 businessmen from Africa and 150 from China, indicates the significant support that Beijing provides African businesses with interests in China. The most recent forum was held in Beijing in October 2004.

This cooperation between Chinese and African businesses is part of a long history of China providing aid to African countries, and thereby building goodwill and political support. Chinese assistance to African countries includes grants as well as low and no-interest loans. China is also very effective at leveraging loans a second time, forgiving debt for the poorest countries at the high-profile FOCACs. China's aid and debt forgiveness earns it significant political capital among African countries, ensuring their support in the UN and other multilateral forums.

Moreover, Chinese technical aid to Africa is becoming increasingly important in building China's influence in the region. Medical, agricultural and engineering teams have provided technical aid to African countries for decades to support everything from building projects to treating AIDS patients. Since 1963, some 15,000 Chinese doctors have worked in 47 African states treating nearly 180 million cases of HIV/AIDS. At the end of 2003, 940 Chinese doctors were still working throughout the continent. Beijing prefers technical support over financial aid to African countries for obvious reasons. Financial aid stretches resources and diverts capital from significant needs at home, therefore investments in trade and projects that have a chance at providing returns are more popular than direct aid and loan programs.

China's efforts to encourage African governments to fashion their economic systems after their own is an important indication of the soft power that China hopes to ultimately project in Africa.

Finally, the Chinese government has also actively promoted its own brand of economic development and reform model to African countries, encouraging government counterparts in several countries to visit China and learn from their experience. China's efforts to encourage African governments to fashion their economic systems after its own is an important indication of the soft power that China hopes to ultimately project in Africa.

China's soft power gambit can also be seen in its heavy investments in Africa's educational systems, both by sending teachers to Africa and providing scholarships to African students from across the continent to study in Chinese universities. Between the start of the educational exchanges in the mid-1950s and 2000, 5,582 African students had enrolled in Chinese universities. These students typically spend two years learning Chinese, then study technical subjects, particularly engineering disciplines. Currently, about half of African students are pursuing advanced degrees. This support for education improves China's image in many countries and builds grassroots support in local communities and a better understanding of China among the educated elite. But more than just increasing goodwill toward Beijing, these educational programs help to provide China with the kind of workforce it requires to expand its own high-tech industries. As China's space program expands and matures, it is seeking to improve its space-tracking capabilities in the southern hemisphere. China operates a space tracking station in Namibia, and utilizes South African ports of call to support space-tracking ships.

China's investments in Africa pay an added dividend in the diplomatic effort to deny Taiwan international space through recognition by individual countries and their resulting support in multilateral forums, such as the UN. For example, China's deployment of 90 peacekeepers to Liberia in December of 2003 occurred two months after Liberia switched its diplomatic recognition from Taiwan to China, illustrating the strategic importance that African nations hold in the ongoing diplomatic struggle between Taiwan and China. Five countries in Africa currently recognize Taiwan, making up one quarter of the total. However, several African countries have played China and Taiwan against one another, seeking massive aid packages and switching recognition. In order to compete with China's dominating presence on the continent and support in international forums, Taiwan must offer substantial aid packages to its African allies. Taipei is able to concentrate its greater financial resources on the small number of countries that recognize it, while methodically approaching other countries that might consider switching recognition to it. Beijing, with more countries to support, must carefully consider its investments in countries that are likely to provide it with a stable return.

Beijing's Investment in Sudan Paying Off

China's rapidly growing demand for imported oil and other raw materials surprised world commodity and financial markets and revealed the extent to which China has invested in extractives industries in Africa in order to "lock up barrels" at their source. China, through the China National Petroleum Corporation (CNPC), is the most visible and significant investor in Sudanese oil exploration, transportation and production infrastructure. These investments enabled Sudan to begin exporting oil in 1999 and eventually become a net oil exporter. Though Sudan's production capacity of 310,000 barrels per day (bpd) in 2004 is relatively insignificant compared to the global production of approximately 82 million bpd (2004), its product is of a high quality. According to Angelina Tany, Minister of State for Mines and Energy, Sudan plans to be producing one million bbl/d of crude oil by the end of 2008. Such so-called "light-sweet crude" is in short supply in global markets, and sells at a premium over Middle Eastern crude, which has a higher sulfur content. China's investment in Sudanese oil production capacity has resulted in Sudan's output now amounting to five percent of China's total imports. Significantly, China is Sudan's single largest customer of oil, taking over half of Sudan's exports in 2003. This relationship with Sudan provides Beijing with significant diplomatic leverage over Khartoum, and puts China in a strong position to encourage Sudan to take measures to stop the violence in Darfur and even invest in social programs to promote domestic security and stability.

China's experience in promoting trade and investment relations with Sudan illustrates its broader interests in Africa, as well as some of the competitive advantages Beijing enjoys when operating in difficult environments. African countries represent a significant market for cheap Chinese-made products, which helps China maintain a favorable global balance of trade and creates jobs in China. Several African countries also present Chinese firms with an investment environment where they can compete effectively against Western multinational corporations that enjoy greater access to international capital and technology. Chinese companies have been very active investors in African infrastructure (including hydropower plants, pipelines, factories and hospitals) and are particularly competitive in countries where unreliable political situations, sanctions or other potential liabilities keep large multinationals from committing themselves. Chinese firms are not hindered at home by legal challenges from non-governmental organizations or concerned about corporate-image liabilities when investing in high-risk markets with unsavory regimes or where severe human rights abuses take place. In fact, Chinese companies are attracted to the potential for large profits in markets with less competition from multinational firms.

Conclusion

China's interests in Africa represent an opportunity for the United States and the international community. China maintains friendly relations with most African nations, particularly nations that the United States has limited contact with or diplomatic leverage over, such as Libya and Sudan. If President Bush seeks to address U.S. national security interests around the world, promoting social, political and economic development in Africa will have to become a significant priority for the administration. China can potentially be a strong ally in this effort.

But, as the United States and China seek to further their interests in Africa, whether they work together or at cross-purposes remain an open question. The United States could see China as a competitor, and become increasingly concerned about its growing spheres of influence, while China could see U.S. efforts to promote stability and democracy in Africa as an effort to cut off its access to raw materials and further contain China's professed "peaceful rise." Of course, China is always cautious of U.S. intentions, which might lead to suspicion of any overtures made to it to cooperate on issues, particularly involving other nations' internal affairs. China is likely to be initially reluctant to work with the United States on any efforts to coerce African countries to conform to a Western-centric global strategy. Concerns about the subjugation of its own interests, as well as any precedent such cooperation would set regarding a code of conduct for nations that China enjoys close relationships with, are sure to dominate Beijing's thinking on these issues. The Chinese remain wary that their cooperation on the North Korean nuclear issue might encourage Washington to seek to use their leverage on Sudan, Libya, Syria and Iran, without tangible benefits on the table for Beijing. U.S. assertions that China's effort to defuse the North Korean crisis is in its best interest might not translate as easily to problems in Africa.

Originally published in *China Brief* Volume 4 Issue 24 on December 7, 2004.

CHINA'S SOFT POWER IN AFRICA: FROM THE "BEIJING CONSENSUS" TO HEALTH DIPLOMACY

By Drew Thompson

China's relations with Africa have steadily deepened and strengthened since the founding of "new China" in 1949. Evolving from ideologically-driven interactions during the Cold War, today's China-Africa relations combine pragmatic economic and political means to achieve China's objective of establishing a world order that is peaceful and conducive to continued economic growth and stability at home. In the 1960s and 1970s, China supported liberation movements in several African countries, gave aid to socialist nations to build stadiums, hospitals, railroads and other infrastructure and cemented relations through a steady stream of expert engineers, teachers and doctors. Today, Chinese officials travel to Africa accompanied by bankers and businesspeople, promoting political and economic commerce that expands China-Africa ties in a sustainable fashion. While trade and diplomacy are driven by China's newfound economic strength and subsequent demand for raw materials, China continues to support longstanding programs that deliver aid to underserved African citizens, such as sending teams of doctors and providing medicines. Following the framework set out by the first Forum on China-Africa Cooperation Forum (FOCAC) in 2000, China-Africa relations are set to advance through a combination of traditional financial aid and technical support programs, along with rapidly growing bilateral trade and investment.

China is an appealing partner for many African countries for a variety of reasons. China's approach to bilateral relations and economic development, characterized by Joshua Cooper Ramo as the "Beijing Consensus," provides an alternative to development and political economic reforms espoused by "the West" and typified by the "Washington Consensus" of the World Bank and IMF. Beijing's consistent respect for other nations' sovereignty and steadfast refusal to criticize or involve itself in the internal affairs of African nations earns it the respect of leaders and elites who have benefited from poor governance and opaque political systems and are reluctant to implement painful economic or political reforms demanded by the West. African leaders' embrace of the "Beijing Consensus" reflects perhaps what is most attractive about Beijing's "soft power": a long-standing history of friendly ties, provision of appreciated, "no-strings-attached" financial and technical aid to both elites and the most needy, and growing commerce between the world's largest developing nation and the continent with the most developing nations.

China's Soft Power and the "Beijing Consensus"

"Soft power," following Joseph Nye's formulation, includes a country's culture, political values, foreign policies, and economic attraction as essential components of national strength, providing the capacity to persuade other nations to willingly adopt the same goals. While China's culture prevailed for centuries from the Tang Dynasty through the mid-Qing, it no longer competes with cultural icons emanating from the United States. Undeterred, Chinese leaders and businesspeople have leveraged China's strengths, which include a pragmatic approach to international relations based on the principle of non-interference in domestic affairs. China's economic development model, the "Beijing Consensus," refutes Western notions of political liberalization or economic reforms as indispensable for long-term, sustained development. China has effectively exported its notion of economic development with Chinese characteristics to its African trading partners, encouraging them to develop their economies through trade and investment in infrastructure and social institutions, without dictating terms for political or economic reforms. With an expanding manufacturing sector, China's growing need for raw materials, energy and new markets for cheap consumer goods make its economy relatively complementary to many African ones. While the light industrial manufacturing sectors in many African nations are suffering from growing imports from China, the dominant extractives industries are benefiting from Chinese capital investment as well as a seemingly bottomless market. China's respect for national sovereignty is attractive not only to Zimbabwe's

Robert Mugabe, but scores of other African nations that are reluctant to implement economic and political reforms considered necessary by Western donor institutions and countries.

China has effectively exported its notion of economic development with Chinese characteristics to its African trading partners, encouraging them to develop their economies through trade and investment in infrastructure and social institutions, without dictating terms for political or economic reforms.

The principle of non-interference does not mean that China rejects political and economic reform per se in Africa. Indeed, China is careful to support African-led efforts to develop sound governance and sustainable development throughout the continent. Recognizing that good governance and political reforms are vital to the long-term development of African nations, 19 nations have joined the "New Partnership for Africa's Development" (NEPAD), a consensus framework of the member countries to promote sustainable development, good governance and poverty reduction, and stop the marginalization of African economies in an increasingly globalized world. While China supports NEPAD, it repeatedly stresses that it does so through the framework of FOCAC, thereby avoiding the potentially awkward position of having to support the key structural elements that are ultimately necessary for NEPAD's success: transparency, democracy, free press, civil society, independent judiciary, and rule of law—all areas where China has resisted substantial reform and has relatively little to contribute technologically.

The strength of China's African relations and the source of much of its soft power stem from more than just the relatively recent growth in trade and investment. Throughout its history of cooperation with African nations, China has emphasized that it has "given what it could" in terms of financial aid and technical support and it continues to do so even as its ability to promote relations through economic incentives—primarily trade, tourism, and investment—has grown. Technical support, without political "strings attached" (other than affirmation of a "one-China policy") has remained a significant aspect of China's support for African states. Under the auspices of the FOCAC, China has committed to contributing to the development of human resources in Africa by establishing a fund that is jointly administered and used by various Chinese ministries (Foreign Affairs, Commerce, Education, Science and Technology, Agriculture and Health) in order to train African personnel. As of 2003, over 6,000 Africans had been trained as part of the program (*Beijing Review*, January 20, 2005). Scholarships for over 1,500 African students are annually awarded by China, while many Chinese universities have established relationships with African institutions (Xinhua, December 16, 2003). These programs create enduring bonds between Chinese and African institutions and individuals. While university scholarships promote closer ties between China and African elites, China has also promoted "health diplomacy" with African partners, establishing a relationship between Chinese doctors and millions of ordinary Africans, and earning the gratitude of many African leaders eager to be seen providing public goods to their citizens.

Medical Teams and Health Diplomacy as Soft Power

China has a long history of conducting active "heath diplomacy" programs with African and Middle Eastern countries. China's early relations with many African nations included significant aid in the form of infrastructure, scholarships for African elites to study in Chinese universities and the deployment of teams of doctors. Today, these institutions remain, either as direct government support or under the auspices of the FOCAC. While China's growing trade and infrastructure investments in Africa have been the subject of increasing discourse, there has been little discussion of a long-standing and still influential segment of China's soft power in Africa: health diplomacy.

Today, China regularly conducts cooperation in the field of health, including numerous ministerial visits with African leaders to facilitate the regular exchange of medical teams and training for medical professionals. China also provides medicine and medical equipment free of charge to several African countries, and has active programs to jointly prevent and treat infectious diseases including malaria and HIV/AIDS. In 2002, the Chinese Ministry of Health conducted a two-part international training course in techniques for the prevention and treatment of malaria and tropical diseases, in which 30 students from 17 African countries participated (1st International Training Course on Malaria Control, September 10, 2002). That same year, as part of the FOCAC, China convened a Sino-African forum on traditional medicine and pharmaceuticals which was attended by participants from 21 African countries (World Health Association, October 31, 2002).

China deployed its first medical team in 1964 at the invitation of the Algerian government. Since then, China has cumulatively sent over 15,000 doctors to more than 47 African countries and treated approximately 180 million African patients with cases of HIV/AIDS. In 2003, China deployed a total of 860 medical personnel in 35 teams to 34 countries (Xinhua, December 16, 2004). Chinese doctors that are part of the medical teams, known as *yiliaodui*, normally spend up to two years in-country. Many doctors have served on medical teams more than once. Additionally, Chinese military medical units have been deployed on UN Peacekeeping operations in Africa, providing medical assistance to other peacekeepers (many of whom are from African nations), as well as civilians. The PLA Navy's number 401 hospital in Qingdao has also sent medical teams to Zambia in the past. Civilian medical cooperation is institutionalized with the health bureaus of individual Chinese provinces, thus maintaining long-term commitments to provide medical workers and aid to specific countries.

Chinese Provincial Health Bureau Medical Team Cooperation with African Countries*

Table:

Chinese Province	African State
Fujian	Botswana
Gansu	Madagascar
Guangdong	Equatorial Guinea
Guangxi	Niger, Comoro
Henan	Zambia, Eritrea, Ethiopia
Hubei	Algeria, Lesotho
Hunan	Sierra Leone, Cape Verde, Zimbabwe
Inner Mongolia	Rwanda
Jiangxi	Tunisia
Ningxia	Benin
Qinghai	Burundi
Shaanxi	Mauritania, Guinea, Sudan
Shandong	Tanzania, Seychelles
Shanghai	Morocco
Shanxi	Togo, Cameroon, Djibouti
Sichuan	Mozambique, Guinea Bissau
Tianjin	Republic of Congo (Brazzaville)
Yunnan	Uganda
Zhejiang	Mali, Namibia, Central Africa

*Tibet, Xinjiang, Guizhou and Hainan do not dispatch medical teams abroad. Other Chinese provinces not listed here dispatch medical teams to other developing countries outside of Africa.

This long-term medical cooperation builds person-to-person relations between Africans and Chinese, and brings benefits to both sides. Like the many sports stadiums, highways, and other infrastructure such as the Tanzania-Zambia Railroad built in 1976 (and refurbished in 2005) by the Chinese, the medical teams are publicized by both Chinese and African leaders as a tangible public good. Yet China's capacity to send large numbers of medical doctors to Africa is limited, and the program faces an uncertain future over the long term. Many provincial budgets are increasingly stretched by a shrinking tax base since rural tax reforms have been implemented. The health needs of many Chinese are also not being met, and government doctors are increasingly called upon to deal with public health issues at home. Additionally, given that the Chinese medical system is increasingly privatized, more doctors are less inclined to accept a two-year posting in Africa, particularly because they currently subsidize their meager government stipend with income generated through patient fees and medicine sales. Medical bureaus in some wealthy provinces have reportedly been forced to recruit doctors from inland provinces in order to fulfill their *yilaodui* obligations.

The ability to "see no evil" is a convenient aspect of the "Beijing Consensus," and its rejection of unpalatable aspects, such as economic "shock therapy" or political reform, makes China all the more welcome in many African capitals.

African support for the program remains strong, however, as evidenced by the willingness of participating countries to sign biannual treaties that invite the teams and settle the terms of the mission. According to the treaties negotiated between China and the countries receiving medical teams, all but the poorest of the recipient countries pay the medical team's expenses, such as international airfares, doctor and support staff stipends (including Chinese cooks), as well as the cost of some medicine and equipment that is brought by the team. For the poorest countries, China covers the costs of the team's travel and the equipment and medicines that the teams import with them, permitting the hospitals where they work to sell the drugs to help the countries cover the cost of hosting the medical teams. Granted, while many countries offset the costs of paying the expenses and salaries of the medical teams with grants and loans from China or other donor nations, host nations repeatedly demonstrate their appreciation by continuing the program and covering the expenses of the team out of national budgets. Medical teams are also regularly given national awards in Africa and China for their contributions.

China's influence and sound relationships in Africa are the result of many years of investment in building relations through aid, trade, and cultural and technical exchange—not just the byproduct of China's recently booming economy and soaring demand for African raw materials. China's strong sense of national sovereignty and willingness to conduct commerce without political "strings" certainly contribute to its success. The ability to "see no evil" is a convenient aspect of the "Beijing Consensus," and its rejection of unpalatable aspects, such as economic "shock therapy" or political reform, makes China all the more welcome in many African capitals. China's approach to Africa, including the way it conducts business and the provision of aid, technical support, and the dispatch of medical teams, comprises key components of China's influence on the continent.

Originally published in *China Brief* Volume 5 Issue 21 on October 13, 2005.

HU'S SAFARI: CHINA'S EMERGING STRATEGIC PARTNERSHIPS IN AFRICA

By Wenran Jiang

Chinese President Hu Jintao wrapped up his eight-country, twelve-day African tour in February 2007 in the midst of controversy regarding China's role in the continent. Government officials from the countries that received China's leader expressed gratitude for their guest's generous offers of aid, cancellations of debt and promises of trade and investment. Critics, however, charge that China's actions in Africa are nothing less than neocolonialism, as it seizes a new sphere of influence, grabs oil and other resources, props up repressive regimes and leaves individual African countries on the losing end. Beijing has refuted such characterizations by identifying itself with the developing world, stressing the reciprocal nature of its interactions with Africa and promising a new paradigm of China-Africa partnership based on traditional friendship.

Beijing's Unprecedented Focus on Africa

The international attention on China's relations with Africa is in part a result of the Chinese leadership's decision to make the resource-rich continent one of its foreign policy priorities in recent years. Hu's February 2007 trip to Africa is his second within a span of one year, the third as China's president and the fifth since he became a member of the Politburo in the early 1990s. In the summer of 2006, Chinese Premier Wen Jiabao toured seven African countries. Since 2004, six senior Chinese leaders from the nine-member Politburo Standing Committee of the Chinese Communist Party (CCP) have visited Africa, covering most of the countries on the continent [1]. The Chinese foreign minister's decision to select an African country as his first foreign trip of each year since 1991 indicates the extensive focus that Chinese leaders have placed upon Africa and, in doing so, reveals the importance that Beijing has attached to that part of the world.

The watershed event in Sino-African relations was the elaborate Forum on China-Africa Cooperation (FOCAC) summit held in Beijing in November 2006. As a part of the 2006 "China's Year of Africa" and in commemoration of the 50th anniversary of China's diplomatic relationship with Africa, 48 out of the 53 African countries sent their leaders to Beijing for a gathering that no other country in the world has yet been able to assemble. Beijing's streets and subways were filled with celebratory signs; President Hu, standing at the Great Hall of the People, received all 48 African leaders, most of them presidents or prime ministers; and over the course of the following days, promised a long list of future initiatives of cooperation bundled with generous financial incentives:

- A "new type of China-Africa strategic partnership," characterized by "political equality and mutual trust, economic win-win cooperation and cultural exchanges," was announced as an overall framework in bilateral relations.

- Additional high-level bilateral visits in order to maintain the positive momentum of Sino-African relations were proposed. The foreign ministers of China and the African countries "will hold political consultations in New York on the sideline of the UN General Assembly to exchange views on major issues of common interest."

- China and Africa will work to more than double the current trade volumes by 2010, reaching $100 billion in bilateral trade.

- China will encourage investment in Africa by setting up a China-Africa development fund amounting to $5 billion and establishing special economic zones in Africa.

- Beijing will provide African countries with $3 billion in preferential loans in the next three years, while also canceling $1 billion of debt from African countries.

- Trade deals signed between Chinese and African corporations during the summit totaled $1.9 billion.

- In addition to providing a $37.5 million grant for anti-malarial drugs in the next three years, Beijing will assist African countries in building 30 hospitals and 30 demonstration centers for the prevention and treatment of malaria

- China will build 100 rural schools in Africa over the next three years and double the number of current scholarships given to African students to study in China from 2,000 to 4,000 by 2009 [2].

The Three Notables: Sudan, Zambia and South Africa

President Hu's much publicized African trip is clearly a strategic step and a committed follow-up to the FOCAC summit. To carry out Beijing's promise of enhanced cooperation, Hu delivered offers and initiatives at every stop of his eight-country tour. Three particular countries on Hu's itinerary, however, generated more headlines than the others: Sudan, Zambia and South Africa. Each country represents a specific challenge that Beijing faces in its African diplomacy.

Of the three countries, China has the most significant energy interests in Sudan, and its oil companies have been operating in the country since the departure of the Western oil majors in the mid-1990s. The state-owned China National Petroleum Corporation (CNPC) has the largest overseas production in Sudan, and other Chinese firms have also invested heavily in refineries, pipelines and other infrastructure projects. Bilateral trade reached $2.9 billion in the first eleven months of 2006. China is Sudan's largest trading partner, while Sudan is China's third-largest trading partner in Africa (Reuters, January 24, 2007). In recent years, Beijing has been facing increased international criticism for its unwillingness to use its significant economic leverage to persuade the Sudanese government to cease its sponsorship of atrocities in the Darfur region. In what seemed to be a response to the criticism and possibly a departure from China's traditional policy of non-interference in other countries' domestic affairs, Hu presented a four-point proposal on seeking a resolution on Darfur during his meeting with Sudanese President Omar Hassan Ahmed al-Bashir. The most important point was Hu's support of a United Nations peacekeeping mission in Darfur (*People's Daily*, February 3, 2007). While it is too early to conclude from such a mild case of "interference" that there are any major changes in China's foreign policy tenets, Hu's Sudan encounter clearly reflects Beijing's desire to stabilize Sudan and to be perceived as a responsible power by the international community.

In Zambia, the rapid influx of Chinese businessmen and investment in the country's rich copper and other commodity sectors has resulted in accusations that many of the Chinese owners have exploited the local workers. Not long ago, the opposition leader in Zambia's election ran on an anti-China platform, and though he lost the election, accusations of low wages and other mistreatment in Chinese-owned mines linger. Hu's stop in Zambia was marked by efforts from both sides to defuse criticisms, with Beijing offering Zambia $800 million in special loans and canceling $350 million in debts that Zambia owed to China. The two governments also announced the establishment of a special economic zone (*Xingdao Huanqiu*, February 4, 2007). While Hu emphatically rejected the view that China is simply replacing the old colonial powers, interested in extracting Africa's resources for its own economic benefits, China's own record of labor protection during the past three decades is a troubling one; extraordinary efforts will be required if fair labor laws are to be strictly enforced abroad.

China's presence in South Africa is likewise being questioned, though the debate has been centered upon the extent to which bilateral economic ties between the two countries are competitive or complementary. South Africa is China's largest trading partner on the continent, with bilateral trade totaling $6.3 billion in 2005, up 42.4 percent year-on-year (*China Daily*, January 30, 2007). As the most advanced economy in Africa, South Africa's domestic economy has received serious challenges from the arrival of Chinese products. There are significant concerns that Chinese imports are resulting in the loss of manufacturing jobs in South Africa. Facing concerns that South Africa may end up in a neocolonial relationship, exporting resources to China and receiving more expensive valued-added manufacturing goods in return—a familiar pattern that characterizes Africa's past colonial trade relations with Europe—Hu pledged to address the issue of trade imbalances between China and Africa, which are heavily in China's favor.

Africa a Zero-Sum Game?

Regarding the prospects of further China-Africa cooperation, the issues raised during Hu's Feburary 2007 trip to Africa will almost certainly surface again. *Zhongnanhai's* economic interests in the continent as well as its global aspirations guarantee that China will not be disengaging from Africa in the near future. In fact, China's policymakers and academics will pay even closer attention to these contentious problems, and Beijing is likely to continue to adjust its policies toward Africa in order to both advance its relations with the continent and to fend off international criticism.

Zhongnanhai's economic interests in the continent as well as its global aspirations guarantee that China will not be disengaging from Africa in the near future.

Such resolve may only be reinforced, rather than weakened, by the recent decision of the U.S. military to create an Africa Command (USAFRICOM). The fact that the announcement coincided with President Hu's tour of Africa may lead China to believe that the United States intends to compete with it for both geopolitical influence and resources on the continent. Yet, such a move is likely to reinforce Beijing's awareness of the current limitations of its global reach, and could strengthen the voices inside China's military and policymaking circles that call for the development of even greater power projection capabilities.

The irony is that both China and the United States have similar interests in gaining access to Africa's vast energy and raw material resources, and both require a stable environment on the continent in order for them to achieve their objectives. The two major powers could also work together to tackle many of the development problems facing African countries. It is therefore in Beijing's interests to forge a truly "win-win" situation in its relations with Africa, while exploring a cooperative framework with the United States and the EU countries to ensure that the major powers do not engage in hostile policies that harm both the African people as well as their own interests.

Originally published in *China Brief* Volume 7 Issue 4 on February 21, 2007.

Notes

1. Data assembled by the author through the special report on Hu Jintao's Africa trip at http://politics.people.com.cn/GB/1024/5388818.html.
2. "Action plan adopted at China-Africa summit, mapping cooperation course" Beijing Summit & Third Ministerial Conference of Forum on China-Africa Cooperation, http://english.focacsummit.org/2006-11/05/content_5167.htm, (English); http://www.focacsummit.org/zxbd/2006-11/05/content_5186.htm (Chinese).

CHINA AND AFRICA: A NEW SCRAMBLE?

By Mauro De Lorenzo

While the question of China's growing role in Africa has attracted wide attention over recent years, the intensity of the debate has not always been proportional to the actual extent of China's role on the continent. China's footprint in Africa is indeed expanding, as is that of the United States, Europe, India and many other countries that are looking to Africa as a trade and investment partner. Since 2001, every industrialized country has markedly increased its trade with Africa, principally with oil and gas purchases. As more and more African conflicts find resolution and as African governments continue to improve their regulatory environment, this growth of foreign— including Chinese— activities is a predictable consequence.

What distinguishes China's involvement in Africa from that of other nations is that it is accompanied by a clear government policy in support of African commercial ventures, abundant financing and tax benefits for Chinese firms operating abroad and robust diplomacy toward the region [1]. State-owned Chinese companies can depend on the Ministry of Commerce, which manages most Chinese aid programs, to add sweeteners to bids for African government contracts or assets. A $5 billion oil-backed concessional loan was a prominent feature of the massive energy deals struck in Angola in 2005-2006, for example. With the announcement of a $5 billion investment fund for Africa at the Beijing Summit of the Forum on China-Africa Cooperation (FOCAC) in November 2006, we can expect more deals that combine aid and investment.

Meanwhile, thanks to the pageantry associated with the Beijing Summit in November 2006 and the numerous extended visits paid to Africa by President Hu Jintao, Premier Wen Jiabao and Foreign Minister Li Zhaoxing, the high visibility of China's new profile in Africa has served as a target for Western concerns about the consequences of China's economic and military rise, and of its true intentions in regions where it previously had few interests and little influence. While China proclaims benign intentions—"mutual benefit" and "win-win cooperation" are the catchphrases—it may not fully appreciate the possible consequences of its methods of delivering aid upon African politics.

Trade, Investment and Aid

There are three main components to China's economic engagement in Africa that are not always distinguished: trade, investment and aid. First, Chinese trade with Africa increased from $11 billion to $40 billion between 2000 and 2005, becoming Africa's third largest trading partner [2]. Most of the increase comes from oil imports from Sudan, where China's companies have been active since 1995, and Angola, where they made major energy investments in 2003-2004. It is, however, important to consider these figures together with Africa's increased trade with Europe and North America. It has also grown, though less slowly, and continues to constitute the destination for the majority of Africa's exports. An important difference, however, is that the increase in Chinese trade with Africa is driven by "complementarities" between the two economies, whereas increased trade with North America and Europe has resulted from preferential trade arrangements, such as the African Growth and Opportunity Act (AGOA).

There are three main components to China's economic engagement in Africa that are not always distinguished: trade, investment and aid.

Second, Chinese investment in Africa is increasing, but still represents a small fraction of China's total Foreign Direct Investment (FDI) stock. The stock of Chinese FDI in Africa in 2005 was $1.6 billion, which represented only 3 percent of China's total FDI. Most Chinese investment was directed to Asia (53 percent) and Latin America (37 percent). The period 2003-2005 saw massive increases of Chinese FDI outflows to all parts of the world, not just to Africa [3].

Third, Chinese aid is now set to increase dramatically as well, and it is here that we can expect to see the most profound challenges to Africa's relationships with the rest of the world. China has had aid programs in Africa since the 1960s, but with the exception of the rail line between Tanzania and Zambia and a number of stadiums around the continent, the impact left by Chinese aid was not great. World Bank chief Paul Wolfowitz has called China to account for lending to countries that have recently benefited from the Heavily Indebted Poor Countries (HIPC) loan forgiveness program. The value of Chinese aid in Africa is set to overtake World Bank assistance in 2007 with $8.1 billion on offer compared with only $2.3 billion from the Bank (Bloomberg, November 3, 2006).

The Chinese "aid" now on offer is intimately tied to its commercial expansion and often comes in the form of credits from the Export-Import Bank of China (China Exim Bank). The Beijing Summit also announced a token expansion of more purely humanitarian aid programs, such as the dispatching of 300 "young volunteers" to Africa and the pledge of establishing 100 rural schools in the continent before 2009. Beijing sees aid-giving as a way of generating positive sentiment toward China, and seems unaware of the consequences it can have on governance and economic performance, particularly when channeled through weak and undemocratic national governments. To the extent that Western donors have begun to learn some of the lessons from the poor performance of their previous aid programs, increased Chinese aid-giving could be a setback for sound economic policy-making and democratic accountability in Africa.

A View from the Great Lakes of Africa

With no energy resources, Rwanda and Burundi are not high priorities for China, but they are strategically situated next to the resource-rich Democratic Republic of the Congo, where China has growing interests. Discussions are underway to start a Confucius Institute at the Kigali Institute of Science and Technology in 2007, and Rwanda would like to entice Chinese companies doing business in the sub-region to locate their headquarters in Kigali [4]. However, though China's engagement in both countries is on the increase, it has hardly reached the tsunami-like proportions that breathless media reports about China re-colonizing Africa would suggest.

In Rwanda, there has actually been little new Chinese investment since 2004. The Rwanda Investment and Export Promotion Agency (RIEPA) has issued no incentive-qualification certificates to Chinese companies over the past year or so. Most of the Chinese companies that are active in Rwanda are in the construction sector and have been working there since the 1970s or 1980s, such as the China National Road and Bridge Company, which has won significant contracts from the Rwandan government. New entrants include telecommunications companies *Zhongxing* and *Huawei*, with which the U.S.-Rwandan telephone company, Terracom, recently signed a deal to upgrade its network technology. The number of Chinese restaurants has expanded by 50 percent: from two to three.

Many of the Chinese actors on the ground are small-scale, private entrepreneurs or traders [5]. The owner of the new Chinese restaurant in Kigali first came to the country in 1996—to open a medical clinic; Chinese medicine has been extremely popular in East Africa since at least the 1980s. This tallies with UN Conference on Trade and Development's (UNCTAD) finding that most Chinese investments in Africa are small and medium-sized enterprises (SMEs)—and thus only indirectly motivated by the high-level Chinese "go abroad" policy and its attendant incentives. Chinese firms are present in the Rwandan market, but they are not particularly central and hardly dominant. There are also none of the complaints about Chinese traders that are commonly heard in Zambia or South Africa. Chinese diplomats lament how "conservative" and "short-sighted" their compatriots are: very few end up investing despite promises of embassy support in bidding for contracts.

Rwanda was the first African country to open a permanent trade office in China. It is based in Shenzhen, and staffed by two Rwandans, one of whom has lived in China for 12 years and speaks Mandarin fluently. It assists Rwandan importers who visit Hong Kong and the factories of Guangdong in search of electronics and textiles that sell well in Rwanda and the sub-region. The office has had less success in enticing Chinese entrepreneurs to invest in Rwanda, though a mobile-phone assembly facility for the local market is being planned in Rwanda by a Chinese-Rwandan joint venture. The office found that its most urgent task in China was much more basic: reassuring Chinese businesspeople that Rwandans did not live in trees, that Chinese visitors would not be hacked to death in a flare-up of the genocide, and that there is food to eat. A poster showing a bare-chested Rwandan traditional dancer was removed from the office because it was giving visitors the wrong impression about how most Rwandans dress.

The views of senior Rwandan officials toward China are positive and welcoming, but do not rise to adulation. They had a good experience at the Beijing Summit, but are waiting to see how China's promises of increased cooperation will be translated into action. While they are concerned that Rwandans might be taken advantage of by Chinese firms and prefer Chinese investment over aid, Rwanda is allowing China to build the new headquarters for its foreign ministry. The rest of China's aid program in Rwanda—some small health and agriculture programs and the management of a government-owned cement plant—is not significant enough that it would give the government significant "leverage" with the World Bank or bilateral donors. Even with the increased commitments announced in Beijing, there is little chance that China will soon rival the hundreds of millions of dollars a year that Rwanda receives from U.S. and European sources. A Chinese diplomat stated privately that there were no plans to respond to one of the Rwandan government's top infrastructure priorities—a railway to Tanzania and the coast—because it would be "uneconomical." China is financing the equally uneconomical Benguela Railroad rehabilitation in Angola, a major oil supplier.

In neighboring Burundi, where a gleaming new Chinese embassy was recently completed by a company brought in from China, an embassy official expressed his disappointment that the company had decided to return to China rather than establish a permanent presence in the region; the company saw high risks and few returns. Tianshi Health Products, however, proudly flies the Chinese flag over their new office in Bujumbura. In line with paragraph 4.4 of China's January 2006 Africa Policy, which declared that "it is necessary to increase intelligence exchange," some members of the Burundian intelligence service have undergone training in China, according to a foreign human rights researcher who saw photographs of the training in the offices of the Burundian security service. At the official opening of parliament in February 2007, Burundi's only admiral proudly wore a pin he had received during an exchange visit to China. Whether such military and intelligence cooperation is as practical as it is ceremonial is difficult to ascertain.

Though not representative of the continent as a whole, China's engagement in Rwanda and Burundi has not dramatically increased over the past three years. Yet, neither is the engagement of China in oil-producing states like Angola and Sudan representative of the rest of the continent. The China-Africa question is not spontaneously discussed, and is not often in the media. With the exception of some importers, the countries' political and economic elites continue to be oriented primarily to the United States, Europe and South Africa [6].

A View from Beijing

Foreign delegations visiting Beijing to discuss China-Africa relations tend to interact primarily with a community of Africanists and aid specialists based at the Chinese Academy of Social Sciences (CASS), the China Institutes of Contemporary International Relations (CICIR) and other government-affiliated think tanks [6]. They tend to portray China as a selfless friend of African countries and make frequent reference to China's Cold War aid programs and support for African liberation movements. These scholars tend to believe that aid really can buy friendship and goodwill abroad, and also that China needs to systematize its aid apparatus if it is to be able to deliver upon the large commitments made at the Beijing Summit. There is little awareness that aid can have negative economic and political effects in the countries that receive it. There do not seem to be any mechanisms in place to monitor the effectiveness of Chinese aid, even at the most basic level of ensuring that the money is not stolen.

In discussions with U.S. delegations, the focus is often a competition to show which side is more genuinely concerned with Africa's well-being. To the frustration of African interlocutors, the discussion is rarely focused on what Africa should do to take advantage of the new opportunities that China's expanded commitment to Africa offers. To China's experts, criticism of the country's intentions and investments in Africa seems like part of a strategy by Western countries to "thwart China's development," as one scholar put it. One rumor in circulation in PLA circles suggests that U.S. intelligence agencies are planning to foment local unrest toward Chinese ventures in Africa and elsewhere in the developing world.

In off-the-record discussions, two senior Chinese scholars conceded that China should indeed "do something" when faced with genocide in Africa—though they seemed to be referring to private exchanges with African leaders rather than public denunciation or military action. China's intransigent position on Sudan seems to derive not only from China's traditional adherence to a doctrine of "non-interference in internal affairs of sovereign states," but also from a desire to thwart U.S. foreign policy, and less from any specific concern about the security of Chinese energy investments in Sudan: Sudan needs China more than China needs it. One of China's undisclosed requirements for agreeing to pressure the Sudanese government to accept the deployment of a robust UN peacekeeping force may be that Hu Jintao, rather than George W. Bush, takes the credit. As one Chinese blogger exulted during President Hu's trip to Africa in February 2007: "Our brother Hu thawed the Darfur crisis with his cordial smile! The United Nations peacekeeping force is going to station in Darfur with his cordial smile! Bush failed, brother Hu succeeded with a smile! Sino-Africa friendship is true friendship!" [7].

Originally published in *China Brief*: Volume 7 Issue 7 on April 5, 2007.

Notes

1. See the "Forum on China-Africa Cooperation Beijing Action Plan (2007-2009)," the key document emanating from the Beijing Summit in November 2006. It recapitulates and expands the Chinese government white paper on policy towards Africa issued in January 2006.
2. *Asian Foreign Direct Investment in Africa: Towards a New Era of Cooperation among Developing Nations*, UNCTAD/UNDP, (New York: March 2007), 56.
3. Ibid.
4. "Confucius Institute at Kigali Institute of Education," The Office of Chinese Language Council International, January 20, 2007, http://www.hanban.edu.cn/en_hanban/content.php?id=2439.
5. Based upon this author's observations during his several visits to the Great Lakes region.
6. For a good indication of Rwanda's priorities, see this article about President Kagame's address to the Starbucks board of directors in March 2007 and his expanding relations with American CEOs: Marc Gunther, "Why CEOs love Rwanda," *Fortune*, April 3, 2007, http://money.cnn.com/2007/03/28/news/companies/pluggedin_Gunther_Rwanda.fortune/?postversion=2007032910.
7. Jennifer Brea, "Chinese Perceptions of Hu's Visit to Africa," Africabeat, http://jenbrea.typepad.com/africabeat/2007/02/who_is_visiting.html.

RESOURCES, SECURITY AND INFLUENCE: THE ROLE OF THE MILITARY IN CHINA'S AFRICA STRATEGY

By Susan M. Puska

Of all the elements of growing national power China now wields to promote its national interests in Africa, its military's role raises the most anxiety. Beijing's Africa strategy to promote China's economic (resource access and trade) and political (One China recognition) interests explicitly tie in the People's Liberation Army (PLA) to support overall peace and security for its interests in Africa. The strategy tasks the PLA with conducting high-level and technological military cooperation and exchanges, training African military personnel and "support[ing] defense and army building" in African countries [1]. Additionally, the PLA (and police) support China's Africa strategy through participation in United Nations Peacekeeping Operations (PKO), and non-traditional missions, such as combating terrorism, small arms smuggling, drug trafficking and transnational economic crimes. Consequently, the PLA now maintains a growing military presence on the African continent. The estimates range from approximately 1,200 soldiers, including PKO forces, to over 5,000 [2]. Its military-to-military contacts extend throughout the continent, reaching at least 43 countries to provide a network of military relations from which to shape its future role in Africa.

Defense Attaché Representation

Chinese Embassy defense attaché offices throughout Africa provide the diplomatic foundation for China's military contacts. Accredited defense attaches link the PLA to host country militaries. Defense attaché duties vary, but as a minimum, Chinese attaches report on local matters from a military and/or security perspective, and facilitate contacts with local armed forces. China currently maintains bilateral diplomatic military relations with at least 25 African countries, spread across the main regions of the continent.

At least 14 out of the 107 Chinese military attaché offices worldwide are in African countries. Collectively, these offices hold at least 30 diplomatically accredited military officers, in addition to support personnel. They are located in Algeria, Democratic Republic of the Congo, Egypt, Ethiopia, Liberia, Libya, Morocco, Mozambique, Namibia, Nigeria, Sudan, Tunisia, Zambia and Zimbabwe. In Beijing, 18 African countries maintain permanent defense attaché offices [3]. Six of these offices were directly reciprocal: Algeria (which has continuously maintained a defense attaché in Beijing since January 1971), Egypt, Namibia, Nigeria, Sudan, Zambia, and Zimbabwe. The eleven remaining countries that do not have known Chinese resident equivalents in Africa include Burundi, Cameroon, Republic of Congo, Cote d'Ivoire, Equatorial Guinea, Guinea-Bissau, Kenya, Mali, Niger, South Africa and Tanzania.

Since 1985, China has almost doubled the number of defense attaché offices worldwide from 59 to 107 [4]. In Africa, however, the number of Chinese defense attaché offices increased quite modestly from only nine to 14, maintaining an average of 15 percent of all of China's defense attaché offices over the past 20 years. In contrast, China has a defense attaché office in practically every capital in Europe.

Reported Defense-to-Military Activities

China divides its primary bilateral military activities with foreign countries into four main categories [5]:

1. Major Military Exchanges: Between 2001 and 2006, Chinese military leaders visited Africa over 30 times, touring virtually every country that recognizes China. These visits often included more than one country, but several of the countries received multiple stopovers by Chinese military leaders. Of

these, Egypt, by far, welcomed the highest number of Chinese senior delegations—15 during the course of these six years. Additionally, China's still rare naval ship visits have included stops in Africa. Rear Admiral Huang Jiang led the first PLA Navy (PLAN) ship visit, consisting of the *Shenzhen*, China's newest Luhai-class guided missile destroyer at the time, and the *Nancang* supply ship to Africa in July 2000 (*People's Daily*, May 29, 2000). A 2002 naval ship visit by a fleet composed of a guided missile destroyer, the *Qingdao*, and a supply ship, the *Taicang*, included Egypt (*People's Daily*, June 18, 2002).

2. Chinese Bilateral Security Consultations: Between 2001 and 2006, China conducted 110 bilateral security-related meetings and consultations. The number of biannual bilateral defense-related talks jumped from 33 between 2003 and 2004, to 46 during 2005 and 2006. Despites this overall increase, South Africa is the only African country that holds security consultations with China [6]. South Africa and China initiated the Meeting of the Sino-South African Defense Committee on April 2003 in Pretoria, where Xiong Guangkai, Deputy Chief of the General Staff, represented the Chinese. Since then, South Africa and China have had three subsequent meetings that have alternated between South Africa and China. The most recent meeting was held in December 2006 in Pretoria.

3. Joint Exercises: Between August 2005 and December 2006, China conducted joint military exercises (including maritime search and rescue and counter-terrorism scenarios) with India, Pakistan, Russia, Tajikistan, Thailand, Shanghai Cooperation Organization (SCO), and the United States. No African states have yet been included in the joint exercises with China, either bilaterally or multilaterally.

4. Peacekeeping Operations: China has participated in United Nations PKOs since 1990 [7]. As of March 2007, China ranked 13th as a contributor of military and police to UN missions worldwide. Its support includes 1,572 troops, 63 military observers and 174 police. During this same period, Pakistan ranked first with over 10,000 personal; the United States ranked 43rd [8]. China's largest contributions include the United Nations Interim Force in Lebanon (343), and three of the six African PKO missions:

United Nations Mission in the Sudan (UNMIS) – Established in March 2005 to support the implementation of the January 2005 Comprehensive Peace Agreement between the Government of Sudan and the Sudan People's Liberation Movement/Army. It was expanded in August 2006 to include the implementation of the Darfur Peace Agreement. UNMIS provides some humanitarian assistance, as well as protection and promotion of human rights. China contributes 446 out of the 8,766 soldiers, 9 of the 662 police, and 14 of the 599 military observers.

United Nations Operation in Cote d'Ivoire (UNOCI) – Established in April 2004 to facilitate the implementation of the peace agreement signed by Ivorian parties in January 2003. China contributes seven out of the 200 military observers. UNOCI also includes 7,854 soldiers and 1,187 police.

United Nations Mission in Liberia (UNMIL) – Established in September 2003 to support the Comprehensive Peace Agreement, it protects UN staff, facilities and civilians; supports humanitarian and human rights activities; and assists in national security reform, including national police training and the formation of a restructured military. China contributes 565 out of the 13,841 soldiers, 18 of the 1,201 police and three of the 214 military observers.

United Nations Mission in the Democratic Republic of the Congo (MONUC) – Established in November 1999 to support the implementation of the Lusaka Accord, its current mission is to carry out disarmament, demobilization, repatriation, resettlement and reintegration (DDRRR). The final phase of its mission, concurrently in process, is to facilitate transition to "credible" elections. China contributes 218 out of the 16,594 soldiers and 12 of the 713 military observers. The mission also has 1,029 police.

United Nations Mission in Ethiopia and Eritrea (UNMEE) – Established in July 2000 to verify the ceasefire agreement between Eritrea and Ethiopia, brokered by Algeria and the Organization of African Unity. China contributes seven out of the 202 military observers. The mission also has 1,594 soldiers.

United Nations Mission for the Referendum in Western Sahara (MINURSO) – The mission was set up in September 1991 to monitor the ceasefire between the Government of Morocco and the Frente Polisario, and to organize and conduct a referendum on the territory's status. The UN mandate was recently extended until October 2007 [9]. China contributes 13 out of the 195 military observers. MINURSO also includes 28 soldiers and 6 police.

Other Chinese Military Activities in Africa

China's military-to-military activities in Africa also include working level professional contacts, such as military aid and assistance to local militaries in the form of "donations" and technical support, training, and exchanges; arms sales related support; and professional education. Military cooperation in Africa has almost exclusively focused on bilateral cooperation, but in 2003, China participated in a multilateral military environmental protection conference hosted by South Africa, which may indicate a future direction for multilateral military engagement in selected areas [10].

Potential for an Expanded Chinese Military Role in the Future

China's military-to-military activities in Africa, including defense attaché presence, naval ship visits, arms sales, and other missions to support military cooperation can be expected to expand to keep pace with China's growing national interests throughout the region. An increase in its diplomatic military representation and overall presence may inadvertently be encouraged by the establishment of the new United States Africa Combatant Command, if China feels a new combatant command impinges on China's security interests in the region.

If China's limited number of defense attaché offices in Africa do grow, the potential list of countries would likely begin among the eleven that have already established offices in Beijing, but lack a reciprocal counterpart in Africa, as discussed above. Resource access and associated security needs would likely influence any expansion of China's defense attaché offices in Africa. Four of the six countries that China currently maintains reciprocal, resident defense attaché offices with—Algeria, Egypt, Nigeria, and Sudan—are among those countries that China has interests in petroleum and other resources. Gabon and Equatorial Guinea, who are among the main producers of petroleum in Africa and already have established defense attaché offices in Beijing, would be logical additions to China's resident defense attaché offices.

China will increasingly be challenged to respond to security threats to Chinese property and personnel in the region that may necessitate a re-evaluation of the role of China's military.

Military and naval ship visits are also expected to develop. China may enter into agreements with African countries beyond South Africa to establish bilateral defense consultations, and joint exercises under the framework of anti-terrorist or maritime safety scenarios could be an outcome of China's increased military capability and overall interest in Africa.

Finally, China will increasingly be challenged to respond to security threats to Chinese property and personnel in the region that may necessitate a re-evaluation of the role of China's military. The recent kidnappings and killings of Chinese workers in Ethiopia and Nigeria painfully demonstrated that China can no longer depend upon local security forces to protect its oil interests (personnel and facilities) in areas such as Ethiopia and the Niger

Delta. Potential attacks by local insurgents, criminals, and even terrorists, demand skilled defense practitioners. The PLA could provide this either directly and openly in tailored military units with or without Chinese police force participation, through quasi-military or "outsourced" rent-a-soldier security entities that would be manned by trained soldiers who may retain loose association with the PLA as demobilized soldiers, or through other mechanisms based on negotiations with the host African countries.

Implications of Chinese Military Presence in Africa for the United States

While China's military-to-military contacts with Africa have been quite modest, anxiety over China's activities in Africa exceeds the present extent of military activities for several reasons. Among these are questions about China's future military capabilities and its intentions in the region. China's arms sale practices, particularly to Sudan, demonstrate its willingness to look the other way when sovereign states commit genocide and persecution of its citizenry, if it serves China's national interests—in this case, access to oil. Even as China has responded to international pressure to nudge the Sudanese regime toward the settlement of the Darfur crisis, it is woefully late. Furthermore, China's newfound support for the resolution of the Darfur tragedy may be short-lived and ineffective, merely a tactical move to counter the bad press that could overshadow the 2008 Olympics in Beijing. There is certainly no indication China will fundamentally reassess its indiscriminant arms sale practices in Sudan.

China's modern self-identity as a leader of the developing world moralistically insists it could never exploit weaker states. As its power and wealth grow, however, China will be increasingly judged for its actions.

Although China is not alone in placing its national interests and growing demand for resources above the interests of African states, China's modern self-identity as a leader of the developing world moralistically insists it could never exploit weaker states. As its power and wealth grow, however, China will be increasingly judged for its actions.

The implications for U.S. interests in Africa need not lead to a confrontational competition in response to China's growing military profile. There is plenty of work to do in Africa, and the Africans themselves will ultimately decide what courses to follow. China has a constructive role to play in Africa and provides both a useful model for the successful modernization of a developing country, and also has a long-standing relationship, including military-to-military contacts, with many nations on the continent. The United States and others will do well to continue to press China on issues of concern, such as Darfur, but also to look for opportunities to work bilaterally and multilaterally with China and its military in the region.

Originally published in *China Brief*, Volume 7 Issue 11 on May 30, 2007.

Notes

1. "China's African Policy," Embassy of the People's Republic of China in the Republic of South Africa, January 2006, http://www.china-embassy.org.za/eng/zfgx/zgyfzgx/t230687.htm [accessed July 13, 2006].
2. For the high end of this estimate, see Peter Brookes and Ji Hye Shin, "China's Influence in Africa: Implications for the United States," Backgrounder, No. 1916, The Heritage Foundation, February 22, 2003. Estimates of 1,200 soldiers are based primarily on UN PKO statistics, as of March 2007, and an estimate of Chinese military attaché representation throughout the continent.
3. Information is accurate as of March 2007. Beijing Military Attaché Corps in Beijing, http://www.bjmac.org [accessed April 29, 2007].

4. China's National Defense in 2006, http://news.xinhuaanet.com/english/2006-12/29/conten_5547029_22.htm [accessed May 11, 2007]; Directory of PRC Military Personalities, October 2006; Kenneth W. Allen and Eric A. McVadon, "China's Foreign Military Relations," Report #32, The Henry Stimson Center, Washington, D.C., October 1999.

5. The 2004 and 2006 National Defense White Papers provide detailed information on China's military-to-military activities by country and type of contact. Available online at http://www.china.org.cn/e-white/

6. Among African countries, it is highly likely that China also conducts ongoing bilateral defense consultations with Sudan, and possibly Zimbabwe, as a minimum to support arms sales.

7. United Nations Peacekeeping, http://www.un.org/Depts/dpko/dpko/ [accessed April 2007] and Appendix V, China's National Defense in 2006, Information Office of the Sate Council of the People's Republic of China, December 2006, Beijing.

8. Contribution statistics are accurate as of March 2007. Available online at http://www.un.org/Depts/dpko/dpko/contributors/ [accessed April 24, 2007].

9. United Nations Security Council Resolution 1754 (2007) adopted by the Security Council on April 30, 2007.

10. Attendee List of the August 4-8, 2003 Military Integrated Environmental Management Conference is available online at https://www.denix.osd.mil/denix/Public/Intl/S-African/Miem/Documents/namelists.html.

Appendix 1

Military High-Level Visits to Africa 2001-2006

PLA leaders, who visited Africa between 2001-2002 included:
- Minister of National Defense – Cote d'Ivoire, Nigeria
- Deputy Chief of the General Staff - Tanzania (2), Nigeria, Cameroon, Angola, South Africa, Zambia, Kenya, Namibia, Lesotho, and Mozambique
- Chief, General Armaments Department - South Africa
- Political Commissar, General Armaments Department – Egypt
- Deputy Chief, General Political Department - Zimbabwe and Mozambique
- Political Commissar, Beijing Military Region - Sudan, Djibouti, and Zambia
- Political Commissar, Shenyang Military Region - Cameroon, Benin, and Gabon
- President, Academy of Military Sciences – Egypt
- Commander, Jinan Military Region - Guinea, Mali, and Mauritania

PLA leaders, who visited Africa between 2003-2004 included:
- Vice-Chairman of the Central Military Commission – Egypt and South Africa
- Chief of the General Staff – Tanzania (2), South Africa, Morocco, Egypt, Zimbabwe, and Namibia
- Deputy Chief of the General Political Department – Zambia and Uganda
- Commander, Air Force – Egypt, Sudan
- Political Commissar, Air Force – Egypt and Tanzania
- Political Commissar, Academy of Military Sciences – Egypt
- Political Commissar, General Logistics Department – Zambia, Tunisia, and Zimbabwe
- Assistant to Chief of the General Political Department – Tanzania and Egypt
- Commander, Lanzhou Military Region – Zambia and Angola
- Political Commissar, Nanjing Military Region – Ethiopia, Uganda, and Botswana
- Political Commissar, Jinan Military Region – Egypt

PLA leaders, who visited Africa between 2005-2006 included:

- Vice-chairman, Central Military Commission – Sudan
- Minister of National Defense – Egypt and Tanzania
- Deputy Chief of the General Staff, General Logistics Department – Egypt, Kenya, Tanzania, Cameroon
- Assistant Chief of the General Staff Department – South Africa
- Deputy Chief of the General Political Department – Egypt and Uganda
- Commander, Second Artillery – Algeria and Tunisia
- Commander, Nanjing Military Region – Ethiopia and Eritrea
- Political Commissar, General Armaments Department – Namibia and Algeria
- Political Commissar, Beijing Military Region – Egypt
- Political Commissar, Jinan Military Region – Togo, Benin, and Tanzania
- President, Academy of Military Sciences – Egypt and South Africa
- Political Commissar, National Defense University – Egypt, Tanzania, and Zambia

PARTNERS OR PREDATORS? CHINA IN AFRICA

By Greg Mills and Christopher Thompson

The conventional wisdom is that China presents Africa with major threats and opportunities, and that there is growing tension between the United States and China over the latter's evolving African interests.

On paper, at least, the nascent interest of China in Africa looks to the latter's advantage. China's trade with Africa has dramatically increased from $11 billion in 2000 to $56 billion in 2006, making it the continent's third largest trade partner behind the United States and France. Beijing also has an African trade target of $100 billion by 2010 (*Business Day* [South Africa], December 2006). Africa is a new continental market for lesser-priced Chinese exports, while it is a major source of raw materials, especially oil. China has rapidly become the most assertive investor nation in Africa. Over 800 Chinese state-owned enterprises are today active on the continent, while Angola has now become China's largest supplier of oil. Chinese firms have already invested more than $6 billion in Africa in 900 projects—notably in the oil sector (*Asia Times*, July 13, 2007). This, however, still represents only 3 percent of Chinese overseas foreign direct investment (FDI) stock, illustrating the potential for future growth [1].

Reflecting this growing level of engagement, President Hu Jintao visited 17 African states during 2006-2007—more than any other head of state. The November 2006 Beijing Summit on the Forum on China-Africa Cooperation (FOCAC) was the largest diplomatic gathering ever in China. China has diplomatic relations with 48 of Africa's 53 states—Gambia, Malawi, Burkina Faso, Swaziland and Sao Tome apart. At the Beijing summit, the hosts pledged to double African aid and to offer $5 billion in loans and credits by 2009, while it has granted government scholarships to almost 20,000 people from 50 African countries and sent some 16,000 medical professionals to 47 African countries. Beijing has also remitted a combined 10.9 billion yuan ($1.42 billion) in debt owed by African countries and on top of that, more than 10 billion yuan in debt cuts is under way [2]. In May 2007, it was announced that China is to ramp up infrastructure and trade financing to Africa to $20 billion over the next three years via its Exim Bank (Reuters, June 1, 2007). As one recent indicator of the scale and type of Chinese involvement in Africa, in September 2007, China announced that it would lend the Democratic Republic of the Congo $5 billion to modernize its infrastructure and mining sector. Under a draft accord, Beijing earmarked the funds for major road and rail construction projects and for rehabilitation of Congo's mining sector, while the repayment terms proposed included mining concessions and toll revenue deals to be given to Chinese companies (*International Herald Tribune*, September 21, 2007).

An August 2006 high-level meeting of African, U.S. and Chinese specialists held at Tswalu in the Kalahari found that there is no strategic conflict between the United States and China, though this situation is dynamic and could change. In addition, the prospects for such conflict may heighten due to the pursuit of China's African commercial interests almost exclusively through state-owned firms.

Strategic Competition or Co-operation?

There is less clarity, however, on whether there is conflict between African interests on the one hand, and those of China and United States on the other.

African countries face a conundrum with regard to China's changing relationship with the continent. African domestic industries, in textiles and other areas, risk being swamped by cheaper Chinese products. Such concerns are raised by the investment trends of China—as well as the United States—in Africa, which have tended to be in the oil sector. This type of investment traditionally has not benefited African citizens for a range of reasons, including the nature of governance in those countries and macro-economic effects such as the overvaluation of currencies. Oil booms have generally enriched African elites and not their populations [3].

These concerns relate to Africa's emergence as a commodity superpower in a commodity super-cycle. Currently the United States imports two-thirds of its oil needs, 15 percent of which comes from Africa. This figure could increase to 25 percent by 2015 (BBC, September 13, 2002). Africa produced 6.8 million barrels of oil per day in 1979. In 2005, this increased to over 9.8 million bpd. The second-largest global energy importer behind the United States, China currently imports over six million bpd (*International Herald Tribune*, November 13, 2005). This figure is expected to double in the next 15 years. With only half of its energy needs now supplied by domestic sources, China is aggressively pursuing fresh oil interests in Africa, notably in the Sudan, which comprises one-tenth of all Chinese oil imports. Today the China National Petroleum Corporation (CNPC) is the largest investor in the Sudan.

China also agreed to a $3 billion credit line for the Angolan government in 2004, subsequently increased to as much as $11 billion (*The Brunei Times*, October 30, 2007). In 2006 China made a $2.3 billion investment in Nigeria's oil industry, paying 45 percent for a stake in a local field (The Associated Press, January 9, 2006).

In Southern Africa, Angola is at the center of the oil boom, with its output increasing from 722,000 barrels a day in 2001 to 930,000 in 2003 (BBC, September 13, 2002). By 2020, it is expected to reach 3.3 million barrels a day. Nigeria's output is predicted to double to 4.4 million barrels a day by 2020 (BBC, September 13, 2002). Today's minor oil producers—such as Equatorial Guinea, Chad and the Sudan—could more than triple their output given this demand. Today's dozen African oil producers could include five more in the next few years—Tanzania, Kenya, Uganda, Mozambique and Madagascar—if current exploration efforts prove fertile.

The benefit Africa generates from such investment depends more on what they themselves do than what China and the United States can do for Africa. Good governance is a prerequisite for the higher-order investments in Africa that its citizens consider essential, such as beneficiation of natural resources. It is of course crucial that Chinese and U.S. economic activities not implicitly or unconsciously undermine good governance. One of the best guarantees that a venture will promote African interests is the length of its engagement: A company that builds factories and mine shafts has a greater stake in stability and responsible government than does the short-term speculator [4].

It is of course crucial that Chinese and U.S. economic activities not implicitly or unconsciously undermine good governance. One of the best guarantees that a venture will promote African interests is the length of its engagement: A company that builds factories and mine shafts has a greater stake in stability and responsible government than does the short-term speculator.

In addition, low human capacity, poor infrastructure and Africa's small market size—Africa has an economy the same size as the state of Ohio—reduces its attractiveness for foreign investors. More importantly, however, such investors will follow the lead of their local African counterparts. The fact that Africans themselves are seen to be significant divestors in their own countries—around 40 percent of African capital has fled the continent—gives foreign investors scant confidence and comfort [5].

Contrary to the general assertion that there is a contradiction between China's Africa activities and improved standards of African governance and democracy, good governance is also in China's best interest as it was the easiest means to ensure that investor interests could be safeguarded—a realization that Western countries had long since arrived at in Africa. Similarly, democracies have consistently performed better economically than autocracies—outside of East Asia about 50 percent faster growth from 1960-2003—hence their promotion would be in the investor's enlightened self-interest. Moreover, support for autocratic governments by external powers was likely to pit them against African citizens who had consistently fought for such rights.

Given the combination of high domestic investment (45 percent) and savings (50 percent) rates, China is likely to be able to sustain its current high growth phase and appetite for raw materials for the next two decades. This highlights the need for an Africa-China-U.S. "win-win-win" strategy [6].

Conclusion: A Win-Win-Win Strategy?

China's rise poses a tremendous challenge for African development. Given China's industrial pre-eminence, African development is unlikely to come from high-volume manufacturing. Asian countries will probably dominate industries like cheap clothing or footwear for a generation or more, thereby inhibiting most African countries from climbing the traditional first step of the industrialization ladder. A combination of natural resource exploitation, agricultural self-sufficiency and high-value agro-exports, and the expansion of its unique range of service industries including tourism, would seem to be the most likely and rewarding growth path for many African states. This makes it imperative that more value from commodity investments in Africa stays on the continent.

Three issues stand out whereby China, Africa and the United States could together promote Africa's development.

First is the need to raise the levels of transparency and corporate governance in Africa. Here African governments need to improve their legal and regulatory environments. U.S. and Chinese firms—and governments—have a role to play in ensuring that the terms and conditions of deals are transparent so as to minimize opportunities for corruption, patronage and rent-seeking. There is a need to develop and transparently apply continent-wide principles of corporate good behavior.

Second, both Chinese and U.S. aid money should be strategically targeted at projects that will stimulate growth by reducing the costs of doing business. In many countries, this will mean infrastructure investments in electricity, broadband internet, roads, and ports. It may also mean funding for legal and administrative reform, or the hiring of foreign expertise including commercial judges.

Third, while they should ensure the conditions for business are increasingly easy and competitive through better policy and fewer bureaucratic encumbrances, African governments should seek to make technology transfer and value addition a condition in their contract and concession negotiations with foreign firms. This will help to ensure more value stays in Africa, creating employment and delivering development.

Originally published in *China Brief*: Volume 8 Issue 2 on January 17, 2008.

Notes

* The Brenthurst Foundation in Johannesburg which, along with the New York-based Council on Foreign Relations, the Leon H Sullivan Foundation and the Chinese Academy for Social Science (CASS), hosted the three meetings in the Africa-China-U.S. Trilateral Dialogue in South Africa, Beijing and Washington D.C. in August 2006, and February and September 2007 respectively.
1. At present, most Chinese investment is directed at Asia (53 percent) and Latin American (37 percent).

2. These figures were cited during the African Development Bank meetings held in May 2007 unusually in Shanghai. See http://www.blackwell-synergy.com/doi/abs/10.1111/j.1467-6346.2007.00908.x?cookieSet=1&journalCode=arbe; also http://www.uofaweb.ualberta.ca/chinainstitute/nav03.cfm?nav03=55896&nav02=43782&nav01=4 3092

3. Just as China did in the 1970s and 1980s when it negotiated access to China with foreign companies, African governments should—without overplaying their hand—seek to make technology transfer and value addition a condition in their contract and concession negotiations with foreign firms.

4. Paul Collier, Anke Hoeffler and Catherine A Pattillo, "Flight capital as a portfolio choice," World Bank Policy Research Working Paper No 2066, February 1999, http://papers.ssrn.com/sol3/papers.cfm?abstract_id=569197.

5. Ibid.

6. These areas were promoted by the African delegation at the aforementioned trilateral meeting in Washington. See also Lopo do Nascimento, William Lyakurwa, Patrick Mazimhaka, Greg Mills, Joe Mollo, Sydney Mufamadi, Michael Spicer, "Business Principles for a Strong Africa," Brenthurst Discussion Paper 6/2007, September 2007.

ENERGY & ARMS RELATIONS

CHINA'S ARMS SALES TO AFRICA

By Ian Taylor

If current trends continue, Chinese actors will become major players in Africa and ones that may challenge traditional Western interests. Concerns have been voiced over Beijing's apparent willingness to support some of the continent's authoritarian regimes—many of which have poor human rights and governance records. A number of case studies demonstrate that Beijing has been at times quite active in supporting states that are regarded by other international players as "rogue regimes." Growing Chinese activity on the continent thus merits particular attention by the United States and other Western countries, whilst at the same time compelling policymakers to engage rather than confront.

Certainly, Africa's economic involvement in Africa is rapidly increasing. In 1996, the value of China's official trade with Africa was $4 billion; by 2004, this had grown to $29.6 billion, in 2005 reached $39.7 billion, and in 2006 hit $55.5 billion. It is predicted that trade volume between China and Africa will top the $100 billion mark in the next five years. In fact, China has emerged as Africa's third most important trading partner after the United States and France and ahead of the United Kingdom. This is a remarkable development given the pace and timeframe within which this has occurred.

Beijing's economic interest in Africa is based on three factors. First, Beijing asserts that the macroeconomic situation in Africa is taking a favorable turn. This analysis is based on the belief that African countries have adopted a set of active measures to push forward the pace of privatization, open to international trade, and reform their economies. Chinese traders believe this affords great opportunities to their businesses and companies. Second, Chinese manufacturers and shopkeepers believe that the types of goods they produce and sell have immense potential in Africa. They believe that the economy in Africa is not yet as developed as in Western nations and consumers are perceived to be more receptive to the type of inexpensive products that Chinese factories typically produce. Third, the Chinese government encourages Chinese businesses look to secure access to Africa's abundant natural resources, particularly crude oil, non-ferrous metals and fisheries.

Indeed, China's rapidly developing oil requirements have helped propel Sino-African trade in recent years. In 1993, according to the Energy Information Administration in the U.S. Department of Energy, China became a net importer of oil and China is projected to rely on imports for 45 percent of its oil use by 2010. As a result, Beijing has been faithfully encouraging the development of linkages by its National Oil Corporations (NOCs) with oil-rich countries in Africa such as Angola, Nigeria and Sudan. Since around 1995, the Chinese government has begun an "outward-looking oil economy" policy. This is for primarily economic reasons, as the average production cost of Chinese onshore oil is very expensive compared to African or Middle Eastern oil. As a result, Chinese NOCs now have a presence in places in Africa as diverse as Nigeria, Gabon and Sudan. One way by which this policy has been cemented is to use what China refers to as "special relationships." Arms sales are one part of this policy and help offset costs.

Chinese economic interests in Africa have been manifest through increased joint ventures, investment and economic interaction. An emphasis on trade and economic affairs now dominates Sino-African relations and Chinese trade with Africa is growing speedily. Traditionally, Sino-African trade has been vastly unbalanced in China's favor. However, with the massive consumption of Africa's oil by China, the trade balance is now in favor of Africa.

Whilst there are certainly favorable aspects of Sino-African relations, for instance, investment in infrastructure, higher commodity prices fuelled by Chinese demand, it does have to be said that a key negative aspect of the relationship is the sale of Chinese-made arms to the continent. Arms sales to the continent are based on what can only be regarded as irresponsible principles that undermine Beijing's claims that it is qualitatively different from Africa's previous Western colonizers and exploiters. Unfortunately, the track record in Chinese arms sales to the continent thus far may be regarded as damaging to the continent's long-term security, as well as the human security of the average African.

It has been apparent for some time that Beijing hopes to turn the country's arms industry into a top arms exporter by 2020. Concerned that the People's Liberation Army (PLA) was becoming far too influential in the Chinese economy, in 1998, President Jiang Zemin declared that all businesses were being officially de-linked from the PLA. These were accompanied by the defense industry reforms in 1999, when China divided its top five defense corporations (space, aviation, shipbuilding, conventional arms and nuclear) into ten separate enterprises. Prior to the reforms and the divestment of the PLA's business operations, China's military industrial enterprises carried out a "contract responsibility system"—enterprises paid the state both taxes and a segment of their profits. Profits that remained from the production of civilian goods were either reinvested and/or were transferred to the budgets of the military management. With the PLA forced to withdraw from openly operating civilian businesses, however, the search for profits has largely been concentrated in increased arms sales since then. While most major Chinese weapons manufactures are no longer owned by the PLA, but rather by one of the civilian ministries, the remuneration from arms sales continue to return to the Chinese state. In fact, the state ostensibly controls all exports of conventional military items, including small arms, in accordance with its Regulations on Control of Military Product Exports [1].

The central state's ambitions regarding China's arms manufacturers mean that exporters have not only taken on the guise of providing military supplies and weaponry to the continent, but have also involved an active participation in actual conflicts. Remarkably, such involvement has passed with relatively little international attention, although the recent civil society focus in America on the "genocide Olympics" of Beijing 2008 mean that China's arguable laissez-faire attitude to relations with regimes such as in Sudan is starting to haunt Chinese foreign policy and has stimulated somewhat of a rethink.

The central state's ambitions regarding China's arms manufacturers means that exporters have not only taken on the guise of providing military supplies and weaponry to the continent, but have also involved an active participation in actual conflicts.

The classic example of Beijing's weapons exporting policy in Africa was China's involvement in Sudan's long-running civil war, which has claimed nearly two million lives so far. China pursued a policy that was entirely based on narrow economic interests and was keen to supply the Sudanese government with fighter aircraft and an assortment of weaponry. Apart from the profits accrued from these arms sales, the policy helped consolidate and protect Chinese investment in Sudan's oil reserves. Reliable reports from Aviation Week & Space Technology say that Sudan obtained 34 new fighter jets from China, and that the Sudan air force is equipped with $100 million worth of Shenyang fighter planes, including a dozen supersonic F-7 jets [2].

The motivation for such supplies is simple. The state-owned China National Petroleum Corporation (CNPC) owns the largest share (i.e. 40 percent) in Sudan's largest oil venture. The Sino-Sudanese oilfield project covers 50,000 square miles in the southern non-Muslim region of the country and is expected to produce 15 million tons of crude oil annually. With proven reserves of 220 million tons, the project has been among the largest China has undertaken overseas. At the same time, Sudanese government forces, armed with Chinese weapons, used Chinese facilities as a base from which to attack and dislodge southerners in the vicinity of the new oil fields. According to Lam Akol, former Transportation Minister (a southerner who temporarily served in the government during a period of reconciliation), helicopter gunships deployed in attacks on civilians were Chinese-made and were based at airstrips controlled by Chinese oil companies. Such a statement confirms findings from the charity World Vision who spoke to survivors of such attacks, as well as government military deserters (*The Washington Post*, December 23, 2004). A Christian Aid report in 2001 noted that CNPC's oil roads and airstrips were used to conduct bombing raids on southern Sudanese villages and hospitals. The charity accused the Chinese, through their activities in Sudan, of being complicit in scorched earth policies. Beijing, for its part, repeatedly deployed its "alternative" reading of human rights to block United Nations action against Sudan and consistently opposed any intervention by the United Nations with regard to Khartoum's affairs.

Amnesty International said in its June 2006 report that China's relations with Sudan have adversely affected the human rights situation in the country. Arms deliveries from China to Sudan have included ammunition, tanks, helicopters and fighter aircraft, and many of these weapons have been used by Khartoum and pro-state militias to commit massive atrocities in both southern Sudan and Darfur. Chinese-supplied aircraft have been used to launch bombing raids on villages, conduct reconnaissance prior to attacks and ferry ground troops [3]. Amnesty also reported that in 1996, Beijing supplied Z-6 troop-carrying helicopters, while in 2001, a Chinese company repaired Sudan's Mi-8 helicopters. Chinese military trucks, used in attacks on villages, have also been spotted in Sudan. In fact, the UN Panel of Experts investigating arms embargo violations in Sudan documented that Dong Feng military trucks were stored at the Port of Sudan and similar vehicles were observed in Darfur at a Sudanese air force base [4].

An equally notorious example of Beijing's indiscriminate arms sales has been the arms and security equipment that Chinese manufacturer have sold to Robert Mugabe's regime in Zimbabwe, ensuring that Harare is able to maintain its control over the populace. A $240 million deal between China and Zimbabwe is the most obvious example of this and accounts for China's most advanced military aircraft order to any African nation.

Harare's defense minister told parliamentarians in June 2004 that the deal included 12 jet fighters and 100 military vehicles (Johannesburg Radio 702 [English], June 10, 2004). Such purchases are required to replace existing Zimbabwean vehicles and aircraft that are no longer operational due to the Western sanctions that have prevented imports of spare parts and maintenance equipment. The order was kept covert until it was exposed by the state procurement board, which had previously been in charge of Zimbabwe's $136 million defense budget. According to a testimony given by Commissioner Carolyn Bartholomew of the U.S.-China Economic and Security Review Commission, this move enraged South Africa, with many political analysts fearing that such transfers could spark an arms race in southern Africa [5].

Since then, rumors that Beijing has allowed the sale of Chinese-made water cannons and cell phone bugging equipment to Harare's internal security personnel have emerged. In addition, Mugabe's government pursued legislation, notably the Interception of Communications Bill, to monitor internet use, with Zimbabwe obtaining Chinese expertise and technology to monitor the internet [6]. It should be noted that in 2006, Mugabe told an audience that "We want to remind those who might harbor any plans of turning against the government: be warned, we have armed men and women who can pull the trigger…The defense forces have benefited from the government's Look East policy through which they have not only acquired new equipment, but also learned new military strategies" (*Business Day* [Johannesburg], August 16, 2006). As an aside, previously, it was widely reported that Chinese small arms were exchanged for eight tons of Zimbabwean elephant ivory in May 2000. There is little doubt that, as Mugabe's regime comes under increasing pressure from the opposition movement, Chinese arms and equipment are likely to be seen with greater frequency on the streets of Zimbabwe. And it is unlikely that the Zimbabwean people will forget this fact once Mugabe and his cronies go for good.

It has also been reported that Chinese weapons have been traded in exchange for Liberian timber, in contravention of the then-UN arms embargo on Liberia. Such sales helped shore up warlord Charles Taylor until his ignominious flight into exile in August 2003. Nigeria has likewise turned to Chinese suppliers for military supplies to protect its oil fields after Washington was tardy in its response to the decreasing security situation in the Niger Delta (*Financial Times*, February 27, 2006). The Nigerian government was disappointed by Washington's reluctance to provide more support; Nigeria had requested 200 boats to guard the Delta. Washington, although offering military technical assistance and training, has so far provided only four old coastal patrol boats. The United States' reluctance is explained by its anxiety over the corruption within Nigeria's security forces and the widespread human rights violations committed by the Nigerian military. Nigerian security forces have been responsible for "politically motivated killings; the use of lethal force against suspected criminals and hostage-seizing militants in the Niger Delta; beatings and even torture of suspects, detainees, and convicts; and extortion of civilians," as well as "child labor and prostitution, and human trafficking" (AllAfrica.com, March 12).

The apparent lack of regard for the effect such policies may have on Africa is further exemplified by the willingness to supply arms to countries already at war. According to the Congressional Research Service, Chinese exports to Africa made up 10 percent of total conventional arms transfers to Africa between 1996 and 2003. While Ethiopia and Eritrea were edging toward war, Chinese corporations transferred a substantial share of $1 billion in weapons dispatched to both countries between 1998 and 2000. In 1995, a Chinese ship carrying 152 tons of ammunition and light weapons was refused permission to unload in Tanzania as the cargo was destined for the Tutsi-dominated army of Burundi (Agence France-Presse, May 3, 1995). At least thirteen covert shipments of weapons from China were delivered to Dar-es-Salaam, with the final destinations mislabeled and the weapons disguised as agricultural equipment. These were almost certainly destined for the war-torn Great Lakes region (Overseas Development Institute, May 1998).

Business is Business

Beijing proposes three guiding principles in its international arms transfer policy. First, the exports should boost the legitimate self-defense needs of any recipient. Second, the sales should not damage regional and/or international peace and stability. And third, China should not interfere in the domestic affairs of recipient countries. The inherent problem with such a policy, however, is that in Africa, it is often difficult to determine who or what constitutes a legitimate government. In many African countries, power is fundamentally dependent upon "capturing" the state—or at least being linked favorably to those within the state. Therefore, in many places where Chinese companies conduct arms sales, they are often dealing with governments that are little more than glorified kleptocracies and quasi-states whose principal aim is ensuring the survival and enrichment of the elite. For instance, while Mugabe's government may indeed be officially recognized at the United Nations, can Chinese policymakers state that the self-defense needs of an oppressive government, such as the one found in Harare, are indeed legitimate? And as Zimbabwe's denouement continues, are Chinese arms sales to the country not damaging to the regional stability of southern Africa? Finally, in places such as Zimbabwe or Sudan, is it credible for Beijing to claim that humanitarian abuses and gross violations of human rights are simply domestic affairs that cannot and should not be commented upon?

A key aspect of China's policies toward the continent that attracts certain African leaders' support is its stance on "non-interference in domestic affairs." Beijing consistently casts talk of democracy and human rights as a tool of neo-imperialism and demands that internal matters remain outside the concern of external actors. Central to this is the assertion that all countries have the right to choose their own definition of human rights. Beijing has gone so far as to state that good governance conditionalities, which include discussion of democracy and human rights, constitute a violation of the human rights of the receiving country. It is axiomatic that such a stance grants the rulers of each country the right to define their own version of "human rights" and also, how such rights should be protected (or not, as the case may be). China rarely attaches any political strings to its assistance to Africa. This has opened up space to deal quite profitably with some of the more heinous regimes on the continent—something which Western states and manufacturers have long been accused of.

It is no coincidence that Sudan and Zimbabwe now play host to a very large Chinese economic presence. In short, by advancing the theme of non-interference in domestic affairs and promoting a culturally relativist notion of human rights, China has been able to appeal to numerous African leaders. At the same time it secures African support for Beijing whenever China's own human rights record is put under the spotlight in forums such as the United Nations.

The Bottom Line

To be certain, the Chinese are hardly the only arms exporting country guilty of weapons sales to repressive African countries. Arms exports from China pale in significance to those of the United States, and are even less than those of Russia, France or Britain. Indeed, under Tony Blair, British arms sales to Africa have quadrupled and many exports have involved the selling of arms to authoritarian states on the continent with poor human rights records. Yet, elements of civil society in many of these Western countries have actively engaged their governments in order to influence policies and arms export regulations toward such countries. Such groups are non-existent in China and consequently, there is little pressure upon Beijing to adopt more responsible policies regarding its arms sales abroad. Compounding this challenge is the fact that China has refused to sign any multilateral agreements governing arms sales, and Beijing's policies remain arguably ambiguous, stymieing effective regulation and control of its arms exports. That China does not publish information about its arms exports—and last submitted data to the UN Register on Conventional Arms (UNROCA) covering its exports in 1996—makes Chinese arms sales activities highly opaque and arouses suspicions. There is a very real danger that Beijing's supposed "non-political" stance merely masks the bottom line for Chinese arms manufacturers: the chase for profits. Unmoved by ideological concerns and without fear of political consequences, Chinese arms exporters stand accused of at times being willing to deliver arms to, and conduct business with, African despots.

However, Beijing's desire to be recognized as a responsible stakeholder in the international arena and one that is qualitatively distinct from the former colonial powers has made it sensitive to external criticism and pressure. These aspirations provide the international community with an opportunity to influence Chinese behavior regarding arms sales and shape Beijing's ever-maturing policy toward Africa. It is certainly true that aspects of China's engagement towards Africa are problematic. Arms sales are one such example. But China's links with Africa also have positive aspects to it. The task for policymakers is to engage and encourage the positive features, whilst pointing out to Beijing that China's global reputation as a responsible great power is threatened by its current stance towards arms sales and that in the long-run, Chinese interests are best-served by a stable and conflict-free Africa. Policy-makers in Beijing are starting to realize this, and this opens up space for constructive dialogue between China, Africa and the West.

Originally published as two articles in *China Brief:* Volume 7 Issue 7 on April 5, 2007, and Volume 5, Issue 21 on October 13, 2005.

Notes

1. "Regulations on Control of Military Products Export," James Martin Center for Nonproliferation Studies, http://cns.miis.edu/research/china/chiexp/regmpe.htm
2. See also Daniel L. Byman and Roger Cliff, "China's Arms Sales: Motivations and Implications," The RAND Corporation, 1999.
3. "China: Sustaining Conflict and Human Rights Abuses: The Flow of Arms Continues," Amnesty International, http://web.amnesty.org/library/Index/ENGASA170302006
4. Ibid.
5. U.S. China Economic and Security Review Commission, *Testimony of Carolyn Bartholomew, Commissioner; U.S. China Economic and Security Review Commission Hearing on China's Influence In Africa; U.S. House of Representatives, Committee on International Relations, Subcommittee on Africa, Global Human Rights and International Operations*, Carolyn Bartholomew, (Washington, D.C.: July 28, 2005). http://www.uscc.gov/testimonies_speeches/testimonies/2005/05_07_29_bartholomew.php
6. Sami Ben Gharbia, "Zimbabwe: The Interception of the Communications Bill," Global Voices Advocacy, http://advocacy.globalvoicesonline.org/2007/06/18/zimbabwe-the-interception-of-communications-bill/

CHINA'S BOOMING ENERGY RELATIONS WITH AFRICA

By Wenran Jiang

With continuous economic growth averaging an astonishing annual rate of 10 percent over the past quarter century, China has transformed its landscape to become one of the largest economic powerhouses on earth, created development opportunities for its trading partners around the world and, in the process, generated huge demands for new sources of energy and other resources. Africa, on the other hand, has been left behind in the global quest for industrial modernization, economic prosperity and political stability. Yet, into Africa the Chinese are coming. They are coming for trade, investment and joint ventures, and they are consuming all the energy, minerals and other raw materials that the continent can offer.

An Evolution of Traditional Sino-African Ties

Africa's importance to China is reflected by Chinese Premier Wen Jiabao's June 2006 tour of Africa. According to China's Ministry of Commerce, the seven countries on his itinerary—Egypt, Ghana, the Republic of Congo, Angola, South Africa, Tanzania and Uganda—have a combined trade volume of over $20 billion with China, or 50.6 percent of total China-Africa trade last year. Only two months earlier to Premier Wen's trip, Chinese President Hu Jintao visited three other African states—Morocco, Nigeria and Kenya—following his trip to the United States and Saudi Arabia.

Such high-profile visits, a recurring practice over the past few years, have aroused speculation that Beijing's pursuit of great power status may include a new grand strategy regarding Africa. After all, top Chinese leaders have done the same extensive tours to Latin American countries since late 2004 when President Hu first visited Brazil, Argentina, Chile and Cuba. China's ties with African countries, however, can be traced back to the 1950s when newly emerging African states declared their independence. From the 1950s to 1970s, China developed close relations with many of these countries based primarily on shared ideological belief and political identity: anti-colonialism, national independence, economic self-reliance and Third World cooperation. Beijing provided substantial aid and other assistance to struggling African states in order to demonstrate that China was on the side of the Third World.

Things changed in the late 1970s. China's economic reforms gradually moved China away from its radical revolutionary worldview of the past. Beijing's open-door policy, primarily designed to attract foreign trade, investment and joint-venture opportunities from Western countries and to facilitate China's entry into the World Trade Organization (WTO), moved China much closer to a market economy where profits, not political agendas, drove most of the economic and trade activities. In this process, China's relations with African and other Third World countries have also evolved from anti-colonial brothers-in-arms to economic and trade partners based on market principles. Yet, many things have remained the same. Beijing continues to pay and train young African diplomats in the Chinese Foreign Ministry's prestigious Foreign Affairs University, a practice that has continued for many years; China continues to present itself as a member of the Third World; and since 1991, every Chinese foreign minister's first visit abroad each year has been to an African country. Beijing has even named 2006 the "Year of Africa," and it hosted a Sino-African summit toward the end of 2006. Furthermore, according to Beijing's report to the National People's Congress (NPC), most of China's foreign aid—totaling 7.5 billion yuan ($950 million) last year—has gone to more than 50 African countries. In fact, Wen claimed that China has offered Africa more than $44 billion in aid over the past 50 years to finance 900 infrastructure projects (The Associated Press, June 18, 2006). Meanwhile, all signs indicate that China-African relations are entering a new phase centered on energy and raw materials.

The New Focus on Energy

China's relentless pursuit of economic development turned the country into a net petroleum importer in 1993, and by the turn of the new century, its dependency on foreign oil had jumped to about 40 percent of its demand. Beijing's new target is to quadruple its economy again by 2020, as it did from the late 1970s to the mid-1990s. To achieve this goal, however, China must rely even more on external energy supplies as the Middle Kingdom already burns through 6.3 million barrels of oil a day. Although still far behind the United States, which consumes some 20 million barrels a day, the International Energy Bureau projects that Chinese consumption will reach a daily level of 10 million barrels within the next two decades or so.

Thus, China's quest for energy and other resources has brought China to Africa with urgency. Chinese customs statistics reveal that from 2001 to 2005, China's trade with Africa increased 268 percent, slower only than the growth of China's trade with the Middle East in the same period (367 percent), but faster than China's trade growth with Latin America (238 percent), ASEAN (170 percent), European Union (184 percent) and North America (163 percent). In the first quarter of 2006, the Ministry of Commerce reported that China's trade with the seven countries on Premier Wen's current African touring list amounted to $6.56 billion dollars, a surge of 168.2 percent. It is not surprising, therefore, that in such a broad economic context, Africa has turned into a major energy supplier to China in recent years. Back in 2003, both President Hu and Premier Wen visited several oil-producing African states with Chinese energy company executives, and since then China has become involved in an increasing number of energy deals on the continent that bear a number of unique characteristics.

Energy Security with Chinese Characteristics

First, Beijing is willing to get into the "troubled zones" with bold investment and aid packages in exchange for energy. When Angola ended its 27-year civil war in 2002, few foreign countries and firms were willing to invest in the country. China, on the other hand, committed a $3 billion oil-backed credit line to rebuild the country's shattered infrastructure. Beijing also made Angola its largest foreign aid destination. Now, Angola is the second largest oil producer after Nigeria in sub-Saharan Africa, producing 1.4 million barrels per day with one-third of its oil exports—13 percent of total Chinese imports—going to China. In the first four months of this year, Angola was also the largest supplier of crude to the Chinese market after Saudi Arabia (AFP, June 20). Similar arrangements have been made with Nigeria and other countries as well.

Second, Chinese energy companies are committing large amounts of funding and labor for exploration and development rights in resource-rich countries. Sudan is one of the earliest and largest overseas energy projects by China's major energy companies. Chinese operations in Sudan include investment, development, pipeline building and a large number of Chinese labor deployments. Today, China has $4 billion of investment in the country. The China National Petroleum Corporation (CNPC) has a 40 percent controlling stake in Greater Nile Petroleum that dominates Sudan's oilfields. Last year, China purchased more than half of Sudan's oil exports, and earlier this year, China National Offshore Oil Corporation (CNOOC) announced that it had bought a 45 percent stake in a Nigerian oil-and-gas field for $2.27 billion and also purchased 35 percent of an exploration license in the Niger Delta for $60 million. Chinese companies have made similar investments in Angola and other countries.

It appears that the Chinese companies are often willing to outbid their competitors in major contracts awarded by African governments because their concerns are not in short-term returns but rather in strategic positioning for the future.

Third, Chinese energy companies enter into joint-ventures with national governments, state-controlled energy companies or individual enterprises in order to establish a long-term local presence. It appears that the Chinese companies are often willing to outbid their competitors in major contracts awarded by African governments because their concerns are not in short-term returns but rather in strategic positioning for the future.

Fourth, China does not take into consideration the particular concerns of the United States or other Western countries when selecting energy cooperation partners and has a different set of standards on how to advance political reform and human rights in Africa. Most notoriously, China has been willing to engage in energy deals with the Sudanese government despite the ongoing crisis in Darfur. Likewise, China has just reached an energy and mining deal worth $1.3 billion with Zimbabwe. In exchange for building three coal-fired thermal power stations, Zimbabwe is likely to repay the Chinese investment with its rich deposits of platinum, gold, coal nickel and diamonds (*The Guardian*, June 16, 2006).

A Model for Future Cooperation or a Return to the Past?

In the past few years, the demands from China and other developing economies for oil and natural gas have become the major factor, although not the only one, that has driven up world energy prices. Chinese energy companies' extensive activities in Africa, Latin America, the Middle East and Central Asia in search of oil and gas assets have created anxiety regarding the world's future supply of energy. Discussions of a new "great game"—a term traditionally associated with competition among major world powers for the control of Eurasian oil resources since the late nineteenth century—have become frequent among observers of energy security.

Today, Africa supplies China with nearly a third of its oil imports. Beijing's extensive engagement and its ascending status in Africa also raises important questions on the nature of China's involvement in the continent as well as Beijing's long-term objectives in the region. Critics charge that China has pursued mercantilist policies in the region for pure economic benefits without human rights or environmental concerns. Due to China's support, they argue, the Sudanese government has been able to continue its genocidal policy in the Darfur region, and the Mugabe regime has been able to survive and carry on its abuses of human rights in Zimbabwe.

Officially, Beijing rejects the criticism with two arguments. The first is China's trademark policy of non-interference in domestic affairs. As Premier Wen stated, "We believe that people in different regions and countries, including those in Africa, have their right and ability to handle their own issues" (*South China Morning Post*, June 19, 2006). The second is China's emphasis that its involvement in Africa is different from the colonialism of the past, and that an affluent China is now putting money back into the local African economy. As Chinese leaders like to say, it is a win-win situation.

With China speedily expanding its activities in Africa, international concerns over Chinese behavior are also deepening and calls for Beijing to be a more responsible world power are becoming stronger. There are also indications that Chinese policy makers, academics, NGOs and even enterprises are beginning to reflect upon China's role in Africa. Many African countries are benefiting from a "China boom," but they would be better served if Beijing were to take further steps in balancing between economic interests and the welfare of the African people. Only by doing so would China be able to demonstrate to the world that its arrival in Africa is indeed different from the old colonial powers.

Originally published in *China Brief*: Volume 6 Issue 13 on June 21, 2006.

Note: Special thanks to Taikun Ji and Simin Yu of the China Institute at the University of Alberta for data collection.

FEEDING THE DRAGON: CHINA'S QUEST FOR AFRICAN MINERALS

By John C. K. Daly

While much of the attention on China's emergence onto the global economic stage as an industrial powerhouse has focused on the accumulation of its massive trade surpluses, most Western observers probing Beijing's interest in Africa's rich natural resources have concentrated on the Middle Kingdom's seemingly insatiable appetite for energy resources. Africa currently contributes 12 percent of the world's liquid hydrocarbon (oil) production. In 2013, African oil production is projected to rise to 10.7-11.4 million barrels per day (bpd), and by 2018 to 12.4-14.5 million bpd [1]. In 2007, African oil constituted more than 22 percent of the United States' total usage and 28 percent of China's—the latter case including approximately 60 percent of the Sudan's oil export—compared to the 2006 figures of 9 percent for China, 33 percent for the United States and 36 percent for Europe.

A less mainstream but perhaps more significant issue for Sino-African relations is China's growing interest in Africa's rich mineral resources—where Beijing's shopping list literally runs the gamut, from aluminum to zirconium [2]. Considering China's dynamic economy and robust growth, its interest in African minerals may well prove in the long run more strategically important in its grand strategy than African oil—especially if China's deals with Central Asian energy exporters prove successful. The minerals sought by China affect every aspect of its economy, from the minerals like titanium needed for producing military aircraft to the iron ore needed to fuel its export of consumer goods, to its surging diamond trade for the country's growing appetite for luxury items.

Considering China's dynamic economy and robust growth, its interest in African minerals may well prove in the long run more strategically important in its grand strategy than African oil—especially if China's deals with Central Asian energy exporters prove successful.

Although China possesses an abundant supply of colored metal mineral resources, most of it is of low-grade ores and only one-third of the total amount of mineral ores can be processed through available technology. While China's rapid economic growth drives up demand for colored metal resources, the growing demand and supply gap could put a serious strain on the Chinese economy (*Beijing Review*, December 14, 2007).

Chen Qiyuan, a professor at Central South University, oversees the project in the 973 Program that is charged with implementing the 11th Five-year Plan (2006-2010), in particular, toward researching and developing essential minerals. Chen said that the project has strategic significance not only for sustaining economic development but also for national security. Chen estimates that the research that his project is undertaking would increase the lifespan of China's mineral resources. If metal output and recycling levels stay at the 2005 level, Chen's research indicates China's copper resources will last another 12 years, nickel for 40 years and zinc for 18 years (*Beijing Review*, December 14, 2007).

China-Africa Overall Trade

During the 1990s, trade between China and Africa grew by 700 percent, doubling from 2002 to 2003 and in 2005 almost doubled again. In 1995, Chinese imports from Africa were worth $1.4 billion; 11 years later, their value soared to $28.7 billion, a 2,000 percent increase [3].

Unlike virtually all of China's significant trading partners, in 2006, Africa as a whole actually ran a modest trade surplus, sending China $28.8 billion in goods while importing $26.7 billion [4]. In

January 2006, China released its first policy paper on Africa—China's African Policy—elaborating its future objectives on the continent, noting that "China is willing to negotiate a Free Trade Agreement (FTA) with African countries and African regional organizations when conditions are ripe" (Xinhua, January 14, 2006)

By 2010, China will overtake the United States and France as Africa's biggest trading partner (BBC, July 4, 2007). Current African exports are extensively resource-based, with oil accounting for 73 percent of African exports to China; followed by iron ore, totaling 4.03 percent of China's global supply, which was worth $131.8 million in 1995 and $839.16 million in 2006; cotton; diamonds, which constituted $151.3 million in 1996 and $704.5 million in 2006, aggregating 29 percent of Chinese global supplies; and timber. For 2006, China's top 10 African import countries were Angola ($10.9 billion), South Africa ($4.09 billion), the Democratic Republic of the Congo ($2.78 billion), Equatorial Guinea ($2.53 billion), the Sudan ($1.94 billion), Libya ($1.69 billion), Gabon ($816.8 million), Mauritania ($402.02 million), Morocco ($359.47 million) and Zambia ($269.13 million) [5].

China and South Africa

Out of the 54 countries and the island territories in Africa, Beijing regards South Africa as the continent's mineralogical treasure house. South Africa is the largest producer of gold—currently accounting for 14 percent of total global production and containing 40.1 percent of the world's known reserves—and contains 87.7 percent of the world's platinum reserves, 80 percent of its manganese ore, 72.4 percent of its chrome ore and 27 percent of its vanadium [6]. In 2006, gold accounted for 20 percent of South Africa's exports, while coal, platinum and other minerals made up an additional 25 percent [7]. South Africa also has substantial reserves of other industrially important metals and minerals [8].

Between 1996 and 2005, South African exports to China increased to well over $1.25 billion. China reciprocally has invested $130 million in South Africa, mostly in the Buffelsfontein chromium mine (BuaNews, January 9). According to South African Revenue Service trade data, in 2007, South African exports to China rose 195 percent compared with the same period in 2006, to $2.26 billion, behind Japan, the United States, Germany and Britain (*Business Report* [South Africa], September 14, 2007). South Africa accounts for about 75 percent of world ferrochrome, and China now imports over 90 percent of the ferrochrome consumed by its voracious stainless steel industry.

China is not alone in its interest in South African minerals; the United States is also heavily dependent upon South Africa for key minerals including chrome, manganese, vanadium and platinum. In February 1987, then President Ronald Reagan certified andalusite, antimony, chrysotile asbestos, chromium, cobalt, industrial diamonds, manganese, platinum group metals, rutile and vanadium as "strategic" minerals that were considered essential for supplying military, industrial and civilian needs of the United States at the time of a national emergency; moreover, they are not sufficiently found or produced in the United States [9].

China's Voracious Appetite for Minerals

China's outreach for minerals and resources to supply its economy have had a global impact; since 2005, many commodity prices have soared—gold and silver are again reaching price heights not seen since the late 1970s, while in 2007 prices for copper, zinc, lead, tin, chromium, platinum, molybdenum, coal, oil and uranium also set multi-year or all-time highs (africa-investor.com, March 1, 2006).

China now consumes 30 percent of the global total for zinc and 25 percent of that of lead, while since 1996 China's consumption of refined copper has risen from less than 10 percent of world demand to 22 percent, and the Chinese economy absorbs 27 percent of the globe's iron and steel and

25 percent of its aluminum. China already produces one-third of the world's steel, and its iron ore imports are expected to double by 2012. In 2003, China passed the United States to become the world's largest copper consumer and by the following year consumed 46 percent more than the United States. In 2006, China announced plans to set up Strategic Mineral Reserve to stockpile uranium, copper, aluminum, iron ore and other minerals. The reserves are critical for providing China with a buffer to adjust to market fluctuations, manage emergencies and guarantee the security of resource supplies [10].

China's African Resource Acquisition Investment Strategy

The general patterns of Chinese investment in Africa are discernible and differ in many respects from Western attitudes. First and foremost, China in its long-term view has concluded that Africa's overall macroeconomic situation is improving, despite the problems wracking the continent—from corruption to civil war—giving it a much bolder position on investment than more cautious Western investors. Chinese producers also see Africa as a continent of immense opportunity for their low-cost products, which in most cases undercut higher-priced Western imports. The final element in Beijing's perception of Africa is a keenly focused awareness of the continent's rich resource base; while Western competitors also covet Africa's mineralogical resources, Chinese investment strategy benefits from Western deficits and therefore holds advantages over European and American approaches. Western investors arrive with ideological baggage and domestic constraints in the form of economic reform, anti-corruption and human rights campaigns—a key aspect of China's policies toward the continent is its avowedly apolitical and amoral stance described as "non-interference in domestic affairs." Adding to the appeal of China's "soft power" is an appreciation of a half-century history of friendly ties and past Chinese support for liberation movements in Africa, topped off with the provision of "no-strings-attached" financial and technical aid to African countries. These deals often include low-interest or interest-free loans and additional funding for both developing infrastructure and civil projects.

Western investors arrive with ideological baggage and domestic constraints in the form of economic reform, anti-corruption and human rights campaigns—a key aspect of China's policies toward the continent is its avowedly apolitical and amoral stance described as "non-interference in domestic affairs."

A prime example is Chinese investment in Angola. China invested in Angola's oil industry even as civil war raged, in 1995 exporting $135.7 million worth of hydrocarbons. Since the nation ended a 27-year civil war in 2002, Angola has become China's largest trading partner, in 2006 surpassing Saudi Arabia as China's leading oil exporter, and has the fastest-growing economy on the continent with a projected 2007 gross domestic product (GDP) growth rate of over 20 percent. In 2006, Angola exported $10.93 billion of oil to China and joined OPEC, but two-thirds of the population is estimated to earn less than a dollar a day. This has provided an opportunity for the opposition, with Unita party leader Isaias Samakuva commenting, "What we have seen is that Angolans have not benefited from the accords with China. These are aspects that need to be looked at carefully and see how they can be bettered" (*Cruzeiro do Sul* [Brazil], January 12, 2007).

China has landed some impressive deals throughout Africa, including winning a majority stake in the Democratic Republic of the Congo's (DRC) Gecamines joint venture. In return for a $5 billion loan, the DRC government is giving four Chinese state enterprises a 68 percent stake in a joint venture with Gecamines, the state-owned mining company, in addition to China Overseas Engineering's $300 million investment in two Congolese copper and cobalt mining projects (*The China Monitor*, November 2007). In another coup, in June 2006, China beat out Brazil's Vale do Rio Doce—the world's top iron ore producer—and French company Eramet to secure a $3 billion contract to develop massive iron ore reserves in Belinga, Gabon. During the Forum on China-Africa Cooperation (FOCAC) in November 2006, among the agreements concluded by China were a $938 million contract to develop an aluminum plant in Egypt and a $230 million deal for ferrochrome mining and smelting in South Africa.

These investments do not come without risks: on April 24, 2007, a guerrilla attack on a Chinese-run oil field in Ethiopia left 77 people dead. Since 2004, dozens of Chinese workers, engineers and other civilians have been killed or kidnapped in Nigeria, Kenya and other African states. Moreover, African workers in Angola, Zambia, Nigeria and Morocco have demonstrated over Chinese labor policies, most notably at Zambia's Chambishi copper mine, where on January 3, 500 workers went on strike to protest low salaries and poor working conditions, with one worker representative commenting that salaries were as low as $54 per month (*The Times of Zambia*, January 4, 2008).

China's extensive operations in the Sudan have also attracted intense international criticism for fraternizing with a supporter of terrorism involved in a brutal campaign in Darfur, an ongoing legacy of the Sudan's ongoing 24-year civil war. The international community also deplores China's deepening relationship with Mugabe's despotic regime, but Beijing instead focuses on projections that in 2008 trade between Zimbabwe and China is set to increase to $500 million (*The Herald* [Zimbabwe], January 7, 2008). In December 2007, Sinosteel Corporation acquired a 67 percent stake in Zimbabwe's leading ferrochrome producer and exporter Zimasco Holdings (*The Herald* [Zimbabwe], December 20, 2007).

Despite the problems enumerated above, the possibilities for the future of Chinese-African trade seem limitless. According to South African mining executive Sir Sam Jonah, only 30 percent of Africa has been explored for mineral wealth (*The Gibbs Review*, January 2006). The only question, in an increasingly resource-hungry world, is whether Africa's riches go East or West.

Conclusion

China's Africa strategy—which is tied to over 50 years of ideological solidarity, beginning when the continent was struggling to liberate itself from colonialism—is now paying immense economic dividends. China's willingness to invest heavily in African nations either currently wracked by civil war—such as the Sudan and the Democratic Republic of the Congo—or recently emerged from chaos—such as Angola—has given it a leading position in development projects that more timorous Western investors up to now have largely avoided. Given the relative political stability of Africa, it remains a high-risk strategy. For Beijing to maintain China's impressive growth record, however, there is really little choice, as American and European investors have already locked up many of the globe's more stable sources of raw materials. It remains to be seen whether China's Africa policy will ultimately become a system that pacifies the continent, or possibly leads to either covert or overt "resource wars" for the limited supply of both hydrocarbons and strategic minerals. China's policy, at least as regards what Washington defines as strategic minerals, could certainly become a disruptive influence in Washington-Beijing relations. Given China's oft-stated commitment to global peaceful development, it remains to be seen how such a confrontation might play out. Considering Washington's establishment last year of its AFRICOM military command, there seems little doubt that in the event of armed confrontation Beijing would be the loser. China clearly prefers the economic benefits of peaceful trade; as the wars in Afghanistan and Iraq so vividly illustrate, armed conflict is a net consumer of men, material and money and it is obvious that for the present Beijing is trying to avoid such a path.

Originally published in *China Brief* Volume 8 Issue 3 on January 31, 2008.

Notes

1. "Fuelling Africa's Sustainable Development: The Oil and Gas Perspectives," African Union, http://www.africa-union.org/root/AU/Conferences/Past/2006/November/infrastructure/doc/en/AU_EXP_OG_5_Fuelling_Eng.doc.
2. China's extensive shopping list for African minerals includes: aluminum; asbestos; basalt; boric acids and oxides; carbonates; chromium ore and concentrates; coal; cobalt ore and concentrates; diamonds; feldspar; ferroalloys; fluorspar; gold; granite; iron ores and concentrates; lead ore and concentrates; leucite; manganese ores and concentrates, including ferrous manganese iron ore; lime; molybdenum ore and concentrates; nepheline; nickel; niobium; syenite; oxometallic and peroxometallic acid salts; platinum; porphyry; silver; slacked lime; tin ore and concentrates; titanium oxides; tungsten ore and concentrates; quartz; quartzite; quicklime; tantalium; vanadium; zinc and zirconium ore and concentrates (see source in Note 3).
3. World Trade Atlas, "Index for Chinese Trade Data–Dec. Years (ranked by Chinese imports)," Trade Law Centre for Southern Africa, http://www.tralac.org/pdf/20070220_China_Africa_top20s2007.xls
4. Ibid.
5. Ibid.
6. South Africa Yearbook "South Africa's mineral reserves 2005," South African Minerals Bureau, www.gcis.gov.za/docs/publications/yearbook/chapter16.pdf
7. EU SADC Investment Promotion Programme, "SADC Mining Industry Review" Mines 2006, www.mines2006.com/Downloads/EN/SADC%20Mining%20Industry%20Review_MINES%202006.pdf
8. These minerals include antimony, asbestos, diamonds, coal, fluorspar, phosphates, iron ore, lead, zinc, uranium, vermiculite and zirconium. South Africa is the world's largest producer of gold, platinum group metals, vanadium and alumino-silicates, as well as one of the world's top five producers of antimony, chromite, diamonds, ferrochrome, ferro-manganese, fluorspar, manganese, titanium, vermiculite and zirconium.
9. Natalie Johnson, "Strategic Minerals in the United States," Emporia State University, http://www.emporia.edu/earthsci/amber/go336/natalie/newindex.htm
10. Metals prices have completed the sixth year of a bull-pricing phase that started in 2002. Since the end of 2001, a market basket of six basic nonferrous metals (aluminum, copper, lead, nickel, tin and zinc) has increased in a supercycle pricing surge of 338 percent (Source: Tom Stundza, "Metals: here's what you'll pay this year," Purchasing.com, January 17, 2008, http://www.purchasing.com/article/CA6518773.html?industryid=48405).

COUNTRY/REGION SPECIFIC RELATIONS

ANGOLA:

CHINA IN ANGOLA: AN EMERGING ENERGY PARTNERSHIP

By Paul Hare

Despite the impressive economic ties between China and Angola in recent years, their historical relations have suffered periods of strain and volatility. During Angola's struggle against Portuguese colonial rule, China provided training and assistance to National Union for the Total Independence of Angola (UNITA), one of the three rival national liberation movements in Angola, while the Soviets supported the Popular Movement for the Liberation of Angola (MPLA) and the United States initially backed the National Front for the Liberation of Angola (FNLA). When independence was achieved in November 1975, the MPLA controlled the capital, and its leader, Agnostinho Neto, became the first president of Angola. Although China subsequently severed its ties to UNITA, the two countries did not establish diplomatic relations until 1983, a reflection, perhaps, of the previously strained relationship between the two governments. During the next two decades, China maintained a fairly low profile in Angola, providing only small-scale assistance. There were reports that Beijing had helped establish fishing cooperative, an electric appliance factory and a low-cost housing project. In light of what was to come, however, the Chinese role during these two decades was modest.

The Turnaround

Relations between the two countries took an about face in March 2004 when China's Export-Import Bank (Exim Bank) offered a $2 billion oil-backed loan to Angola on very favorable terms (*Financial Times*, March 4, 2006). The reasons for an offer of this magnitude soon became clear. Shell had divested itself of its oil interests in Angola and had negotiated a deal with Indian oil companies to take over its 50 percent equity-stake in deep-water Bloc 18, operated by BP. Sonangol, Angola's national oil company, exercised its right of first refusal and instead, gave the equity stake to Sinopec, one of China's national oil companies (*The Financial Express*, March 8, 2005). In another development reflecting China's increased clout, Sonangol refused to extend France-based Total's concession over one part of offshore oil Bloc 3, presumably because of an Angolan pique with the French government over the "Angolagate" affair; Sinopec was the end beneficiary of the new arrangement.

In a round of bidding in 2006, the Sonangol-Sinopec consortium (SSI) made record breaking bids amounting to $2.2 billion in signature bonuses to obtain rights in relinquished areas of deep-water Blocs 17 and 18 (*Business Week*, June 7, 2006). The Chinese were not the only ones bidding high. In an earlier round in April, ENI, the Italian oil company, bid over $900,000 to win operating rights for the relinquished areas of Bloc 15. SSI received a 20 percent share in that bloc. Although SSI has the major equity stake in the relinquished areas of Bloc 18 (40 percent), Petrobras, the Brazilian oil company, will be the operator because the Chinese lack the capability to develop deep-water areas (*Latin American News*, November 6, 2006).

China's motivations to strategically target Angola for investment are multifaceted, ranging from the level of political stability to its natural resources. Angola enjoys a large measure of political stability, especially since the death of Jonas Savimbi, UNITA's leader, in February 2002. Furthermore, in April of that year, new peace accords were signed between the government and UNITA; most observers believe that in contrast to previous agreements, the peace will last this time around. Even during the years of war, the major oil companies had established good working relations with Sonangol and were able to carry out operations off the coast of Angola without interruption. A further consideration for China was that Angola's oil production has surged in recent years and is expected to reach 2 million barrels per day (bpd) in 2008. The deep-water blocs have been especially prolific, and even though the oil majors (BP, ExxonMobil and Total) have presumably explored and developed the best parts of Blocs 15, 17, and 18, there is the promise of additional oil to be found in the relinquished areas.

In addition to acquiring equity-stakes in oil concessions, the Chinese have also invested in the development of Angola's oil processing infrastructure. Sinopec and Sonangol have formed a consortium to build a major new refinery in Lobito. Sonangol and the Ministry of Petroleum had previously attempted to attract the oil majors to invest in the project but were unsuccessful because of concerns about the project's financial viability. Emblematic of the burgeoning relationship between the two countries, Angola surpassed the Saudis and became the number one oil exporter to China in February 2006 (*Financial Times*, October 26, 2006).

Beyond the Oil Sector

Under the ambit of the $2 billion loan, Chinese companies are engaged in a host of projects throughout Angola, constructing schools, clinics, hospitals and low-cost housing and building basic infrastructure, such as roads and bridges. The most ambitious undertaking is the rehabilitation of the Benguela Railroad, linking the port of Lobito on the Atlantic with the Democratic Republic of the Congo and Zambia, the old copper route. Other major projects include a new airport and a railroad linking Luanda with Malange, a major town in the interior of the country. The Chinese telecommunications company, ZTE, is modernizing and expanding Angola Telecom's fixed line telephone network, as well as investing in military communications and establishing a telecommunications training facility. Another Chinese company is working on the production center for Angola's television station (Afrol News, March 7, 2005).

Indicative of the growing Chinese business presence, 26 Chinese companies established a Chamber of Commerce in Luanda in 2006. At this point, the bulk of Chinese projects are of the "brick and mortar type" and are focused on infrastructure rehabilitation, which correspond to the Angolan government's strategy of giving top priority to reopening the country's transportation corridors devastated by the 27 years of war. Investments or assistance to promote long-term sustainable development and capacity building are thus far minimal, though there have been reports of Chinese involvement in funding a $40 million cotton growing project (Angola Press Agency, November 6, 2006).

Lack of Transparency in Activities

In spite of the magnitude of China's projects in the country, very little is known about them. For instance, it is unclear exactly how much money in the form of aid and loans has been offered by Beijing; estimates vary from $2 billion to $9 billion. The Angolan government maintains that the level is currently $2 billion, which most likely reflects the fact that the original Exim Bank loan of $2 billion has not yet been used up, but that further monies will become available once it is. It is also unclear exactly how many Chinese nationals are currently residing in Angola, with reports citing anywhere between 10,000 to 80,000. While Angolan officials have dismissed the upper end of the estimates, they themselves do not offer an official count.

The bidding process for the lucrative contracts is likewise opaque, as it is unclear how many Angolan companies have received contracts under the Chinese loan, though according to the terms of the Exim Bank agreement, 30 percent are supposed to go to the Angolans. Nor is it known how many Angolans are employed by the Chinese, though once again this is stipulated in the agreement. Whatever the facts may be, the popular perception is that the Chinese have gotten the lion's share of the loan money and have brought large numbers of Chinese workers to carry out their projects.

Challenges and Opportunities Ahead

Unlike Sudan or Zimbabwe, Angola's growing partnership with China should not be viewed as a serious threat to the interests of the West or the United States. Although China's propensity to lock into oil supplies runs counter to the West's preference for it to rely on market supply and demand mechanisms, it is at a high cost to the Chinese and does not seriously degrade U.S. energy security. Of more immediate concern is the competitive advantage that Chinese oil companies enjoy because of credit lines and other incentives offered by the Chinese government and its agencies. Angola is not yet an exclusive Chinese market, however, and Angola does not look at China as its sole or even most important partner. Angolans want high quality goods and services from the West and the United States and welcome western investments in the non-oil sectors. The recent purchase of Boeing aircraft, amounting to almost $1 billion, by TAAG, Angola's national airline, underlines this point. Five of the aircraft are scheduled to arrive in Luanda on November 11, Angola's Independence Day. Similarly, GE may be supplying locomotives to Angola's railroad system.

The infusion of money and lines of credit from China certainly diminishes the influence of the International Monetary Fund (IMF) and other actors that would like to promote economic reform and liberalization in Angola. Yet this should not be exaggerated, as Angola remains interested in having its debt rescheduled at the Paris Club and continues to maintain a dialogue with the IMF. An IMF mission went to Luanda at the end of November 2006 to engage in further discussions. The World Bank also remains engaged in a number of areas, including the organization of petroleum management workshops in Angola in May 2006, which high-ranking Angolan officials attended.

The massive influx of Chinese businesspersons and companies into Angola has been received with a mixed response. Anecdotal evidence suggests that there is already a growing resentment of the Chinese presence in Angola. There has been talk of the "Chinese Invasion" and complaints that the Chinese are taking jobs and contracts away from the Angolans. Moreover, the Chinese have not been transferring skills or technology to the Angolans, raising the question of what happens once a project is completed. Others, including those at high levels of government, have criticized the quality of the goods and services that Angola has been receiving from China. As potential evidence of the growing tensions between the two countries, President José E. dos Santos chose to visit Moscow with a high-powered delegation, while sending his Prime Minister to the recent Forum on China-Africa Cooperation (FOCAC) summit in his stead. Whether or not this was a signal to China is difficult to tell. President dos Santos does not particularly like to sit in large meetings of leaders wherever they might gather, but one would understand if the Chinese were to interpret his absence as a rebuff.

China is in Angola for the long haul—or at least as long as the oil continues to flow—but the same can be said about other countries. The Chinese now have significant equity-stakes in offshore oil and in the construction of an oil refinery, which will remain even if their other construction projects were to taper off. At the same time, the Chinese can expect the Angolans to become more insistent on quality performance and the transfer of skills and technology in the same way that the oil companies are expected to train Angolan nationals and outsource to Angolan companies. If anything, the absence of President dos Santos at the FOCAC summit was a warning to Beijing that nothing should be taken for granted in Angola, even by China.

Originally published in *China Brief* Volume 6 Issue 22 on November 8, 2006.

EGYPT:

A BURGEONING STRATEGIC PARTNERSHIP: ASSESSING SINO-EGYPTIAN RELATIONS

By Chris Zambelis

China has undertaken an ambitious effort to enhance its energy security and access to vital natural resources to sustain its economic growth in recent years, concluding a number of economic and trade agreements with leading oil and gas producers in Africa and the Middle East. An oft-overlooked objective of this strategy, however, is Beijing's aim of enhancing its position as a rising global power, which would require developing the capability of projecting influence outside of its immediate regional periphery. To this end, China is busy cultivating multifaceted relationships with regional powers throughout Africa and the Middle East—beyond the energy and business sectors—to include cooperation in the political and security spheres, as well as science and cultural exchanges. Shoring up regional support for the "One China" principle also tops Beijing's agenda.

Beijing is also fashioning itself as an alternative source of economic development aid, a role traditionally dominated by the United States, Europe and Western-led institutions such as the World Bank and International Monetary Fund (IMF). The performance of these development organizations has fostered deep-seated resentment among regional governments and populations. In contrast, as a developing country untainted by the colonial legacy of its Western counterparts in the region, Beijing is able to portray itself as a champion of the developing world. This approach has reaped great dividends for China on many fronts.

In this context, Egypt figures prominently into China's strategic calculus. While Beijing has pursued closer economic ties with Cairo, growing political and military relations with Egypt indicate a geopolitical dimension that is leading to a strategic partnership between the two countries.

The Roots of Modern Sino-Egyptian Ties

Modern Sino-Egyptian ties date back to the first meeting between Egyptian President Gamal Abdel Nasser and Chinese Premier Zhou Enlai during the historic 1955 Afro-Asian summit in Bandung, Indonesia that inaugurated the international Non-Aligned Movement (NAM). At the time, Cairo did not yet recognize the PRC. Nevertheless, Zhou Enlai admired Nasser for his vocal support for national liberation movements in Africa and Asia, vision for an independent and strong Egypt free of foreign interference, and ability to mobilize the Egyptian and Arab masses (*People's Daily*, May 29, 2001). The Chinese quickly realized that the charismatic Nasser's attitude toward China would have far reaching implications for China's position in the Arab world, Africa, and beyond.

Egypt's recognition of the PRC in 1956—the first country to do so since 1950—proved critical to China's pursuit of worldwide recognition [1]. Nasser was inspired by China and looked to Beijing for international support, especially after Washington declined his repeated requests for American arms. Zhou Enlai would soon play an integral role in negotiating an arms shipment from the Soviet Union to Egypt. China also supported Egypt's position during the Suez Crisis in 1956. Egypt applauded China's successful detonation of its atomic bomb in 1964 as a victory for the non-aligned nations. Nasser is also reported to have approached Beijing for assistance in developing an Egyptian nuclear weapons program [2].

China Courts Egypt

Egypt, the most populous Arab country, is the political and cultural center of gravity of the Arab world, and Cairo is increasingly using its regional clout to assert itself as the prime advocate for issues affecting the region. Among other things, Egypt is an outspoken proponent of reforming the UN Security Council, and has expressed a strong interest in assuming the role of representing Africa and the Middle East alongside the five permanent members—a position backed by Beijing (*People's Daily*, September 25, 2004).

On the surface, Beijing's efforts to court Cairo reflect a pattern of relations rooted in China's strategy to shore up energy sources in the region. China has spearheaded a number of joint ventures with Egyptian businesses, especially in the oil and natural gas sectors, namely projects dealing with oil and gas exploration, enhancing the productivity of old wells, and manufacturing equipment for the hydrocarbon industry. Beijing and Cairo have also committed to expanding cooperation to include joint ventures in construction, telecommunications and agriculture [3].

Yet as the growing frequency of the exchange of high-level political and military dignitaries indicates, China's ties to Egypt extend far beyond the energy and trade spheres and include a geopolitical dimension that is leading to a strategic partnership—some aspects of which conflict with the United States. Indeed, Egypt continues to enjoy close political, military and economic relations with the United States and is counted as one of Washington's leading allies in the region. Cairo's staunch ties with Washington are not lost on Beijing, as China treads carefully in maneuvering the complex geopolitics that characterize the U.S.-Egypt strategic partnership and Middle East diplomacy more generally. Likewise, Egypt is not prepared to abandon its staunch pro-U.S. orientation anytime soon (and the associated economic and military aid that comes with it) for a strategic alliance with China. Moreover, there is no evidence to suggest that China is anywhere near living up to such a role in the foreseeable future.

Nevertheless, China is becoming increasingly ambitious in its effort to expand relations with Egypt beyond the energy and economic spheres. For example, Sino-Egyptian cooperation extends to military affairs in the form of regular high-level contacts between Beijing and Cairo, a relationship that stems from the NAM. So far, these contacts reaffirm the growing strategic partnership both countries have built in the political and economic spheres but have yet to translate into more tangible results such as the sale of modern weapons systems, as the United States remains the primary source of advanced weapons platforms for Egypt's armed forces. Significantly, a People's Liberation Army Navy (PLAN) fleet comprised of a guided missile destroyer and a supply ship representing the North China Sea Fleet crossed the Suez Canal in June 2002 and docked in the Egyptian port city of Alexandria during its first around-the-world voyage (Xinhua, June 14, 2002). Egyptian Defense Minister Muhammed Hussein Tantawi also made an official visit to Beijing in April 2005 to meet with his Chinese counterpart Cao Gangchuan in an effort to strengthen bilateral military relations and reiterate each side's commitment to further expanding what they described as strategic cooperation between both countries (*People's Daily*, April 10, 2005).

Despite signing the Nuclear Non-Proliferation Treaty (NPT) and advocating a Nuclear Weapons Free Zone (NWFZ) in the Middle East—in response to Israel's robust nuclear arsenal and Iran's nuclear program—Cairo is often cited as a likely candidate to pursue its own nuclear option down the road. China's history of nuclear cooperation in the region may portend closer ties with Egypt in this area, if Cairo decides on such a course of action. Egypt has already approached China and Russia in 2002 for assistance in the development of a nuclear reactor in Alexandria. In a September 2006 speech, Egyptian President Hosni Mubarak announced that Egypt is once again ready to seriously pursue a nuclear energy program. Cairo's renewed emphasis on developing its nuclear energy capacity was reported to have topped the agenda of Mubarak's November 2006 state visits to Moscow and Beijing (*Al-Ahram Weekly*, January 25-31, 2007).

Beijing's overtures in Cairo are finding many eager and willing partners. China and Egypt see themselves as natural leaders in their respective regions and sharing a legacy as the contemporary heirs of great ancient civilizations. Both countries boast having converging interests on an array of

Beijing's overtures in Cairo are finding many eager and willing partners. China and Egypt see themselves as natural leaders in their respective regions and sharing a legacy as the contemporary heirs of great ancient civilizations.

key foreign policy issues. For example, China and Egypt see virtually eye-to-eye on the issue of Iraq, Afghanistan, and the U.S.-led war on terrorism. Additionally, Beijing and Cairo remain firm in their opposition to the U.S.-led initiative to impose UN Security Council sanctions against Sudan over the crisis in Darfur.

Despite China's controversial defense ties with Israel, Beijing is outspoken in support of the Egyptian and Arab position with respect to the Arab-Israeli conflict, namely in its criticism of Israel's continued occupation of Palestinian territory and expansion of settlements on Palestinian land. Egypt reciprocates with its unwavering support of the "One China" principle and its view that Taiwan constitutes sovereign Chinese territory. Cairo was also a staunch supporter of Beijing's adoption of the Anti-Secession Law aimed at preventing Taiwan from declaring independence (*People's Daily,* March 17, 2005).

China relies on Egypt's influence over fellow Arab and African countries as a means through which to secure support for its position vis-à-vis Taiwan, a strategy meant to marginalize Taipei in international bodies and other institutions. This aspect of Sino-Egyptian ties exemplifies a key facet in China's approach to Africa. Egypt is also a leading advocate of greater Sino-Arab cooperation under the auspices of the Arab League, as well as enhanced ties between the African Union and China.

Beijing has pursued a series of agreements that enhance China's direct access to Egyptian port facilities along the Suez Canal through Hong Kong's Hutchison Whampoa, Limited, a firm reported to have close ties with the Chinese government and the PLA. China has demonstrated an interest in securing a presence in and around strategic trade and communication choke points across the globe, as evidenced by its control of both the Atlantic and Pacific sides of the Panama Canal, also under Hutchison Whampoa, Limited.

The China National Aero-Technology Import and Export Corporation (CATIC) recently partnered with Egypt's A.O.I. Aircraft to jointly produce K-8E flight trainers, the largest joint venture between both countries to date (Xinhua, August 8, 2005). This venture indicates closer ties between both countries' defense industries and military.

By courting Egypt, China enhances its regional influence and, at the same time, is better positioned to check U.S. power in a region of vital strategic significance. Beijing's interest and presence in the Middle East also demonstrates its growing capability to project power deep in a part of the world that remains in the U.S. sphere of influence. A key element of this strategy may also be a reaction to Washington's expanded presence in Central and Southeast Asia, regions China considers to be in its sphere of influence.

Cairo Looks to Beijing

China is not alone in recognizing the long-term benefits of a strong relationship with Egypt. As China's fifth largest trading partner in Africa, Cairo identifies Beijing as a crucial partner to its economic development and a lucrative source of investment. Egypt is also keen on tapping the Chinese market through expanded trade links. Bilateral trade in 2006 reached almost $3.2 billion, an impressive increase of 48 percent from the previous year. Egypt has been aggressive in pursuing even stronger trade links and believes that China can become Egypt's top trade partner by the year 2012 (*People's Daily,* May 22, 2007).

Despite an expansion in bilateral trade, business relations continue to be characterized by a large Egyptian trade deficit. In a gesture indicative of the high priority Beijing places on friendly relations with Cairo, China offers subsidies to Chinese traders to encourage the purchase of Egyptian goods such as textiles and marble in an effort to placate Cairo's concerns over the large trade imbalance. China has also promoted Egypt as an "approved" tourist destination for its burgeoning middle class. This demonstrates another important step in the maturing ties between both sides, especially given the Egyptian economy's heavy reliance on tourist revenue as a source of foreign currency.

Egypt looks to China as an attractive alternative to the West, especially in terms of economic and social progress and political development. In this sense, Cairo sees China as a successful model of modernization that should be emulated in the Arab world and Africa (*Al-Ahram Weekly*, September 16-22, 2004). Cairo also relies on Beijing as a source for new technology and cooperation in the scientific research and development sectors, especially in agriculture. Moreover, Egypt is eager to utilize its strategic location and extensive contacts in the region to serve as a gateway for greater Chinese inroads into the Middle East and Africa. The Egyptian government has also begun encouraging young Egyptians to learn Chinese (China Radio International, October 10, 2004).

On the geopolitical front, Egyptian strategists believe that close ties with an emerging China can act as a potential check on U.S. influence in the region. Although Cairo's stance remains firmly entrenched in the United States and the West, Egypt resents growing U.S. pressure to implement democratic reforms and criticism of its human rights record. Given China's experience with U.S. criticism on these and related issues, Beijing is quite sensitive to Cairo's concerns, bringing both sides together on another important level. The Egyptian public is deeply resentful of its government's strong ties to both the United States and Israel and its perceived inability to influence Washington on topics ranging from the conflict in Iraq and Israel's occupation of Palestinian territory—issues that resonate deeply among ordinary Egyptians. Many Egyptians see their government as an illegitimate and corrupt vassal regime propped up by U.S. economic and political support. Therefore, Cairo sees expanding political and economic ties with China as a way of both enhancing its regional role and decreasing its dependence on the United States, both real and perceived. Egypt also hopes that an emerging China can stand up to the United States on these and related issues that affect the Middle East. This suits China, as Beijing is presenting itself as a potential alternative to the United States.

Public Diplomacy in Sino-Egyptian Relations

Sino-Egyptian relations are firmly rooted in the confluence of tangible mutual interests that encompass economics, geopolitics and security. Nevertheless, it is worth examining the nature of the rhetoric both sides use to characterize their rapidly expanding ties to better understand the trajectory of the Sino-Egyptian relationship. Doing so would provide insight into the power of effective public diplomacy. After all, like all forms of public diplomacy, Sino-Egyptian discourse is calculated to achieve specific objectives and to present a carefully calibrated image for international and domestic consumption.

As mentioned earlier, China and Egypt see themselves as the proud heirs of great civilizations. As a result, they believe that they occupy a privileged place in the world based on their respective ancient heritages. Sino-Egyptian public diplomacy is imbued with this kind of reinforcing rhetoric, in addition to populist themes that emphasize "South-South" cooperation and solidarity. Moreover, discourse highlighting themes such as mutual respect, equality and a shared sense of pride resonates strongly in Africa and the Middle East, especially in societies that continue to be shaped by patron-client relationships with former colonial and Western powers. In contrast, despite its aspirations of global power, China is keen on portraying its inevitable rise as a benign phenomenon and one that is symbolic of the potential harbored by developing countries. This presents China as a positive example worth following for countries like Egypt.

The rhetoric used to mark the 50th anniversary of the establishment of Sino-Egyptian relations in May 2006 is typical of Chinese public diplomacy in Egypt. During a June 2006 press conference in Cairo, Premier Wen stated: "China and Egypt both have great civilizations…and are both creators of human glory and progress and defender [sic] of mankind's cultural heritage, and we both pursue lofty values and ideals" (*People's Daily,* June 19, 2006). He added that China "feels indebted" to the Egyptians, the first nation in Africa to recognize the People's Republic of China (PRC) in 1956. He quoted a Chinese proverb in a sign of heartfelt appreciation: "We should never forget the benefits we are offered or forget the favor received." Premier Wen went on to remind his Egyptian audience that "the hat of neo-colonialism simply doesn't fit China," a response meant to refute reports of Chinese human rights abuses in the African business sector (Xinhua, October 5, 2006).

There are signs that Beijing's calculated rhetoric toward Egypt resonates beyond the official state level and is reaching ordinary Chinese. Zhang Boyin, a retired professor at Beijing University described his first trip to Egypt in 2006 as a "dream come true." He went on to proudly repeat Mao Zedong's adage regarding the significance of Africa to China: "It is our African brothers who carried us into the United Nations" (Xinhua, October 5, 2006). China is tapping this momentum by expanding Sino-Egyptian contacts on the popular level. For example, China and Egypt agreed to establish the Egyptian Chinese University in Cairo, the first Chinese university in the Middle East. Beijing is also encouraging outbound Chinese tourism to Egypt, as well as to Africa more generally. China is also rapidly expanding cultural contacts to include educational exchanges in Egypt and elsewhere in Africa featuring the promotion of the Chinese language and culture through the establishment of local "Confucius Institutes" (Xinhua, October 5, 2006).

Egyptian public diplomacy in China mirrors its counterpart's emphasis on the "special" nature of Sino-Egyptian ties. In a statement just prior to his November 2006 visit to Beijing to attend the Forum on China-Africa Cooperation (FOCAC), President Mubarak stated: "For me, visiting China is like going home. Egypt sees China more as a brother than as an ordinary friendly nation." In a show of appreciation for Beijing's growing engagement in Africa in recent years, President Mubarak added: "The development of Africa-China friendship should be credited to the fact that Africa-China relations are based on equality, mutual respect and reciprocity" (Xinhua, October 31, 2006). In this regard, both China and Egypt are quick to highlight what they label as the revival of "South-South" cooperation, a subtle message meant for U.S. and Western audiences (*Al-Ahram Weekly*, November 9-15, 2006).

Ordinary Egyptians generally harbor positive opinions toward the Chinese. For the most part, Egyptians see China as a potential check on U.S. power in the region, a sentiment stemming from deep-seated opposition to U.S. foreign policy in the Middle East. However, there is evidence that China is attracting popular support and admiration among Egyptians for other reasons. For example, the recent inaugurations of the region's first Confucius Institute, in partnership with Cairo University, and a joint Egyptian-Chinese University are drawing interest among a wide cross-section of Egyptians. Speaking about the Confucius Institute, American University of Cairo Economics Professor Adel Bashai remarked: "We have a lot to learn from the Chinese … the biggest benefit is to know the culture and religion…to know how they got to where they got." The number of Egyptians studying the Chinese language is also growing rapidly. Chinese is now taught at a number of major universities across Egypt, including al-Azhar, one of the world's leading centers of Islamic scholarship (*Daily Star* [Egypt], December 28, 2006).

Conclusion

Relations between China and Egypt will continue to expand and flourish, as both sides reap the benefits of closer ties. This relationship also has the potential to enhance greater Sino-Arab cooperation and Beijing's overall position in Africa, especially as Cairo assumes the de facto leadership role for the region. China will also continue to see Egypt as a strategic springboard to closer ties with other parts of Africa and the Middle East, a role that Cairo welcomes.

Despite the rhetoric, the expansion of Sino-Egyptian ties is driven as much by the intent of ensuring friendly relations with the United States as it is bolstering the existing Sino-Egyptian bond.

Likewise, Egypt will look to China as a means of gaining leverage in its increasingly precarious position vis-à-vis its primary ally, the United States. Egypt will also try to harness China's momentum in assuming a greater leadership role in an attempt to represent Arabs, Muslims and Africans on the global stage. However, despite their mutual emphasis on furthering "South-South" cooperation and enhancing "brotherly ties," there are limits to this relationship. Beijing and Cairo are not prepared or willing to jeopardize friendly and constructive relations with the United States in the foreseeable future in the hopes of cementing closer relations that threaten to directly undermine Washington's stake in the region. Indeed, despite the rhetoric, the expansion of Sino-Egyptian ties is driven as much by the intent of ensuring friendly relations with the United States as it is bolstering the existing Sino-Egyptian bond.

Originally published in *China Brief*, Volume 5 Issue 22 on October 25, 2005.

Notes

1. Dru C. Gladney, *Dislocating China: Muslims, Minorities, and Other Subaltern Topics* (Chicago: University of Chicago Press, 2004), 313.
2. For an intimate account of Nasser's relationship with Zhou Enlai, including his reported request for Chinese assistance to help develop an Egyptian nuclear program to counter Israel after it threatened to develop atomic weapons, see Mohammed Heikal, *The Cairo Documents: The Inside Story of Nasser and His Relationship with World Leaders, Rebels, and Statesmen* (New York: Doubleday & Company, Inc., 1973), 301-317.
3. U.S. China Economic and Security Review Commission, *Testimony before the U.S.-China Economic and Security Review Commission; China's Global Influence: Objectives and Strategies*, David H. Shinn, (Washington, D.C.: July 21, 2005),
http://www.uscc.gov/hearings/2005hearings/written_testimonies/05_07_21_22wrts/shinn_david_wrts.php

NIGER:

MINING FOR ENERGY: CHINA'S RELATIONS WITH NIGER

By Andrew McGregor

A latecomer to the exploitation of foreign energy resources, China has resorted to developing economic relationships with high-risk yet energy-rich nations like Niger in order to maintain its extraordinary pace of development. According to the International Energy Agency, with China's demand for energy resources steadily increasing, it faces the possibility of having to import 80 percent of its energy needs by 2030 [1]. Demand for oil products in China is expected to grow by at least 5.6 percent each year for the next five years (Xinhua, October 25, 2005). For several years now, China has looked to Africa for its energy future, and the continent already supplies 25 percent of China's oil needs. Niger, an impoverished former French colony, has been targeted by China for energy resource development due to its potential reserves of petroleum and its vast confirmed reserves of uranium. Uranium production in Niger (until recently dominated by France) represents 8-10 percent of the world's supply (3,400 tons in 2006) and accounts for nearly 70 percent of the country's exports. Given China's recent emphasis on developing additional nuclear power plants, such a supply of uranium has proven to be incredibly attractive for China's state-owned energy companies.

The Diplomatic Front

China and Niger first established diplomatic relations in 1974. After a four-year hiatus due to Niger's short-lived diplomatic recognition of Taiwan, China resumed official relations with Niger in 1996. Since then, Nigerien and Chinese leaders have been frequent visitors to each other's capitals. The groundwork for the resumption of relations between the two nations was laid during meetings between Niger's President Mamadou Tandja and Chinese President Jiang Zemin in 2001. During the same visit, Tandja became the first foreign head of state to visit the Ningxia Hui Autonomous Region of northwest China, a largely Muslim province that has had experience in anti-desertification and irrigation techniques (*People's Daily*, June 6, 2001).

China's main exports to Niger include textiles, communications equipment and rice. Niger, like most other African countries, supplies China with raw materials but has had great difficulty in establishing a Chinese market for its own manufactured goods. China's booming export industry tends to suppress the manufacturing sector in many African countries, hindering local development. Sino-Nigerien economic relations are governed by a bilateral trade agreement and a joint economic and trade commission. China also provides scholarships for Nigerien students to Chinese universities and medical assistance in the form of a 36-member medical team. In addition, Chinese goodwill has also been expressed through prestige development efforts like the Zinder water supply project, completed in May 2006.

A Strategic Energy Supply

Niger presents the most promising source of uranium to fuel China's program to dramatically increase its use of nuclear power. China's current reliance on coal-powered energy plants is quickly choking its cities in layers of toxic smog. To remedy this, China plans to build one nuclear plant a year until 2020, mostly in the rapidly expanding industrial centers along the Chinese coast. The project will increase China's

China's attempt to develop cleaner energy sources, however, could come at a cost to Niger's environment, a cost Niger seems willing to bear given its desperate need for capital.

nuclear generating capacity from its current nine gigawatts (GW) to 40 GW (Reuters, September 20, 2007). China's attempt to develop cleaner energy sources, however, could come at a cost to Niger's environment, a cost Niger seems willing to bear given its desperate need for capital.

Chinese firms active in Niger's energy sector include the China National Petroleum Corporation (CNPC), the China Nuclear International Uranium Corporation (Sino-Uranium), the China National Uranium Corporation (CNUC) and the Société des Mines d'Agelik, a Chinese prospecting company owned by the China Nuclear Engineering and Construction (Group) Corporation. The CNUC is developing two sites in the Agadez region of Niger, Teguidda and the smaller Madaouela. Production was scheduled to begin in 2010, though this is now threatened by rebel activity. The CNPC is currently exploring for oil in the Agadez region's Bilma and Tenere concessions.

Domestic Instability

Rebel activity in Niger's resource-rich north has threatened the short-term development of its resource industry and has made it much more difficult for Chinese firms to operate in the region. A Tuareg-led rebel group, Le Mouvement des Nigeriens pour la Justice (MNJ), is demanding an end to economic marginalization, environmental degradation and ethnic discrimination. Under pressure from the elusive rebels, the northern region of the country has reverted to military rule. While President Tandja has attempted to stifle all news coming out of the north, Niger's rebel movement has been effective in capitalizing upon modern communications technology as a medium for public relations [2].

Already, the rebels have already begun harassing Chinese companies, and the July kidnapping of a Sino-Uranium executive by the MNJ was intended as a warning to foreign mineral firms that their disregard for the environment and their present arrangements with the Niger government are unacceptable (Xinhua, July 7, 2007)—the executive was later released unharmed. Rebels also attacked an armed supply convoy heading to a CNPC exploration camp in July, killing four soldiers. Following these incidents, the Chinese pulled out of their field operations to return under military escort to Agadez.

The MNJ accuses China of supplying arms to Nigerien military operations in the north in exchange for mineral concessions. They also accuse the government of using mineral revenues to purchase military arms and equipment, including two Russian-made helicopter gunships. Niger's government denies the charges, and the Chinese Foreign Ministry maintains that it takes a "cautious and responsible approach" to arms exports, strictly observing "domestic laws and international obligations" [3]. Yet, rumors abound in West Africa of a Chinese military presence in the region; in January, the Nigeria's Defense Minister was forced to issue a public denial after reports of Chinese troops operating in the Niger Delta under contract from the Lagos government were published in a local newspaper (*The Guardian* [Nigeria], January 24, 2007).

French-Chinese Competition

Until recently, the French uranium company Areva had a virtual monopoly on uranium production since the material was first discovered in Niger in 1957. In early September, several Nigerien civil-society groups organized marches to demand Areva's departure from Niger for allegedly supporting the northern rebels, though no concrete proof was offered to support the charges. The leader of one of the groups involved in the protest suggested that Areva was hiring mercenaries to plant landmines (Voice of America, September 8, 2007). Concurrently, officials of the Niger government have accused Areva of plotting to frighten off their Chinese rivals in the uranium-rich Agadez region by financing MNJ attacks. Even the French government was pulled into the dispute, eventually offering resolution services as well as a team to demine northern Niger. After both the rebels and the French uranium miners denied the accusations of collaboration, Areva increased its payments to the Niger government and committed itself to improving environmental safety measures. It should be noted that Areva has hardly been immune to MNJ activities; on April 30, rebels attacked Areva's Imouraren exploration camp, killing one and wounding four (AFP, April 20, 2007). Areva was subsequently forced to halt operations in the area for a month.

Areva is also making efforts to enter China's nuclear development sector, but there are reports that China has recently cancelled plans for two Areva reactors to be built in Guangdong Province in favor of using domestic technology (though there is still the possibility that the Areva reactors might be relocated) (Reuters, September 20, 2007). France relies heavily on the Areva operations in Niger for uranium to supply its own reactors and nuclear weapons program. Without alternative sources of supply, France will use all of its influence to maintain its leading position in Niger's resource sector. Reflecting energy competition abroad, India has also suddenly emerged as a major competitor for undeveloped energy supplies in the West African region, though in Niger, China may have acted quickly to sideline India's offers to the Niger government (*The Times of India*, September 23, 2007).

Efforts to secure energy resources irrespective of market supply and demand threatens to destabilize global energy markets while perpetuating corrupt and undemocratic regimes that are able to offer protection to Chinese operations, thus leading China into a neo-colonial style relationship it has long tried to avoid in Africa.

Conclusion

The recent international revival of interest in nuclear power has created an opportunity for Niger to break out of the neo-colonial legacy of French rule by broadening its trade and cooperation with countries like China. As Niger's Prime Minister Seyni Oumarou recently said of this shift in patrons, "Nothing is going to be as it was in Niger ... Today the whole world is seeking to profit from the partnership with the Chinese and we should not isolate ourselves from that" (Reuters, August 1, 2007). Yet China's sense of urgency in locking up energy supplies makes it vulnerable to major disruptions from opposition groups, such as Niger's MNJ. Efforts to secure energy resources irrespective of market supply and demand threatens to destabilize global energy markets while perpetuating corrupt and undemocratic regimes that are able to offer protection to Chinese operations, thus leading China into a neo-colonial style relationship it has long tried to avoid in Africa.

Originally published in *China Brief* Volume 7 Issue 18 on October 3, 2007.

Notes

1. Osumi, Yo, "World Energy Outlook, and Energy Security and Cooperation in Northeast Asia," International Energy Agency, http://www.iea.org/textbase/speech/2006/yo_neasia.pdf.
2. The MNJ posts information about itself at: http://m-n-j.blogspot.com/.
3. Chinese Foreign Ministry, http://www.china-embassy.org/eng/gyzg/t339261.htm.

NIGERIA:

SINO-NIGERIAN RELATIONS: FTZS, TEXTILES AND OIL

By Ian Taylor

Nigeria is rapidly becoming one of China's largest trading partners in Africa, with trade between the two countries reaching over $3 billion in 2006. To gauge the exponential rise in Sino-Nigerian trade relations, one may consider the fact that in 1998 its trade volume was $384 million (AllAfrica.com, April 14, 2006). By 2001, this had reached $1 billion and by 2004, $2 billion. Nigerian exports to China—excluding oil—have quadrupled. Signifying Nigeria's importance to China, in January 2006, Beijing signed a Memorandum of Understanding with Abuja on the Establishment of a Strategic Partnership. In doing so, Nigeria became the first African country to sign such an agreement with China. Other anecdotal points emphasize the importance of this bilateral relationship. China's first scheduled direct flight to Africa was inaugurated on December 31, 2006, when China Southern Airlines Company launched its maiden flight from Beijing to Lagos via Dubai. With some 50,000 Chinese now living in Nigeria and a growing Nigerian diaspora in China, the airline's service makes commercial sense. In August 2005, Nigeria also began hosting a Chinese newspaper, *West African United Business Weekly*, the first in West Africa. Such levels of engagement mean that China's links with Nigeria are qualitatively different from the West, and as a result, may potentially produce benefits for the ordinary people of Nigeria.

Nigeria's Markets

In 2006, China announced that it would invest $267 million to establish the first phase of the Lekki Free Trade Zone (FTZ) in Lagos (*People's Daily*, May 9, 2006). Approved by the Chinese government, the Lekki FTZ is the first of its kind that Beijing has constructed overseas. Eventually, the project aims to cover 150 square kilometers with a total investment of $5 billion. Of course, as with other announced Chinese projects in Africa, whether or not Nigeria will ever see a 15 square kilometer FTZ in Lagos where 300,000 Nigerians are employed is a matter of speculation, if not skepticism.

Yet, any development of the FTZ will have to confront the growing concern regarding Chinese work practices. According to a Nigerian report, "Chinese companies are notorious for their tendency to bring in their own workers as opposed to hiring locally. Local content has no meaning to the Chinese-run companies. This policy does not in any way address issues of unemployment in the host nations. Safety standards within their industries are another area of concern. The fire incident at a Chinese-owned industry in Ikorodu Town, Lagos State, revealed that it was standard practice to lock the workers in while on duty. In this particular case, this policy hindered the workers escape route from the fire and resulted in many of them losing their lives" (*This Day* [Lagos], February 15, 2007). Considering the infamous corrupt tendencies of Nigerian government officials, however, it is probable that safety inspectors were bribed to look the other way. There are, nevertheless, genuine issues surrounding Chinese labor practices, in Nigeria as elsewhere in Africa.

As with other announced Chinese projects in Africa, whether or not Nigeria will ever see a 15 square kilometer FTZ in Lagos where 300,000 Nigerians are employed is a matter of speculation, if not skepticism.

The flooding of Nigerian markets with cheap Chinese products, undermining the country's commercial operations, has also become a politically sensitive issue. For example, the enormous influx of inexpensive Chinese textiles has resulted in the shrinking of Nigeria's domestic textile industries as Nigerian fabrics have been unable to compete with their Chinese counterparts. As

General Secretary of the Textile, Tailoring and Garment Union Issa Aremu notes, the mass importation of textiles—both second-hand from Europe and new garments, mostly from China— has led to the closing of 65 Nigerian textile mills and the laying off of a total of 150,000 textile workers over the past ten years (*Koinonia International*, February 15, 2005). Aremu also claims that more than one million others whose jobs are linked to the textile industry, such as traders and cotton farmers, have also lost their means of livelihood because of the closures.

Investing in Nigeria's Oil

As Africa's leading oil producer and the eleventh largest oil producer worldwide, Nigeria has a light, low sulfur grade of oil known as "sweet crude," which is valued for its high gasoline content and relatively cheap processing outlay. Until recently, China had been completely excluded from Nigeria's oil industry by an established presence of Western oil companies in Nigeria. This is rapidly changing, however, through a mix of canny Chinese diplomacy and sweetener development deals.

With regard to specific Chinese oil contracts in Nigeria, in October 2004, it was stated that Nigeria needed an annual investment of $10 billion in order to reach a proven reserve of 40 billion barrels by 2010 (*People's Daily*, April 20, 2005). Consequently, PetroChina signed an agreement with the Nigerian government to locate upstream oil and gas assets that might be incorporated into downstream projects. In July 2005, PetroChina signed an $800 million contract that guaranteed 30,000 barrels per day to China over a five-year period, to be renewed every year (Xinhua, July 9, 2005). Building on such developments, in April 2006, the Nigerian government offered China four oil exploration licenses in exchange for $4 billion worth of investment in Nigeria's infrastructure.

The two countries then signed seven development agreements granting Abuja export credit worth $500 million (Reuters, April 27, 2006). China agreed to repair the Kaduna Refining and Petrochemicals Company, while undertaking other investment projects, such as building a hydropower plant in the Mambila, Plateau State. In return for this, China was permitted to exercise the "right of first refusal" on oil blocs. China National Offshore Oil Corporation (CNOOC) has also taken over the commitments of a contractor of a deepwater bloc that had earlier been assigned to South Atlantic Petroleum Limited, a company owned by a former Nigerian Defense Minister, Theophilus Danjuma (*People's Daily*, January 10, 2006). Reflecting the ties between politics and oil in Nigeria, Danjuma immediately took steps in Nigeria's courts to negate the deal. Claiming that his company's acreage had been revoked for political reasons linked to his non-support for then President Olusegun Obasanjo's attempt to change the Nigerian constitution and run for a third term, Danjuma's case was brought before the Federal High Court, which ruled in favor of Obasanjo's government.

There have been indications that Sino-African ties in the oil sector have not been progressing as smoothly as initially thought. In March 2007, it was announced that the Nigerian Government was reconsidering its plans to hand over the management of the Kaduna refinery to CNOOC since China's promise to invest in the refinery had not materialized. Director General of the Bureau of Public Enterprises Irene Chigbue stated that the plan to get CNOOC to manage the Kaduna refinery, which produces 110,000 barrels per day (bpd), "[ran] into hitches as the CNOOC have not been forthcoming with the takeover plans" (*This Day*, March 6, 2007). Indeed, the Chinese had initially agreed to manage the Kaduna refinery as a pre-condition to winning oil blocks for which Chinese companies were bidding. Chigbue added, "The arrangement which was tied to oil block allocation as a result of the peculiar nature of the refinery, which requires heavy investment, was being considered for review as the Chinese firm had not shown appreciable interest ... No appreciable progress had been made since the allocation took place" (*Vanguard*, March 6, 2007). Such a situation is particularly important for Nigeria—and threatens to sour Sino-Nigerian relations—as Abuja is desperate to offload its former public enterprises to competent management.

Other problems in Sino-Nigerian relations also revolve around the oil industry and threaten to undermine the bilateral links and the "win-win" situation that Beijing boasts about in its discussions of Sino-African ties. In particular, the security situation surrounding the oil industry in the Niger Delta is becoming increasingly problematic. Nigerian militants from the Movement for the Emancipation of the Niger Delta (MEND) have warned Chinese companies to "stay well clear" of the Niger Delta or risk facing attacks. They have also claimed responsibility for a car bomb attack near the port town of Warri, stating that the blast was "a warning against Chinese expansion in the region" and that "the Chinese government, by investing in stolen crude, places its citizens in our line of fire" (*Financial Times*, May 1, 2006).

Complaining of Washington's tardiness in offering security assistance in the form of personnel and hardware, Nigeria has turned to China for military assistance to protect its oil fields.

Complaining of Washington's tardiness in offering security assistance in the form of personnel and hardware, Nigeria has turned to China for military assistance to protect its oil fields. Given that Nigerian security forces are responsible for "politically motivated killings; the use of lethal force against suspected criminals and hostage-seizing militants in the Niger Delta; beatings and even torture of suspects, detainees, and convicts; and extortion of civilians," as well as "child labor and prostitution, and human trafficking," Washington's reluctance to provide such elements with further supplies is perhaps understandable [1]. China, however, needs little compulsion to sell weapons to such actors and is able to fill the gap left by the hesitant Western nations.

Conclusion

Even as China is becoming heavily involved in Nigeria's oil industry, Chinese companies are also penetrating other spheres of Nigeria's economy. In the process, unlike most other foreign actors in the country, they are investing in fixed assets, such as refineries and factories, with the intention of developing a long-term economic relationship. Consequently, stability and good governance in Nigeria is advantageous for Beijing because it is the only way to guarantee that Chinese interests are protected. In such circumstances, the task for the West and for Nigerian civil society is to engage Beijing by cooperating in areas where mutual interests converge and work to advance the well-being of the Nigerian people as a whole.

Originally published in *China Brief*: Volume 7 Issue 11 on May 30, 2007.

Notes

1. Library of Congress – Federal Research Division, *Country Profile: Nigeria*, (Washington D.C.: June 2006), 22.

HORN OF AFRICA:

DUELING PRIORITIES FOR BEIJING IN THE HORN OF AFRICA

By David Shinn and Joshua Eisenman

The Horn of Africa has become an increasingly important region for China. Of the five countries—Sudan, Ethiopia, Eritrea, Djibouti, and Somalia/Somaliland—that constitute the Horn, Sudan looms especially large. In 2005, China receives around 7 percent of its oil from Sudan, has invested millions in Sudan's oil sector, and supports Khartoum as it faces international condemnation for its handling of the crisis in Darfur. China's engagement in tiny Djibouti and the still-struggling state of Somalia and its breakaway sister, Somaliland, is modest. Surprisingly, China's growing ties with neighboring Ethiopia and Eritrea have thus far escaped extensive review. This analysis seeks to fill that void.

On September 13, 2005, United Nations' Secretary General Kofi Annan warned that fighting between Ethiopia and Eritrea threatens to destroy the fragile peace secured in 2000. He explained the need to extend the UN peacekeeping mission along the Eritrean-Ethiopian border, and in a UN press release called on the "international community to spare no effort in bringing the parties together." To underscore the stakes, the Eritrean Minister of Finance Berhane Abrehe, in an address at the UN General Assembly on September 21, said, "the dark clouds of war are again hanging over my country" and that Eritrea is determined "to defend and preserve its territorial integrity by any means possible." Juxtaposed with visits by high-level Chinese military delegations to both Ethiopia and Eritrea in August 2005, these warnings underscore why a discussion of Beijing's relations with the Horn of Africa, especially Ethiopia and Eritrea, is timely.

A Crisis in Ethiopian-Eritrean Relations

Following formal Eritrean independence from Ethiopia in 1993, the two countries initially enjoyed close relations until policy differences and growing tensions culminated in a border incident in May 1998. This incursion by Eritrea, which occurred in the border village of Badme, led to full-scale war, the death of an estimated 100,000 Ethiopian and Eritrean soldiers, and several hundred-thousand displaced persons, mostly Eritrean. The UN Security Council imposed an arms embargo. In 2000, Addis Ababa and Asmara signed an agreement establishing a commission to resolve the border dispute and calling for both forces to withdraw to the positions they held before May 1998. The UN established its Mission in Ethiopia and Eritrea (UNMEE) with several thousand peacekeeping troops to patrol the security zone along the border of the two countries. In 2003, when the Border Commission issued its ruling, Ethiopia rejected the decision primarily because it awarded Badme to Eritrea. For its part, Eritrea has refused to discuss with Ethiopia any changes in the agreement, arguing that both sides agreed at the outset to accept the Commission's binding arbitration. Currently, Ethiopia holds Badme and several other small pieces of territory awarded to Eritrea, and both countries have deployed large numbers of troops in the vicinity of the border. This has resulted in increased tension and threatens to undo the fragile peace.

China's Role in the Horn

China has successfully maintained good relations with all five nations in the Horn of Africa. Beijing has supplied millions of dollars in aid and loans, built infrastructure projects, extended preferential trade agreements, sold military equipment, and offered political support for Horn countries at the UN and in other international fora. China has sent medical teams to the region for many years and worked hard to cultivate relations with future leaders by providing scholarships for Africans to study in China. In 2005, Ethiopia's Minister of Trade Girma Biru was quoted in the *Wall Street Journal* as saying, "China has become our most reliable partner" (*Wall Street Journal,* March 29, 2005). For its part, China has received strong support on contentious human rights issues, unwavering adherence to the "One China" policy, and cultivated profitable trade and investment relationships.

China has formalized its cooperation with the Horn and the rest of Africa through the Forum on China-Africa Cooperation (FOCAC). Created in Beijing in 2000, the second ministerial meeting took place in Addis Ababa in 2003. This resulted in the Addis Ababa Action Plan and solidified China's presence in the region. The third ministerial meeting of the Forum will take place in Beijing in 2006. The Forum provides a venue for Sino-African consultation and dialogue allowing China to extend its soft power throughout the continent. Examples of Chinese programs include a series of training sessions that are intended to develop personal ties and good will.

Trade and Investment

Through its trade promotion and investment programs, China has become one of the Horn of Africa's most important partners. Beijing has supported economic development through low-cost loans, debt relief and preferential tariffs. Investment projects, many of them on commercial terms, are also encouraged to extend China's economic reach throughout the region. Sudan and Ethiopia have been the biggest beneficiaries of Chinese investment. Other than its substantial oil imports from Sudan, China imports mostly raw materials such as coffee, hides, skins, and oil seeds from countries in the Horn. China's top exports to the region are textiles, manufactured goods, machinery, chemicals, medical products, and building materials. According to Chinese statistics, China's trade with the region totaled over $2.8 billion in 2004. By the first six months of 2005, it had already exceeded $2 billion.

With the exception of oil-rich Sudan, China's trade with the region is heavily weighted in Beijing's favor. In 2004, Chinese exports to Ethiopia made up over 93 percent of their bilateral trade. In the first half of 2005, Chinese purchases from Djibouti, Eritrea, and Somalia/Somaliland were negligible. In an attempt to correct the lopsided trade relationship in 2005, Beijing scrapped tariffs on 190 commodities from 25 Africans nations, including all the Horn countries [1]. Yet, despite Chinese government pronouncements claiming the initiative was an "important commitment to help African countries develop their economies," this decision is unlikely to dramatically change China's trade relationships in the region.

One of China's primary contributions to the region's economic development comes in the form of investment. Chinese companies have constructed commercial and assistance projects such as roads and bridges, power and water supply stations, irrigation and telecommunications networks, and housing. These firms—many of them owned by the Chinese state—have been known to submit bids below cost in an effort to break into the market and are aggressive to the point of alienating domestic competitors. Specific examples of Chinese projects include the Oratta Hospital in Asmara, Djibouti's Foreign Ministry, Addis Ababa's circumferential highway, and the $300 million hydroelectric dam and power plant on Ethiopia's Tekeze River. Notably, the Tekeze project is behind schedule and the Ethiopian government is insisting the Chinese construction firm pay for the delays (Addis Tribune, June 9, 2005). In all, scores of Chinese firms are operating in the Horn.

Diplomatic and Military Ties

China has been highly successful in convincing countries in the Horn to support its initiatives in international organizations, while aligning itself with African proposals supported by Horn nations. In March 2005, for example, Ethiopia's Parliament approved a resolution in support of Beijing's Anti-Secession Law (Xinhua, March 15, 2005). China has also supported proposals favored by both Ethiopia and Eritrea on UN Security Council reform. One exception is the Ottawa Treaty banning land mines. China has refused to sign the agreement; most African countries support outlawing land mines.

For Beijing, the support it receives from Horn of Africa countries for China's position on human rights is a valuable contribution. Ethiopia and Eritrea are voting members of the UN Commission on Human Rights until 2006, and Sudan is a member until 2007. In 2004 the U.S. and other Western countries were thwarted in their attempts to censure China for its human rights record, with Sudan, Ethiopia, and Eritrea all siding with China in the commission. The emboldened Chinese Ambassador Sha Zukang claimed: "The truth is that the Chinese people enjoy freedoms of speech, assembly, religion and belief that are guaranteed by law" (Xinhua, April 15, 2004). Beijing has reciprocated by lending its support to the governments of Ethiopia, Eritrea, and Sudan, all of which have been criticized for their human rights records.

One of the most intriguing and difficult to document aspects of China's relations with countries in the Horn of Africa is military cooperation, sales, and assistance. China has supplied significant quantities of military equipment to Sudan for many years and was once an important source of arms for Somalia. China became a major arms seller to Ethiopia and Eritrea during their 1998-2000 conflict. Bypassing a UN arms embargo, Beijing sold over $1 billion in arms to both sides, according to press reports. In September 2005, China and the other four permanent members of the UN Security Council called the unresolved Ethiopia-Eritrea boarder question "inherently destabilizing" and approved the Secretary General's plan to extend the UN mandate for a 3,000 strong peacekeeping force along the Ethiopia/Eritrea border until March 15, 2006.

While world leaders are fearful of new conflict, China continues to encourage military cooperation and extend arms sales to Ethiopia and Eritrea, as well as to Sudan and Djibouti. Ethiopian Prime Minister Meles Zenawi and Chinese Lieutenant General Zhu Wenquan, commander of the Nanjing Military Region, met in Addis Ababa in August 2005. According to the Ethiopian Ministry of Foreign Affairs Seyoum Mesfin, they agreed that "Ethiopia and China shall forge mutual cooperation in military training, exchange of military technologies, and peacekeeping missions, among others." The previous week Lieutenant General Zhu, joined by Vice Admiral Gu Wengen, met with the commander of the Eritrean Air Force, Major General Teklay Habteselassie. At that gathering, Zhu was reported by Eritrean radio to have said that it was China's desire "for the armies of the two sisterly countries to cooperate in various training." China's training of Eritrean military forces is well known; years ago even Eritrea's President Isaias Afewerki received military training in China (*New Straits Times* [Malaysia], July 14, 2005).

While world leaders are fearful of new conflict, China continues to encourage military cooperation and extend arms sales to Ethiopia and Eritrea, as well as to Sudan and Djibouti.

Beijing is also enhancing military cooperation with Djibouti. This interest may relate to the establishment in Djibouti in 2002 of an American counterterrorism base. Known as Combined Joint Task Force–Horn of Africa, it consists of about 1,400 U.S. and coalition military and civilian personnel who monitor the situation in the Horn, East Africa, and Yemen. Djiboutian Chief of General Staff Fathi Houssein met in July with Cao Gangchuan, China's Minister of National Defense, and Liang Guanglie, Chief of General Staff of the People's Liberation Army (PLA). Liang, as quoted in Xinhua on July 22, 2005, said that "China attaches importance to the friendship with Djibouti armed forces and will further increase and deepen the cooperation."

There is limited public information available on Chinese arms sales to countries in the Horn. Beijing is not, however, the only country violating arms embargos in the region. Moscow and several former Soviet republics have also secured contracts with Sudan, Ethiopia, and Eritrea (*The Economist*, April 23, 2005). Unfortunately, many of these weapons find their way surreptitiously to Somalia. This places Beijing and Moscow in the hypocritical position of competing for arms contracts while supporting UN peacekeeping operations in the region. In fact, China has a small number of peacekeepers assigned to UNMEE and a new mission in southern Sudan. Beijing and Moscow, therefore, supply weapons to the region while at the same time voting for resolutions calling on the parties not to use them. One observer called this situation "a windfall for arms merchants on the so-called 'security' council" [2]. In the long-run, arms sales and military contacts will allow Beijing and Moscow to extend their influence in both Addis Ababa and Asmara "turning the potential costs into political dividends," according to one Russian military commentator quoted in Moscow's *Kommersant* (April 15, 2005).

Implications for the Region

While China's economic assistance and investment contribute to the betterment of the Horn of Africa, its arms sales and heavily unbalanced trade relationships do not. A backlash against cheap Chinese textile exports has already begun in neighboring Kenya and several other African countries. Some African leaders have been accused of being complicit in China's pursuit of its self-interest. In order to avoid being portrayed as exploitative, China would be well served to implement policies that go beyond appeals to the region's ruling elites and address the needs of the less fortunate populations in the Horn of Africa. Most hypocritical is China's willingness to arm both Ethiopia and Eritrea while supporting UN Security Council resolutions and even providing peacekeeping troops for UN missions in the region. As northerners and southerners implement a delicate peace in Sudan and tension rises along the border between Ethiopia and Eritrea, this is no time for China to arm the region.

In order to avoid being portrayed as exploitative, China would be well served to implement policies that go beyond appeals to the region's ruling elites and address the needs of the less fortunate populations in the Horn of Africa.

Originally published in *China Brief:* Volume 5 Issue 21 on October 13, 2005.

Notes

1. Forum on China-Africa Cooperation, http://www.focac.org/eng/zt/zfhzltcsh/t196993.htm.
2. John Sorenson, "Lines in the Sand," *Canadian Business and Current Affairs*, June 1, 2005.

SOUTH AFRICA:

SOUTH AFRICA AND CHINA: FORGING AFRICA'S STRATEGIC PARTNERSHIP

By Christopher Alden

Ten years of official diplomatic relations between the People's Republic of China (PRC) and the Republic of South Africa have been marked by a multitude of milestones in both countries. From a period of no official ties to limited interaction between the South African and Chinese governments, the relationship has subsequently grown to become one of the closest between African and Asian states. Underpinning the warm ties between the two countries is growing economic engagement, which has put South Africa amongst China's top three trading partners on the continent. At the same time, the impact of ongoing leadership struggles within the African National Congress (ANC), coupled with endemic crime and xenophobia, has produced an undercurrent that is introducing a degree of uncertainty to this nascent partnership.

With the onset of diplomatic relations with China in 1998, South Africa's foreign policy charted new waters by re-orienting its diplomacy and, increasingly its economy, away from its exclusive focus on Europe and North America. The establishment of the bi-national commission in December 2001, subsequently reinforced through the strategic dialogue process, has ensured that there is systematic government-to-government contact at the deputy president/vice president and ministerial levels, a process that facilitates close cooperation on multiple areas of mutual concern. Since taking up the non-permanent seat on the UN Security Council in 2006, it has become clear that South African positions on matters like Darfur, Zimbabwe and Burma (Myanmar) mirror those of China and are a clear indication of the two governments' shared outlook on the key features of the international system. Indeed, that Pretoria prioritizes its concerns for sovereignty over that of human rights and democracy *Underpinning the warm ties between the two countries is growing economic engagement, which has put South Africa amongst China's top three trading partners on the continent.* suggests that the South Africa's image as a liberal beacon in Africa is waning and moving ever closer to Beijing's perspective on these matters. Regarding the reform of international institutions, South Africa and China also share a common view on the need to transform the UN Security Council and the international financial institutions to better reflect developing country interests (though Beijing has been careful not to alienate other African aspirants to a permanent seat in the Security Council by supporting the African Union's call for a rotating seat).

Military co-operation, though discussed at senior levels by both governments, appears not to have produced the same levels of co-operation as found in the diplomatic and economic spheres. Certainly, the spectacle of joint military exercises with the Indian and Brazilian navies agreed at the last IBSA summit will raise the stakes for those wishing to achieve a closer degree of co-operation between South Africa and China. Moreover, South African weapons producers are by some accounts in competition with their Chinese counterparts for markets in Africa, including Sudan.

These close diplomatic ties have been matched by growing economic engagement. With two way trade rising from $800 million in 1998 to $11.2 billion in October 2007, economic cooperation between the two countries is being realized at ever-increasing rates. Moreover, the once low levels of Chinese investment into South Africa are finally catching up with the high-profile South African investment in China. In particular, Chinese FDI reached new heights with the announcement in November 2007 that the Industrial and Commercial Bank of China (ICBC) would be purchasing a 20 percent stake in Standard Bank worth $5.6 billion. This is complemented by significant South African investment in China, which surpassed $200 million in 2006. Leading the charge are SAB-

Miller, which owns 55 breweries in China; Sasol, which has a joint venture with Ningxia and Shenhua CLC to develop coal-to-oil plants in China; and other resource based companies such as Anglo-American and Kumba Resources. With Chinese demand for foodstuffs growing exponentially, the potential for further development of commercial links between South Africa and China exists.

At the same time, the deepening of economic ties with China has raised important questions as to the uneven impact of trade in certain sectors of the South African economy—with locally produced textiles experiencing sharp reductions while exports of South African agricultural products are soaring—and has created challenges for China and South Africa alike. The emphasis of South Africa-China trade has been on the Chinese acquisition of minerals, agricultural goods and related commodities while South Africa absorbs imports of low-end consumer goods. This is, however, changing and we are beginning to see higher value-added products from China such as automobiles and 'white goods' entering the local market. To demonstrate its sensitivity toward trade relations the Chinese government agreed to impose unilateral restrictions on its own textile and clothing exports in late 2006, in order to give South Africa's manufacturers time to retool their operations in anticipation of a re-opening of trade in this sector. Additional frictions exist over the commercial rivalry between South African firms in areas like construction and mobile phones, where Chinese firms have made inroads into parts of Africa which South African business has traditionally seen as their 'natural' market.

Moreover, there are a host of other factors complicating the process of deepening bilateral ties. Key amongst these is the politics of succession within the ruling ANC, which has pitted President Thabo Mbeki against his former deputy president, Jacob Zuma. The routing of Mbeki and his supporters at the ANC's party congress in December 2007 was owed in large part to the Congress of South African Trade Unions (Cosatu) and other disgruntled elements within the ANC. As Cosatu has been at the forefront of the debate regarding the impact of Chinese investment and imports on labor interests, the spectacle of a Zuma presidency—which owes his position to the trade union—is seen with some trepidation in Beijing. Cosatu's defense of the opposition in neighboring Zimbabwe resulted in the refusal to unload a shipment of Chinese arms in Durban bound for that country in April 2008. The situation, which brought on a public round of condemnation by Southern African leaders, could serve as a harbinger of the trade union's influence on future foreign policy. Furthermore, South Africa has the largest Chinese community—with over 300,000 Chinese in residence, many of whom arrived within the last decade—on the continent, and its high rates of crime are taking a toll on their confidence. Many in the Chinese community believe that they are being specifically targeted by South African criminals and, with the rising tide of xenophobia gripping the country and the failure of the police to stem crime, there is a growing atmosphere of siege that is starting to affect individual entrepreneurs' investment decisions.

The rolling out of Chinese backed infrastructure across the continent —often characterized in the South African press as an outright loss for South African interests and firms—should be recognized for what it is: an unprecedented step aimed at addressing of a key obstacle to African development. partners on the continent.

While strong bilateral engagement between South Africa and China are at the heart of the relationship, the two sides recognize that there are considerable opportunities for greater co-operation in the rest of Africa. In this regard, the rolling out of Chinese backed infrastructure across the continent—often characterized in the South African press as an outright loss for South African interests and firms—should be recognized for what it is: an unprecedented step aimed at addressing of a key obstacle to African development. Indeed, given World Bank estimates that Africa has an infrastructure backlog measured at over $32 billion. The Chinese role is one of contributing to addressing this issue and leaves plenty of opportunity for others, especially South Africans, to play a significant role. Evidence from Ethiopia to Angola, where Chinese financed firms have built transport and communication infrastructure, already links these initiatives to increased economic growth in those countries. Moreover, this opening of previously isolated or closed markets benefits not only Chinese economic interests but provides an opportunity for South African (and others) exporters. In this regard, the ICBC-Standard Bank arrangement is a compelling model of Chinese-South African private/public sector co-operation, promising greater collaboration in provisions for financial services across the African continent through Standard Bank's established presence in 18 countries, in giving the South African bank better access to the Chinese domestic market and providing a new source of capital. According to the Chief Executive Officer of Standard Bank, Jaco Maree, "We will try to keep almost all the (Chinese investment) money that we can outside of South Africa because it is earmarked for growth in Africa and growth outside of Africa" [1].

At the same time, Chinese competitiveness is a phenomenon that is raising concerns not only in certain circles in South Africa but increasingly across the continent as well. While talk of a "de-industrialization" of Africa is certainly exaggerated, nonetheless there are very real fears that in some areas in Africa's hard fought gains in manufacturing will fall victim to the Chinese economic juggernaut. Though overall the balance of trade between China and Africa is in rough parity, individual countries like South Africa are experiencing significant trade imbalances with South African imports of Chinese products valued at $7.5 billion (R49.1 bn) and South Africa exports to China valued at $3.64 billion (R23.7 bn) in 2007. The Chinese are well-aware of this problem, as the South African textile case suggests, and have begun to introduce measures such as zero tariff ratings on selected goods from Africa's poorest countries though there is undoubtedly more that can be done. Other aspects of China's engagement are raising eyebrows in African capitals as well. In particular, the role of Chinese weapons sales in established arenas of conflict around the continent, highlighted by the Zimbabwean case, are increasingly viewed as problematic by South Africa.

Notwithstanding these issues, it is clear that officials on both sides would like relations between South Africa and China to become the linchpin of a new invigorated form of South-South co-operation. Reflecting this is the decision in late 2007 to deepen bilateral co-operation by establishing a Partnership for Growth and Development whose overarching aim is to forge a more equitable relationship between the two countries. Featuring in this arrangement are talks around gaining long term access to South African resources in exchange for investment and greater market access for value-added and beneficiated products [2]. Even the moribund negotiations around a China-SACU preferential trade agreement is back on the table and likely to be re-opened in the coming year. This multifaceted diplomatic collaboration between China and South Africa, coupled with an increasingly strong economic foundation, is poised to become one of the drivers of growth on the African continent. Realising this aim, against the backdrop of an incoming South African administration and pressure from local interests, is the key challenge for this maturing relationship.

Originally published in *China Brief:* Volume 8 Issue 13 on June 18, 2008.

Notes

1. Quoted in: Regis Nyamakanga, "Standard's Chinese boost," *Business Day* (South Africa), http://www.businessday.co.za/Articles/TarkArticle.aspx?ID=3066808
2. Rob Davies, Deputy Minister of Trade and Industry of South Africa, presentation at conference on China and South Africa, May 2, 2008.

SUDAN:

SUDAN: NEO-COLONIALISM WITH CHINESE CHARACTERISTICS

By Yitzhak Shichor

In the 1960s and 1970s, Beijing defined a "superpower" as one that expands overseas both in military and in economic terms, and added that—in that sense—China would never be a "superpower." At the beginning of the 21st century, China is indeed still far away from being a "superpower" in that sense, but there are initial indications in this direction. A substantial Chinese presence (sometime called "overseas bases" (*haiwai jichu*)—not so much military but definitely economic—is already evident in a number of countries such as Burma (Myanmar), Pakistan, and especially in Sudan. Still a far cry from old-style colonialism, China's predominant role in Sudan's economy, military as well as foreign affairs, could be termed neo-colonialism with Chinese characteristics.

Sudan was the fourth African government to establish diplomatic relations with China, on February 4, 1959. There was, however, nothing significant in the relations between the two countries until the mid-1990s when Beijing realized its urgent need to acquire energy resources to supplement its dwindling domestic production and keep pace with the fast economic growth. By that time, a decision had already been made to establish oil bases abroad by PRC investment and participation in the exploration, development and construction of oilfields and pipelines, "to guarantee our country's long term and steady supply of crude oil import" (*quebao woguo jinkou yuanshi de changqi wending gongying*). In the case of Sudan, this policy that had been launched in the mid-1990s has already paid handsome dividends. The PRC has become the predominant actor in Sudan's economy—and international politics.

By 2005, within seven years, China's import from Sudan had grown nearly fifty times, while PRC export to Sudan had grown less than six times and overall trade turnover nearly fourteen times.

In Search of Oil Wells and Power (Plants)

Indeed, China's interest in Sudan had been motivated initially by oil, to be discussed below. The role of oil in Sino-Sudanese relations is amply demonstrated by trade turnover figures, mainly by China's increased import (see Table 1). The turning point came in 2000 when Sudan's export to China suddenly jumped nearly fourteen times compared to 1999, when Chinese "share-oil" (*fen e you*) began to flow out. By 2005, within seven years, China's import from Sudan had grown nearly fifty times, while PRC export to Sudan had grown less than six times and overall trade turnover nearly fourteen times. Sino-Sudanese trade turnover (that declined in 2006) still accounts for no more than 0.2-0.3 percent of China's total foreign trade.

Table 1: China-Sudan Trade, 1999-2006
(In Million US Dollars)

Year	Total	Export	Import	Change in Import
2006	3,353.81	1,410.33	1,934.48	-26.0%
2005	3,908.05	1,293.59	2,614.46	53.3%
2004	2,521.76	815.89	1,705.88	18.3%
2003	1,920.24	478.42	1,441.82	24.6%
2002	1,549.98	392.39	1,157.59	23.4%
2001	1,158.02	219.89	938.13	28.2%
2000	890.11	156.38	731.73	1272.9%
1999	282.65	229.35	53.30	---

Source: Adapted from *China Statistical Yearbook*, various years.

Yet trade is but one aspect of China's economic activity in Sudan. China is involved in extensive construction projects, to be detailed below, which place Sudan as the top partner in China's foreign economic cooperation in 2005 and 2006, up from number four in 2004 (discounting Hong Kong and Macao, see Table 2). Another indication of Sudan's importance to China is the size of Beijing's direct non-financial investment in that country. Again, excluding Hong Kong and Macao (that legally belong to the PRC) as well as Cayman Islands and Virgin Islands (that are tax havens), Sudan has become an attractive market for Chinese net direct investments—number six in 2005, number seven in 2006 and number five in accumulated investment by yearend 2006 (Table 3). According to Dr. Ahmad Majdhub, State Minister in the Ministry of Finance, by June 2007 the total Chinese investment in Sudan had reached $6 billion, invested in fifty different projects (*Ra'y al-Sha'b* [The People's View] (Khartoum), June 21, 2007).

Table 2: China's Foreign Economic Cooperation, Top Partners, 2004-2006
(In Million US Dollars, excluding Hong Kong and Macao)

2004		2005		2006	
Country	Total	Country	Total	Country	Total
1. Singapore	1,085.36	1. Sudan	1,342.78	1. Sudan	1,754.65
2. Japan	859.61	2. Japan	1,189.80	2. Algeria	1,702.74
3. Algeria	829.96	3. Singapore	1,165.90	3. Japan	1,530.93
4. Sudan	748.28	4. Algeria	1,065.35	4. Singapore	1,250.41
5. Pakistan	586.01	5. Nigeria	799.92	5. United States	1,216.33
6. Bangladesh	523.64	6. Pakistan	751.42	6. Nigeria	1,141.05
7. Nigeria	499.02	7. Iran	652.74	7. India	1,133.60

Source: Adapted from *China Statistical Yearbook*, various years.

Table 3: China's Overseas Direct Investment (Non-Financial): Top Receivers
(In Million US Dollars, excluding Hong Kong, Macao, Cayman Is., Virgin Is.)

Net Direct Investment 2005		Net Direct Investment 2006		Accumulated DI, End of 2006	
1. ROK	588.82	1. Russia	452.11	1. US	1,237.87
2. US	231.82	2. US	198.34	2. ROK	949.24
3. Russia	203.33	3. Singapore	132.15	3. Russia	929.76
4. Australia	193.07	4. Algeria	98.93	4. Australia	794.35
5. Germany	128.74	5. Nigeria	67.79	5. Sudan	497.13
6. Sudan	91.13	6. Indonesia	56.94	6. Germany	472.03
7. Algeria	84.87	7. Sudan	50.79	7. Singapore	468.01

Source: Adapted from *China Statistical Yearbook*, various years.

China's dominant presence in Sudan is mostly related to oil. Its assets and investments include a 40 percent majority share that the China National Petroleum Corporation (CNPC) acquired in late 1996 in the Greater Nile Petroleum Operating Company (GNPOC), a newly created consortium. Of a total of $1.047 billion, China paid $441 million. In May 1997, the consortium won a large scale twenty year project for the production and transportation of oil in western Kordofan, covering three blocks of oilfields in the Mughlad Basin: Unity (no. 1), Heglig (no. 2) and Kaikang (no. 4). Precisely two years later, a $1 billion 1,506km export pipeline was inaugurated. Its original output of 150,000 barrels per day was later doubled to 300,000 barrels per day, and could be tripled to 450,000 barrels per day. Again, Beijing played the major role: engineering, equipment and construction of the fields' facilities and the pipeline were provided by the China Petroleum Engineering Construction Corporation (CPECC) while 70 percent of the supplies were provided by the China Petroleum Technology and Development Corporation (CPTDC). On June 23, 1999, oil began to flow into the new pipeline, opening a new chapter in Sino-Sudanese relations [1].

A week later, on June 30, 1999, a new refinery was inaugurated north of Khartoum. It could process 50,000 barrels per day (bpd, about 2.5 million tons a year), increased by June 2004 to 70,000 bpd. CNPC, that provided half of the total investment of $540 million, built and operates the refinery. On August 30, 1999, Sudan exported 600,000 barrels of oil from Port Bashir—a new 2 million ton oil terminal, 25km south of Port Sudan, built by China. This shipment turned Sudan into a net oil exporter for the first time ever. Now, with the infrastructure prepared, China wanted more oil. On October 1, 2001, the Petrodar Operating Company (PDOC) was inaugurated with 41 percent of its shares (again a majority) owned by CNPC. It controls an area of 72,000 square km, covering blocks 3 and 7 in the Melut basin—east of China's other concessions. As of January 2007, these two blocks produced some 165,000 bpd, expected to reach a peak of 200,000 bpd by late 2007. Further, China Petroleum Engineering and Construction Group have been chosen to build a $215 million oil terminal to service blocks 3 and 7. The two blocks are connected to Port Sudan by a 150,000 bpd day capacity pipeline that can reach a maximum of 500,000 bpd.

CNPC's concessions also include the Fula field in block no. 6 (western Kordofan and southern Darfur), which began production in November 2004 at a rate of 10,000 bpd, expected to reach 80,000 bpd (up from its current production of 40,000 bpd). Based on a deal signed in August 2003, CNPC constructed a 730km oil pipeline from the Fula oilfields in western Kordofan to the main oil refinery in Khartoum, and expanded this refinery's capacity to 100,000 bpd, at a cost of $340 million, offered by CNPC. In early July 2007, it was reported that CNPC had signed a 20-year contract with the Sudanese government for exploration right in northern Sudan's block of shallow water in the Red Sea. CNPC will have the majority share at 35-40 percent (since the project is still in its initial stage, the size of the investment would be decided later) with the rest going to five oil companies from other countries, including Sudapet (Sudan) and Pertamina (Indonesia) (AFP, July 2, 2007; *Sudan Tribune*, July 2, 3, 2007).

China is now Sudan's main oil producer, exporter as well as, most important, importer. In 1999, China's oil import from Sudan was modestly launched at 266,126 tons, barely 0.73 percent of its total oil import. Yet a year later, in 2000, oil import from Sudan bounced to 3,312, 591 tons (or 4.72 percent of China's total oil import). By 2002, it nearly doubled to 6,425,447 tons (9.26 percent), turning Sudan into China's fourth largest oil supplier, following Saudi Arabia, Iran and Oman. Although Chinese-controlled oil production in Sudan further increased in 2004 and 2005, Sudan's relative share in China's import declined, meaning that the extra oil was sold elsewhere, perhaps in swap deals, or that China imported more oil from other sources. For example, in 2006 nearly 39 percent of Sudan's crude oil exports were shipped to Japan and only about 31 percent to China (nearly 70 percent to these two countries) [2]. In the first seven months of 2007, Beijing reportedly imported 43 percent of Sudan's total oil production (*Sudan Tribune*, August 30, 2007). Thus, Sudan will remain a major supplier of China's oil, given continued internal stability and the steady growth in output and even more so its reserves.

In 2006, Sudan's oil production reached only 365,000 (414,000 according to the EIA) bpd (*Sudan Tribune*, March 7, 2007), well below the expected 500,000 bpd, causing China's import a 26 percent decline in 2006. If in 2002 Sudan's share in China's oil import had reached 9.25 percent, in 2006 it shrank to 2.86 percent. It is expected that Sudan's oil production would reach an average of 520,000 bpd in 2007 (Table 4). Indeed, between January and July 2007 China imported 6.25 million tons of crude oil to China, a sixfold increase over the same period in 2006 (*Sudan Tribune*, July 2, August 23, 2007). Consequently, the Chinese reported a dramatic increase of 86.2 percent in bilateral trade for the first quarter of 2007 (*Renmin Ribao*, July 19, 2007). This may have reflected Sudan's increased proven reserves, estimated in January 2007 at five billion barrels (compared to 563 million barrels in 2006 and 262 million barrels in 2001) [3]. Based on these estimates, Sudan's oil output could last for many decades. Although Sudan's share in the world's total oil output is no more than 0.4 percent-0.5 percent, oil export to China affects bilateral trade. China's import from Sudan jumped over ten times, from $1.47 million in 1998—before the "oil boom"—to $2.61 billion in 2005, seven years later. In 2006, 76.2 percent (according to other statistics nearly 80 percent) of Sudan's total export is absorbed by China, which is also Sudan's second top source of import (at 18.6 percent) [4]. China is Sudan's top trading partner, as well as top investor, primarily but not only, in oil.

Table 4: Sudan's Oil Production, 1999-2007
(In Barrels per Day)

Year	Volume	Change (%)
1999	63,000	---
2000	174,000	176.2
2001	211,000	21.3
2002	233,000	10.4
2003	255,000	9.4
2004	325,000	27.5
2005	355,000	9.2
2006	397,000	11.8
2007	*520,000	*31.0

Source: *Sudan Tribune*, June 18, 2007.
* Estimate.

In addition to Sudan's oil industry, China is active in other sectors. A subsidiary of the giant Harbin Power Equipment Company built phase one of the El-Gaili Gas Station, an oil-fired power station project (formerly known as Qarre I), about 50km north of Sudan's capital, at a cost of $149 million provided by China's Central Bank. When started operating in August 2004, its 200 megawatt generation capacity accounted for about one third of Sudan's national total at the time. In late July 2007, phase two (known as Qarre II) was about to be completed nearby, altogether producing 330 megawatt, the largest electricity generation project in Sudan (Xinhua, July 15, 2007; *Renmin Ribao*, July 19, 2007). The Chinese are also involved in the construction and funding of hydropower plants including a 75-85 percent investment in the 300 megawatt Kajbar Dam construction and the 1,250 megawatt Merowe (Hamdab) Dam, 400km north of Khartoum, at a total cost of $1.73 billion. China's Export-Import Bank provided $540 million to finance the project—the largest hydropower project currently under construction in Africa—whose contract was signed on June 7, 2003 (AFP, May 18, 2007). Expected to be completed in late 2008, it would reportedly double or even triple Sudan's electricity-generating capacity and increase Sudan's irrigation system and cultivated area by nearly 50 percent. The Chinese admitted that the project has political value and "is not a purely commercial one." In support of the dam China is also constructing a 1,745km power transmission line and transformation stations, the longest ever built in Sudan. Launched in early 2004, they were due for completion in 2007 at a cost of nearly $466 million. In the first quarter of 2007, China signed $1.4 billion worth of new engineering projects contracts. Business turnover for the first half of the year reached $864 million (*Renmin Ribao*, July 19, 2007).

In addition, in early 2002, the Sudan's polypropylene project that was built within one year entirely by China's Petroleum and Natural Gas Exploration and Development Corporation at a cost of $23 million went into operation in Khartoum. In 2002 China also extended to Sudan a $2.5 million grant to rehabilitate a Radiotherapy Hospital. In June 2004, the Chinese signed a $3.6 million preferential loan agreement with Khartoum for a new International Conference Hall and for training Sudan's Ministry of International Cooperation employees. Yet, available funds—and its huge foreign exchange reserves—are not the primary, nor the only, explanation for Beijing's position in Sudan.

A Barrel of a Gun for a Barrel of Oil?

China's predominance in Sudan is an outcome of two complementary processes: eager to reach energy resources, China was practically sucked into Sudan's vacuum. In turn, this vacuum is also an outcome of three interconnected processes: one, the deterioration of internal security conditions in Sudan; two, the growing abuse of human rights; and three, Sudan's alleged support of terrorism. These have driven away American and other Western oil and other companies from Sudan from the 1980s to the early 2000s thereby paving the ground for the Chinese to step in. While Chevron finally abandoned its investments in Sudan's oilfields in 1992 for security reasons, other U.S. companies (like Occidental Petroleum Corporation) have been barred by Congress from dealing with Sudan, one of the countries accused of supporting terrorism. Furthermore, Washington, as well as human rights organizations, have applied pressure also on non-American oil firms (for example, Canada's Talisman, Austria's OMV and Sweden's Lundin) to withdraw from Sudan or drastically cut down their business there. Some companies (e.g. TotalFinaElf, renamed Total in 2003) have failed to develop their concessions due to the internal war. China was quick to fill the gap, in more than one sense, perceived by a number of Western governments and NGOs not only as a money-maker but also as the trouble-maker.

While atrocities in Sudan's Darfur region go on, it has become fashionable to criticize China for the stalemate and thereby for the continued violence. U.S. Secretary of State Condoleezza Rice singled out China as she called for increased pressure on Khartoum to accept a UN peacekeeping force to settle the bloody conflict. Some U.S. lawmakers have accused Beijing of supporting Sudan's intransigence by preferring oil acquisition to resolving the tragedy of Darfur (The Associated Press, February 17, 2007). The UN's special envoy to Sudan, Jan Pronk, said in no nonsense words that "if there is any country which could play an important role [in convincing the Sudanese government], it is China. [However,] China never put a lot of pressure [on Sudan]. The pressure came in particular from the other members of the Security Council (AFP, January 16, 2007). According to certain Western media, the PRC, a permanent member of the UN Security Council, continues to protect Sudan's President al-Bashir—and its invested oil interests—with the threat of using its veto (*International Herald Tribune*, August 4, 2006). Others went as far as claiming that "No other country has more clout on the Khartoum government than China, which absorbs 60 percent of Sudan's total oil output and has repeatedly used its UN Security Council veto power to block further sanctions on the regime" (AFP, February 2, 2007). In a January 2006 report, the U.S. based Council of Foreign Relations said that China is a "major" supplier of weapons to Sudan, a claim elaborated in a June 2006

Although China's interest in Sudan has been primarily economic, its association with the Khartoum government has begun to attract crossfire not only for fraternizing with a supporter of terrorism but also for arming Sudan.

Amnesty International Report titled *China: Sustaining Conflict and Human Right Abuses: the Flow of Arms Accelerates*. It mentioned (pp. 19-20) an unknown number of aircraft and helicopters supplied in the 1990s, and at least 222 "military" trucks, sighted in 2005. Is China a "major" supplier of weapons to Sudan?

Although China's interest in Sudan has been primarily economic, its association with the Khartoum government has begun to attract crossfire not only for fraternizing with a supporter of terrorism but also for arming Sudan. For example, AFP mentions China as "a key supplier of military arms and equipment" in many of its dispatches on Sudan and Darfur. In its May 2007 report Amnesty International accused China of supplying about $81 million of arms, ammunition and spare parts for aircraft and helicopters just in 2005. The Chinese also delivered six K-8 military training/attack aircraft to Sudan's Air Force, with another six to follow, together with flight simulators. After graduation, Sudanese pilots are expected to fly the Q-5 (or A-5) Chinese-made Fantan, a fighter-ground-attack aircraft. Amnesty provided photographs and data of three Q-5s parked at Nyala Airport between January and March 2007. Nyala is the capital of the South Darfur State in western Sudan and Amnesty is concerned that Sudan would use these aircraft "for indiscriminate attacks in Darfur in violation of the UN arms embargo and international humanitarian law" [5].

A few days after Amnesty International's report was issued, Washington blamed the Chinese for exploiting the complexities of the situation in Sudan and taking advantage of Sudan's deficit and need for weapons to buy crude oil at the ridiculous price of $13 per barrel (*Al-Sharq al-Awsat*, May 11, 2007) [6]. Beijing firmly dismissed Amnesty International's claims as "a groundless accusation." It added that China respects the concerned resolutions of the UN Security Council and does not sell or export any arms to any nation or regions under UN bans, nor to organizations or individuals; it sells only to sovereign governments (AFP, May 8, 2007). Beijing maintains steady military relations with Khartoum. Cao Gangchuan, China's Defense Minister, said that the Chinese armed forces attach importance to developing relations with the Sudanese army and are ready to promote cooperation between the two sides in various fields (Xinhua, March 31, 2006). To be sure, in early April 2007, a month before the Amnesty report was published, Beijing had hosted the Chief of the Joint Staff of the Sudanese Armed Forces General Haj Ahmed El Gaili and vowed to further boost military exchanges and cooperation (Xinhua, April 3, 2007; *Jiefangjun Bao* [Liberation Army Daily], April 5, 2007). Whereas this cooperation had begun in the early 1970s, it has gathered momentum since the early 1980s.

Post-Mao China began to supply weapons to Sudan in 1981, reaching a total value of US$342 million by 2006 (see Table 5). Yet China has never been Sudan's number one military supplier; Russia was number one, supplying over two-fifths (41.3 percent) of Sudan's weapons. China was number two, supplying a little over one-fifth of Sudan's total arms acquisitions in that period. The United States was number three (in 1981-1988), providing a little over one-tenth (10.6 percent) of Sudan's arms. The share of all three in Sudan's total arms import for the entire period was 73 percent. In 1982, the United States was Sudan's number one supplier and in 1981-1988, it supplied Sudan with over one quarter (26.3 percent) of it total arms import [7]. Therefore, China's arms supplies to Sudan have been rather limited, especially in view of Sudan's territory (the largest in Africa, ranking ten in the world), and consisted mostly of aircraft and towed guns, as well as fifty armored personnel carriers (APCs) (see Table 6). It appears that China stopped its arms deliveries after the December 2005 UN Security Council vote to impose an arms embargo on Sudan: of the twelve K-8 trainers/combat aircraft ordered by Sudan in 2004, only six were delivered. Although critics of Beijing have linked its arms sales to Sudan to its oil interests there, there are no indications of large-scale Chinese arms sales to Sudan, definitely not since the mid-1990s, when China has become intensively involved in Sudan's oil industry. In fact, no high-level Chinese military delegation has visited Sudan in nearly ten years—until early June 2002. This is another indication of the relatively marginal Sino-Sudanese military relations. Some Chinese now admit that the scale of the Darfur conflict had been upgraded almost to a civil war due to the influx of modern weapons under previous regimes [8]. China's special envoy to Sudan Liu Guijin admitted that China sells weapons to Sudan although, he said, these sales are limited (Interfax, July 5, 2007).

Table 5: China's Arms Sales to Sudan, 1981-2006; by Value
(In million constant 1990 U.S. dollars)

Year	1981	1986	1984	1991	1992	1997	2003	2006	Total	Share
Value	102	27	57	46	6	66	20	14	342	21.5%

Source: Information from the SIPRI *Arms Transfers Database*, URL
http://armstrade.sipri.org/

Table 6: China's Arms Sales to Sudan, 1981-2006; by Types

Number Ordered	Weapon Designation	Weapon Description	Year of Order	Year of Delivery	Number Delivered
(13)	F-6	Fighter aircraft	(1980)	1981	(13) Incl 2 FT-6 trainer
(20)	M-1938/M-30	Towed gun	(1980)	1981	version
(20)	122mm	Towed gun	(1980)	1981	(20) Type 54-1 version
50	Type 59-1 130mm	APC	(1981)	1981	(20)
(9)	YW-531/Type-63	Fighter aircraft	(1986)	1986-7	(50)
10	F-7A	Towed gun	(1988)	1989	(9) Number could be
18	Type 59-1 130mm	Towed gun	(1991)	1992	15
2	D-30 122mm	Transport aircraft	1991	1991	10
(6)	Y-8	Fighter aircraft	(1995)	1997	18, Designation
(3)	F-7M Airguard	FGA aircraft	(2002)	2003	uncertain
(12)	A-5C Fantan	Trainer/combat	(2004)	2006	2 Y-8D version
	K-8 Karakoram-8	ac			(6) Could be 7, status
					uncertain
					(3) Number could be up
					to 20
					(6) Including for
					combat role

Source: Information from the SIPRI *Arms Transfers Database*, URL http://armstrade.sipri.org/.

Nevertheless, Beijing's prominent role in Sudan has led to allegations that the Chinese are not only backing human rights abuse in Sudan but also practically participating in it by cooperating in the forced displacement of peasants resulting from oil concession and dam constructions. Eyewitnesses testified to seeing Chinese-made trucks and armed vehicles at the scene as well as Sudanese troops carrying Chinese-made weapons. At least some—and some say many—of the tens of thousands Chinese workers in Sudan are allegedly demobilized People's Liberation Army (PLA) servicemen. Occasionally, the Chinese are also associated, though indirectly, with the atrocities in Darfur. These allegations, and the intensive Chinese activities in Sudan, have increased the friction coefficient with the United States and have drawn a good deal of criticism. To be sure, it reflects not only moral values but also political, strategic and commercial interests.

To a great extent, its [China] achievements are an outcome of Sudan's domestic instability and international isolation. In this respect, Beijing should be interested in continued unrest in Sudan, and even in human rights abuse that scare away more powerful competitors, primarily Western

Yet, China's position in Sudan is more complex and less secure than we may assume. To a great extent, its achievements are an outcome of Sudan's domestic instability and international isolation. In this respect, Beijing should be interested in continued unrest in Sudan, and even in human rights abuse that scare away more powerful competitors, primarily Western. The Chinese should realize that once Sudan's internal conflicts are settled, Western companies—and governments—would return, at China's expense. It is this concern, perhaps, that had driven Beijing to invest in Sudan as much and as fast as possible, so as to gain a solid long-term foothold and fend off potential rivals. This, however, by no means imply that the Chinese have a long-term interest in instability in Sudan (or elsewhere), let alone in fomenting it. On the contrary, a basic cornerstone of China's post-Mao international behavior is that instability abroad—and at home—is detrimental to China's economic growth. This attitude is also evident in Sudan.

To begin with, Beijing has always considered the Darfur problem as Sudan's internal affair. Therefore, in Sudan—and elsewhere—China has consistently rejected external interference in internal conflicts, sometimes including by the United Nations, and has traditionally avoided taking sides. This policy, that goes back to the 1970s, is reflected in Beijing's attitude toward Sudan's 22-year-old civil war and the more recent Darfur crisis. Still China, that in Mao's time supported national liberation movements, could no longer identify with the separatist agenda of the Sudan People's Liberation Army (SPLA) that fought Khartoum since 1983 for self-determination. Supporting this claim could have had disastrous implications for China's own struggle against separatism at home, not to mention its oil interests. This is why Beijing was pleased by the progress made in the negotiations to restore peace and stability in Sudan, all the more so since rebel forces occasionally targeted Chinese oil pipelines and other facilities.

To be sure, the Chinese in Sudan are exposed to occasional attacks. On October 23, 2007, Darfur rebels called the Justice and Equality Movement (JEM) attacked Defra, a Chinese-run oilfield (one of Sudan's largest sources of crude), and kidnapped two foreign oil workers. JEM commander said: "This is a message to China and Chinese oil companies to stop helping the government with their war in Darfur." Interviewed by Dow Jones Newswires, the leader of the rival rebel group, the Sudan Liberation Movement (SLM) warned two weeks later that foreign oil companies in Sudan "will not be safe." He singled out China that allegedly conducts oil extraction in return for providing weapons: "Any weapon that kills our people comes from China," he said and added that any weapon in Darfur including aircraft, Kalachinkovs and vehicles are Chinese (*Sudan Tribune*, October 25, 2007; December 8, 2007). In another attack on Chinese-run oilfields on December 11, 2007, the JEM reportedly killed and wounded a number of local security troops, seized vehicles and artillery, destroyed oil installation and stopped oil production. The movement's commander insisted: "Our attacks on the oil industry of the Kordofan region east of Darfur would continue until China ended its operations in Sudan" (*Sudan Tribune*, December 13, 2007; *Sudan Tribune*, March 4, 2007). Although Sudan's Armed Forces denied that this attack took place, it has caused deep concern in China.

Peace-keeping for Piece-keeping

Although Sudan's insecurity has driven away scores of competitors thereby paving the ground for China, Beijing must be interested in keeping Sudan's peace and stability in order to create a more convenient environment for its burgeoning economic activities, thereby keeping its piece as well. Notwithstanding the allegations, the Chinese have made considerable peace promotion efforts, both in words and in deeds. China always argued, "That resolving the Darfur issue should be realized through dialogue and peace talks" (Zhongguo Tongxun She, February 3, 2007). Initially, and following its time-honored tradition of non-interference, Beijing prefers that internal conflicts should be settled by the parties directly concerned —the government and its adversaries. If such a domestic attempt failed (or, if an agreement had already been reached but still failed to be implemented), Beijing usually prefers that a regional organization take charge of the process. If it does not work, and only as a last resort, the Chinese would reluctantly agree to a UN intervention, in which they have no choice but to become involved and take sides. This progression is evident in Sudan, first in the south and then in the west.

China's active involvement in Sudan's peace settlement began only after the Sudanese government and the former rebel Sudan People's Liberation Movement on January 9, 2005, signed the Comprehensive Peace Agreement (CPA) thereby ending 21 years of civil war in southern Sudan. On March 24, 2005, a unanimously adopted UN Security Council resolution authorized the dispatch of peacekeeping forces to the region. The Chinese were quick to comply and in May 2005, sent their first group of peacekeepers to Sudan. A more organized PLA detachment had been deployed by May 2006. It was replaced in January 2007 by 435 PLA transportation, engineer and medical troops (Xinhua, January 18, 2007). Stationed in southern Sudan, though, these contingents had nothing to do with Darfur in western Sudan, where the conflict continues.

Following the stalemate in Darfur, the Chinese supported the intervention of African Union peacekeeping forces, as well as the Arab League's efforts. When visiting Sudan in early February 2007, PRC President Hu Jintao said that "the African Union and the United Nations should play constructive roles in a peacekeeping mission in Darfur" (Xinhua, February 2, 2007). But the situation in Darfur is different: the CPA was accepted by the government *and* by the rebels—thereby paving the way for UN peacekeeping operations. However, the Darfur Peace Agreement, signed by Khartoum on May 5, 2006, with a main rebel faction, has been rejected by other rebel groups and, consequently, it has been turned down by Khartoum as well. This affected the PRC voting behavior at the UN Security Council.

Beijing welcomed the May 16, 2006, agreement to hand over the Darfur peacekeeping mission from the African Union Mission in Sudan (AMIS), whose 7,000 troops had been unable to stop the Darfur atrocities and whose mandate was due to expire on September 30, 2006, to the UN Security Council by January 2007. Yet, although he voted for this resolution—adopted unanimously—the PRC delegate still expressed his country's reservations. He clearly stated: "If the United Nations is to deploy a peacekeeping operation in Darfur, the agreement and cooperation of the Sudanese Government must be obtained. That is a basic principle and precondition for the deployment of all peacekeeping operations" (UNSC Resolution 1679). Nevertheless, Beijing announced that it would send a 275-member engineering unit to join the UN-led peacekeeping force in Darfur.

Based on this agreement, on August 31, 2006, the UN Security Council approved the deployment of up to 17,300 troops (and up to 3,300 civilian policemen) to Darfur and "invited the consent of the Sudanese Government […] for that deployment." Although Wang Guangya, China's representative, supported the deployment he insisted that the "consent of the Sudanese Government" should have been obtained *before* the vote and should have been clearly included in the resolution. Since both amendments had been rejected, the PRC abstained (UNSC Resolution 1706; Xinhua, August 31, 2006). Sudan vehemently opposed the UN peacekeeping force deployment in Darfur as "entirely unacceptable." "As it stands, the resolution may be interpreted as allowing UN troop to move into Darfur even without Sudan's consent if needed to halt the humanitarian disaster in the area" (AFP, September 1, 2006). Fully aware of this disaster, the Chinese government offered 40 million yuan ($5.1 million) aid to improve the living conditions and the overall situation in Darfur—as well as a 100 million yuan interest-free loan ($12.8 million) to the Sudanese government (AFP, February 2, 2007). Following the UN resolution, Beijing began, perhaps for the first time in earnest, to apply pressure on Khartoum.

China's Darfur policy makes sense not only in the context of Sudan but also in China. Some noted its perceived concern that the U.S.-led crusade to stop human rights abuse in Sudan (and elsewhere) could be directed at China itself. While already criticized on that score, the Chinese know how to cope with it, but still may be concerned about the implications for their own sovereignty, national unity and territorial integrity (*International Herald Tribune*, August 4, 2006). True, for Beijing these concepts stand above all. While visiting Sudan, President Hu Jintao put forward four principles for handling the Darfur issue, the first of which demanded to "respect Sudan's sovereignty and territorial integrity. Resolution of the Darfur issue will definitely benefit the process of reconciliation among ethnic groups throughout Sudan, benefit safeguarding of national unity in Sudan, and benefit regional peace and stability" (Xinhua, February 2, 2007). Wen Xian, a senior *People's Daily* editor, elaborated that "any program or schemes for the settlement of the Darfur issue, if not favorable to the maintenance of Sudan's national unity, is bound to complicate the problem" (*People's Daily*, February 7, 2007). Special Chinese envoy to Sudan, Liu Guijin, said that "China is categorically opposed to Sudan's breakup" (Interfax, July 5, 2007). No doubt, precedents of eroding the territorial integrity of sovereign states by the UN are unacceptable to the Chinese, yet China is different. In case of a deterioration say, in Tibet or Xinjiang, Beijing would have never allow UN peacekeeping forces on its territory, if needed, by using its veto power. Instead and at once, the Chinese would have mercilessly crushed the rebels. Implicitly, this is exactly what they expect from Sudan: to restore stability at all costs.

It is Sudan's evident inability to do so—combined with the international pressure and the threats to its own economic interests—that have forced Beijing to try and compel Khartoum to accept the UN peacekeeping contingent in Darfur. Beijing has all along reiterated that "[t]he situation has worsened since some western countries are eager to 'internationalize' what had been a pure internal affair of Sudan," and added that "[t]he Darfur issue would not have escalated so fast, we should say, without intervention from external powers driven by their own interests" (*Renmin Ribao*, May 12, 2006). One year later the *Liberation Army Daily* asserted: "It is entirely a Sudanese internal problem. However, the Darfur problem was rapidly 'internationalized' due to malicious stirring and exaggeration by Sudan separatist elements and hostile forces outside the country" (*Jiefabgjun Bao*, May 9, 2007). Denying acting under U.S. pressure to persuade Sudan to accept a UN peacekeeping force in Darfur, Beijing itself—though not terribly enthusiastic about it—ultimately favored an early settlement along these lines. Beijing is not so happy with Khartoum's role in Darfur. Xinhua reported that a Sudanese government Antonov aircraft bombed two villages in Darfur on December 29, 2006 (Xinhua, January 11, 2007). In addition, atrocities committed by the pro-government Janjaweed militia have occasionally been reported by the Chinese media.

Given its insistence that Darfur is Sudan's internal affair, on the one hand, and the U.S. and Western pressure to use its influence in Khartoum, on the other hand, Beijing has been reluctant to force Khartoum to accept the peace proposals. Initially, the Chinese tried to hint cautiously and delicately just before Hu Jintao's visit: "We hope that the Sudanese side could pay attention to the international community's concern" (Zhongguo Tongxun She, January 17, 2007). In its reports about Hu's meeting with al-Bashir, Xinhua mentioned that the talks had been "frank," "candid" and "sincere"— code words that reflect disagreements. Reportedly, Hu Jintao "has advised" al-Bashir that an efficient peacekeeping force is required to restore peace in Darfur (*The Star*, RSA, February 13, 2007). In April 2007, PRC Assistant Foreign Minister Zhai Jun, a seasoned diplomat and special envoy to Sudan, "played a crucial role in persuading Sudan to accept the peace plan over the Darfur issue put forward by former UN chief Kofi Annan [...] [He] has been communicating with various parties through multiple channels to narrow differences [...]" (Xinhua, April 11, 12, 2007).

The U.S. president's envoy to Sudan, Andrew Natsios, commended China's efforts in Sudan: "We have indications at this point that China took steps that are stricter than those it took in the past. So, I believe that we need to encourage China's intervention in Darfur. I also believe that China might have been a decisive factor that made the Sudanese Government reverse its position two days ago concerning Kofi Annan's plan for peace. We have evidence that they exercised pressures for Darfur" (Al-Jazirah Satellite Channel Television, April 12, 2007). The PRC's decision to play a "more constructive role" in the resolution of the Darfur issue is also reflected in the appointment in May 2007 of former Ambassador Liu Guijin—a veteran diplomat with rich experience in Africa—as a as a special representative for African affairs.

Aware of Khartoum's intransigence, Beijing publicly expressed its "hopes that Sudan will show more flexibility" [9]. Praising China's role in improving the Darfur situation, UN Secretary-General Ban

Ki-moon said: to this end, "The Chinese government has been always exerting their utmost efforts" (Xinhua, June 1, 2007). Indeed, following his visit to Sudan, Liu Guijin said that although Beijing had not criticized Sudan in public, "In our own way and through various means and various channels we have tried to advise the Sudanese government to be more flexible [...] Even on certain issues like [whether] to accept the Annan plan [for a joint African Union-UN peacekeeper force] we used very direct language to persuade them" (AFP, June 19, 2007; *Financial Times*). More diplomatic, the PRC Foreign Ministry stated that the Chinese had made "very positive" and "constructive" efforts to peacefully resolve the Darfur issue. He added that China "has done work" on the Sudanese government in the form of high-level mutual visits, the dispatch of special envoys, telephone calls, and correspondence between the two sides (Xinhua, June 19, 2007). These "enormous efforts," though forced on the Chinese, represent a rare experiment in mediation, a measure Beijing has tried to avoid in the past. As Liu Guijin put it, China insists on using "influence without interference" (*China Daily*, July 27, 2007). Sudan's president denied that Hu Jintao applied pressure on Sudan to accept UN peacekeeping troops in Darfur (Sudan Media Center, February 6, 2007), to which Khartoum eventually agreed.

Beijing has always opposed the use of threats to force Sudan to accept peacekeeping forces in Darfur or to pick any particular solution to this problem. "Exerting pressure or imposing sanctions will only further complicate the issue" (Xinhua, January 24, 2007). To illustrate China's stand, Liu said: "Let the Chinese eat with chopsticks, the Americans with a fork and knife, and the Sudanese with their hands. What matter is that they all eat something, and if they have eaten something, then the main goal has been achieved—everyone is full" (Interfax, July 5, 2007). Indeed, China abstained in all UN Security Council that imposed sanctions on Sudan. At the same time, Beijing has never used its veto power to protect Sudan—in spite of occasional allegations—and has been very careful and thrifty in the use of its veto power since joining the United Nations (*China Brief*, September 6, 2006). Therefore, the allegation that Beijing approves of, supports or otherwise disregards, Sudan's Darfur policy, because of its economic and especially oil interests is misleading. While undoubtedly important for China, Sudan is by no means indispensable—and not necessarily a long-term investment. Sudan's proven oil reserves account for less than two percent of those of Saudi Arabia, which has already promised China to supply all its oil needs single-handedly—if necessary. Thus, given the dimensions of China's economic interests in Sudan in relative terms, China could survive easily without Sudan—if worse comes to worst. In other words, this is at best only a partial explanation why Beijing protects Sudan. The fact is, China was left with little choice.

On the one hand they must be disgusted by the Darfur atrocities and aware of Khartoum's involvement in at least some of them. On the other hand they are equally aware of Sudan's sovereign right to settle its internal affairs, or agree to international intervention.

Undoubtedly aware of the unpleasant smell of its oil relations with Khartoum, Beijing pointed frankly that "Chinese oil companies usually target countries that other foreign investors are unwilling to enter, such as Iran, Venezuela and Sudan, because it is too hard to compete with the large Western oil companies" (*Renmin Ribao*, September 15, 2006). Liu Guijin replied to those accusing China that oil drilling in another country and cooperation in the energy field are a normal business activity that should by no means be 'politicized' or "played up." He reiterated that the two sides have carried out transparent, mutually beneficial, and nonexclusive cooperation. Insisting that the root cause of the Darfur issue is poverty and lack of development, addressing these problems will help resolve the Darfur issue "once and for all." He complained that although other oil companies are "even more" active in Sudan, it is CNPC that is always being singled out. "It is unfair" (Xinhua, May 29, 2007). Indeed, a number of other companies, some Western, not only in the field of energy but also in the fields of construction and communications, are active in Sudan.

These include, for example, Lundin (Sweden), ONGC (India), TotalFinaElf (France), White Nile (UK), ABB (Switzerland), Alstom (France), Siemens (Germany), Ericsson (Sweden), PECD Berhad (Malaysia), Petronas (Malaysia) Lahmeyer (Germany), etc., some are China's business partners but hardly mentioned publicly.

In their Darfur policy, the Chinese are walking a tightrope. On the one hand they must be disgusted by the Darfur atrocities and aware of Khartoum's involvement in at least some of them. On the other hand they are equally aware of Sudan's sovereign right to settle its internal affairs, or agree to international intervention. At the same time, as a permanent member of the UN Security Council China has its own responsibility and is interested in achieving peace and stability—but does not want to become associated with the West, least of all with the United States. This is probably the main reason for Beijing to stand by Khartoum. It is difficult to argue with threat perception but China feels threatened. "In Sudan, China has energy source projects in locations far away from Darfur. But some people in the United States insistently lumped China together with the humanitarian crisis in Sudan" (*Zhongguo Qingnian Bao*, May 11, 2006).

The Chinese resent the US attempts to intimidate them into stopping their support of Khartoum. The late U.S. House of Representative Tom Lantos (D-CA), who was chairman of the House International Relations Committee, warned that "If China fails to do its part, it risks being forever known as the host of the 'Genocide Olympics'." The Chinese firmly reject the US Congressional criticism, and any attempt to connect the Olympic Games with politics" (AFP, May 15, 2007). On June 5, 2007, the U.S. House of Representatives adopted a resolution on Sudan's Darfur issue involving China. The Foreign Ministry complained that the resolution had disregarded China's constructive efforts to resolve the Darfur issue, and deliberately criticized China:

> Because of domestic political needs, some Americans stirred up the Darfur issue and deliberately attacked China. They have ulterior motives and their attacks are unjustified. The deliberations and adoption of the above resolution by the US House of Representatives have sent a seriously erroneous signal to the outside world, which is detrimental to Sino-US cooperation on the Darfur issue and will not be helpful in resolving the Darfur issue. China urges the US Congress to objectively and impartially regard China's constructive roles on the Darfur issue, and immediately stop its erroneous act of politically stirring up the Darfur issue and criticizing China without cause (Xinhua, June 7, 2007).

Many in the Middle East, in Africa as well as in Sudan believe that the primary reason for the U.S. insistence on imposing sanctions on Sudan is to undermine the regime, to eliminate the Chinese influence and to block China's penetration into Africa. However, if it keeps on avoiding economic relations with Sudan—the United States will be the loser (*Khartoum Monitor*, June 8, 2007). In the end, the criticism that was directed at China with regard to its policy on Sudan in general, and on Darfur in particular, has been counterproductive. It has only underlined the PRC's role as an upcoming power in international politics that manages to pursue it own policies according to its own priorities, defying Washington, other Western capitals, as well as human rights non-governmental organizations.

Originally published as two articles in *China Brief:* Volume 5 Issue 21 on October 13, 2005, and Volume 7 Issue 7 on April 5, 2007.

Notes

1. Endnotes for this and the following paragraphs are in: Yitzhak Shichor, "Sudan: China's Outpost in Africa," *China Brief*, V:21 (October 13, 2005), 9-11.
2. Energy Information Administration (EIA), *Country Analysis Briefs – Sudan* (April 2007), 4-5.

3. EIA, Sudan., 3. According to BP, Statistical Review of World Energy (June 2007), Sudan's proved oil reserves were 6.4 billion barrels since 2004.

4. http://stat.wto.org/CountryProfiles?SD_e.htm

5. Amnesty International, Sudan: Arms Continuing to Fuel Serious Human Rights Violation in Darfur, AFR 54/019/2007 (May 2007), pp. 7-8, 10, 15-16.

6. It was reported that Sudan sold Chinaoil four cargoes of 1 million barrels each, $3.50-$4.75 a barrel, when the market price was approaching $100 a barrel. Sudan Tribune, November 25, 2007.

7. SIPRI, Arms Trade Database.

8. Jiang Hengkun and Liu Hongwu, "Zhongzu rentong haishi ziyuan zhenduo: Sudan Daerfuer diqu chongtu genyuan tanxi" [Racial Identity or Resource Competition: An Investigation into the Origins of Sudan's Darfur Conflict], Xiya Feizhou [West Asia and Africa], No. 5 (2005), pp. 11-12.

9. Chinese Foreign Ministry website, May 24, 2007.

ZAMBIA:

CHINA AND ZAMBIA: THE ALL-WEATHER FRIENDSHIP HITS STORMY WEATHER

By Paul Hare

When President Hu Jintao visited Zambia in early February 2007, he met with the country's liberation leader and first head of state, Kenneth Kaunda and said, "In China, we say that when you are drinking water, you should not forget the people who dug the well, so we cannot forget the birth of our friendship." Kaunda reciprocated these sentiments, describing China as an "all-weather friend," one of his favorite aphorisms (Xinhua, February 4, 2007). Recalling Chinese assistance during the liberation struggle, he also described how China had stepped forward to build the railroad linking Zambia's Copperbelt with the port of Dar-es-Salaam in Tanzania, when the West rebuffed Tanzanian and Zambian overtures for help (*The Times of Zambia*, February 5, 2007) [1].

Developmental Assistance and the Lure of Copper

China and Zambia continued to enjoy a warm relationship in the years following independence, even when China's fortunes dipped elsewhere on the continent during the Cultural Revolution. In addition to the massive Tazara railway project, China also built roads and a government complex in Lusaka. Another highly touted project was the Mulungushi textile plant established in the late 1970s, which became the biggest textile mill in the country, winning international awards for the quality of its products. In return, Zambia supported Beijing's "One China" policy upon receiving its independence and co-sponsored the UN General Assembly resolution in 1971 to restore China's seat on the Security Council.

When Zambia achieved independence in 1964, it was the third largest copper producer in the world, exporting over 700,000 tons per year and ranked among the most prosperous countries in Africa. Almost 35 years later, however, production fell to a mere 228,000 tons and so did the overall state of the Zambian economy. Low copper prices in global commodities markets, minimal reinvestment in the mines and inefficiencies in the state-controlled enterprise that ran the copper mines all contributed to this precipitous economic decline. When the Zambian government began to privatize its state-controlled enterprises in the 1990s, what is now the state-owned China Non-Ferrous Metal Mining (Group) Co, Limited, acquired ownership of the defunct and bankrupt Chambishi mine in north-central Zambia for $20 million in 1998 and began turning production around. The Chinese committed additional investments into the copper sector when they announced in November 2005 an investment of $200 million in a copper smelter to be located in the newly established Multi-Facility Economic Zone in Chambishi.

Bloom Off the Rose

Despite the long and well-entrenched history of friendship between China and Zambia, the relationship has recently encountered some rough waters. A growing tide of anti-Chinese sentiment surfaced during an unusual and highly volatile election at the end of September 2006, pitting incumbent President Levy Mwanawasa against the veteran, hard slugging opposition candidate, Michael Sata, also known as "King Cobra." Mwanawasa had generally followed a program of economic reform and inducements to attract foreign investment during his first term. Sata, on the other hand, preached a populist message on the campaign trail laced with anti-Chinese references that resonated in the Copperbelt, where Chinese businessmen were accused of paying low wages and ignoring safety procedures. Contributing to the poisoned atmosphere among the miners were two tragic incidents—the death of 49 miners in an explosion at the Chambishi mine in 2005 and the shooting of several miners protesting low wages at the same mine in July 2006.

The growing number of Chinese engaged as traders in the local markets or working in unskilled or semi-skilled positions posed another target for the opposition. Zambian traders complained that the Chinese were importing cheap goods and were driving them out of business. The textile industry was particularly affected, including, ironically, the famed Mulungushi textile factory that the Chinese had helped establish just decades before. Compounding the problem was the fact that that no one could offer an accurate estimate of the number of Chinese in the country. Deputy Minister of Home Affairs Chrispin Musosha told parliament that the 2,300 Chinese living and working in Zambia were expected to double in six months, but others sources claimed that as many as 80,000 Chinese were already residing within the country (UN Integrated Regional Information Networks, February 5, 2007). Dipak Patel, a former minister, warned the government: "We have a lot of Chinese traders selling in the market and displacing local people and causing a lot of friction. You have Chinese laborers here moving wheelbarrows. This needs to be dealt with because you'll end up with a situation with what happened in Uganda with the Indians" (*The Guardian,* February 5, 2007).

The electoral campaign heated up when Sata threatened to chase away the Chinese, Indians and Lebanese, if elected, saying they were "infestors" not "investors." Local media also reported that he had met with Taiwanese businessmen in Malawi to get funding for his campaign and reportedly stated that he would recognize Taiwan as an independent country if he were elected. While Sata denied having received money from Taiwan, he was more ambivalent about his views on the relationship with Taiwan. The Chinese Ambassador to Zambia, Li Baodong, in an unusual departure from diplomatic protocol, responded by calling a press conference at the embassy where he challenged Sata to clarify his position on Taiwan. According to one news report, the ambassador threatened, "We shall have nothing to do with Zambia if Sata wins the elections and goes ahead to recognize Taiwan" (AFP, September 5, 2006). Li also reportedly added that the Chinese business community would halt additional investments until the bilateral relationship between the two countries was clarified. Mwanawasa quickly responded by stating that Sata's comments were unfortunate and appealed to the Chinese to rescind their threat to pull out their investments in Zambia. While some commentators berated what they considered to be Sata's disastrous foray in the international arena, others were incensed that China had poked its nose into the internal affairs of the country.

In retrospect, the most notable feature of the campaign was the degree to which Chinese diplomacy became publicly enmeshed in the internal politics of an African country—an apparent contradiction to China's stated policy of non-interference.

Mwanawasa won the September 28, 2006 elections by a handsome margin, but Sata's party, the Patriotic Front, performed well in the Copperbelt and in Lusaka, where the Chinese presence is most visible. In retrospect, the most notable feature of the campaign was the degree to which Chinese diplomacy became publicly enmeshed in the internal politics of an African country—an apparent contradiction to China's stated policy of non-interference.

Hu's Visit to Zambia

President Hu spent two days in Zambia during his eight-nation trip to Africa in February, more time than in any other country. Some observers attached special significance to this fact, though it is likely that the length of the stopover was prompted more by logistical calculations than by any other considerations. The Chinese leader arrived with the promise of investing $800 million in the new Multi-Facility Economic Zone in Chambishi, the first such zone to be established in Africa. The zone is expected to attract both Chinese and Zambian investors and generate thousands of jobs. Other gifts included cancellations of debt; providing loans for road construction equipment; building a large sports stadium in Ndola, the Copperbelt's largest city; establishing an agricultural technology center, two rural schools, a hospital and a malaria treatment center; and increasing the number of government-funded scholarships. If the purpose of Hu's trip was to cement the bonds between the two governments and their leaders, these goals certainly appear to have been achieved, judging by the fulsome coverage given to the visit in their respective state-controlled media.

Yet, the otherwise smooth façade surrounding the visit cracked due to a number of notable incidents. Hu had intended to visit the Copperbelt to lay the cornerstone for the Ndola stadium and to commission the copper smelter in the new economic zone. Fear of protests by miners over poor working conditions, however, prompted the cancellation of his visit, which was prominently highlighted in the international media. Concerned with possible student protests, the police also sealed off all access roads to the University of Zambia on the day of Hu's arrival. And, finally, there were the workers from the Mulungushi textile factory, who just days before, had staged a protest outside of the Chinese Embassy to complain about the loss of their jobs. The factory's huge financial losses, stemming in part from its inability to compete with cheap Chinese textile imports, forced it to close temporarily.

What Does the Future Hold?

While it seems the Chinese are on the verge of taking over Zambia, starting with the rapacious Chinese companies that seem to be acquiring much of Zambia's rich copper and cobalt resources, the reality of the situation is hardly the case. Vendanta Resources, an Indian-managed company registered in the UK, acquired the country's leading copper producer (Kondola Copper Mines) in 2004. A Swiss company, Glencore International, operates the second-largest producer, Mopani Copper Mines. Other countries involved in copper and cobalt production include Canada, Australia, South Africa, the United States and the United Kingdom. Total copper production reportedly rose to about 427,000 metric tons in 2004, of which the Chinese share represented a little over 10 percent of the total [3].

Likewise, while the Chinese role in Zambia continues to expand, a host of other actors also occupy influential positions. South Africa is Zambia's biggest trading partner, but other African countries—Tanzania, Malawi and Zimbabwe—are also important partners. Moreover, the United States enjoys a good relationship with Zambia and provided some $268 million in assistance through bilateral and multilateral channels in 2006, making it the largest single donor in the country. In December 2005, the two governments signed an agreement canceling $280 million in bilateral debt [4]. A number of multilateral organizations are also involved in the country. The World Bank is the largest multilateral donor and the IMF conducts periodic economic reviews under a three-year Poverty Reduction and Growth Facility. This multitude of external actors, all with significant stakes in the country, serves as evidence that Zambia is unlikely to fall under the exclusive sphere of influence of any particular actor in the near future, including China.

This multitude of external actors, all with significant stakes in the country, serves as evidence that Zambia is unlikely to fall under the exclusive sphere of influence of any particular actor in the near future, including China.

Furthermore, the ripples of anti-Chinese discontent that surfaced in Zambia's election campaign and during Hu's visit flowed from real grievances among the populace; echoes of these, albeit more muted, were also found in Hu's subsequent travels to South Africa and Namibia. South Africa had previously felt the sting of Chinese textile exports crippling local industry and President Thabo Mbeki had warned just in December 2006 that Africa risked becoming an economic colony of China. While Hu received a warm welcome from South African President Mbeki in February 2007, one major South African newspaper pointedly issued a strong critique of China's human rights and labor records; a Namibian newspaper leveled similar criticisms (*The Namibian*, February 5, 2007).

This is not to say that the Chinese position in Zambia and the southern African region is in peril. If one examines the September 2006 election results in Zambia, Michael Sata received 29 percent of the vote; Levy Mwanawasa and a third candidate, Hakainde Hichilema, shared the remainder of more than two-thirds of the vote. Thus, while the anti-Chinese sentiment is certainly troubling for Beijing, it is not immediately threatening toward China's interests. What remains to be seen now is how China will deal with countries that have opposition parties and some degree of freedom of the press, and where labor unions and non-governmental activist groups can make life uncomfortable for those in powerful positions, both domestic and foreign. China can expect growing criticism from these groups if Chinese companies, such as the operators of the Chambishi mine, fail to address the legitimate grievances of their workers. Likewise, if small Chinese traders and unskilled workers continue to multiply and ply their wares and services in African markets, local resentment can be expected to grow, leading, as Dipak Patel warned, to ugly confrontations down the road.

Originally published in *China Brief:* Volume 7 Issue 5 on March 8, 2007.

Notes

1. The Tazara railroad was intended to bypass the use of transportation routes through apartheid South Africa. This was especially important for the export of Zambian copper. The Chinese government offered an interest free loan of about $500 million and work on the project was completed in 1976. On the downside, the Tazara locomotives were underpowered and had to be outfitted with GE engines; and, the roads did not wear well.
2. It is perhaps telling that Sata went to Taiwan, while the Chinese President was visiting Zambia.
3. "The Mineral Industry of Zambia," United States Geological Survey, http://minerals.usgs.gov/minerals/pubs/country/2004/zamyb04.xls.
4. "Background Note on Zambia," U.S. Department of State, http://www.state.gov/r/pa/ei/bgn/2359.htm.

ZIMBABWE:

ZIMBABWE: CHINA'S AFRICAN ALLY

By Joshua Eisenman

Articles about China's foreign policy toward Africa are more commonplace of late, mainly focusing on Beijing's search for petroleum and other resources to power its growing economy. Sino-Sudanese relations, in particular, have taken center stage, which is understandable given the scale of suffering in Sudan and China's contribution to the Khartoum regime's coffers. Despite the international outrage targeted at Beijing over its support for Khartoum, few China watchers have taken adequate notice of China's extensive ties with Zimbabwe. In April 2005, China and Zimbabwe celebrated the 25th anniversary of the establishment of bilateral relations. Juxtaposed with growing repression in Zimbabwe, this lavish state affair underscores why a discussion of China's relationship with Zimbabwe is both necessary and timely.

The History of China—Zimbabwe Relations

Beijing sees a valuable ally in the despotic Robert Mugabe, known the world over for his brutality and communist style agrarian reform. Today's close ties between China and Zimbabwe stem from the Soviet Union's fateful decision to support Joshua Nkomo over Robert Mugabe during Zimbabwe's struggle for independence. Both men opposed colonial rule, but while Nkomo's main arms supplier was the Soviet Union, in October 1978, and again in May 1979, Moscow rebuffed Mugabe's attempts to solicit support. In response, Mugabe's Zanu Party turned profoundly anti-Soviet and extended feelers to Beijing. Beijing identified this growing rift and skillfully developed relations with Zanu prior to Zimbabwe's independence in 1980. Mugabe met with Chinese officials in January 1979 in Mozambique and both sides expressed their intent to deepen ties. With Mugabe's decisive victory in the presidential elections of 1980, China's close ties with Zimbabwe were cemented.

For Harare, an international pariah, China represents its only major international supporter and a patron for its neo-communist land reform policies and resource exploitation.

In June 1980, in one of the first official acts after independence, Zimbabwe's Foreign Minister Simon Muzenda visited Beijing to thank the government for supporting the Zanu Party. The next year, Mugabe himself would visit Beijing. In the years to come trade and cultural exchanges were accompanied by state dinners and good will visits. The close ties between Zanu and the Chinese Communist Party (CCP) that persist today are an extension of these early overtures, which are routinely referred to in each countries' state-run press. As the People's Daily reported, "Relations between China and Zimbabwe started in the days of the liberation struggle in the African country when China aided the liberation fighters in various ways" (*People's Daily*, July 15, 2003).

China and Zimbabwe Today

Sino-Zimbabwean relations have grown apace with the African nation's isolation from the West and its neighbors. Beijing's relations with Harare include diplomatic support, economic and trade deals, and close military ties. For Harare, an international pariah, China represents its only major international supporter and a patron for its neo-communist land reform policies and resource exploitation.

At the ceremony celebrating the 25th anniversary of the establishment of bilateral relations, the Chinese Ambassador Chang Xianyi affirmed Beijing's "profound fraternal relationship" with Harare, describing ties as "an all-weather friendship" (Xinhua, April 23, 2005). At the same event Zimbabwean acting foreign minister Herbert Murerwa recognized that China was now Harare's single largest investor and called for increased efforts to develop Zimbabwe's extensive natural resources.

Given Zimbabwe's severe economic problems and estrangement from western technology, sources of capital and trade, Mugabe is right to see China as a critical ally. At the same time, Mugabe's "Look East Policy" provides Beijing with opportunities to unearth Zimbabwe's valuable natural resources and secure lucrative deals for Chinese state-owned firms.

Trade and Economics

In December 2003, Premier Wen Jiabao said, "China respects and supports efforts by Zimbabwe to bring about social justice through land reform" (The Herald Online [Harare], December 17, 2003). Indeed, Beijing's economic support for Harare remains strong, and through its efforts, Beijing has secured the contracts to develop Zimbabwe's agricultural, mineral and hydroelectric resources.

China supplies Zimbabwe with expertise, technical assistance, and agricultural equipment, including tractors and agro-processing. The Chinese state-owned firm, China International Water and Electric Corporation, has been contracted to farm 250,000 acres in southern Zimbabwe. Chinese and Zimbabwean developers believe the project will yield 2.1 million tons of maize every year, and require the building of a massive irrigation system. It remains unclear how Zimbabwe will pay for the project, although unconfirmed reports claim payment will be made in tobacco, which China purchases in large quantities (Guardian Unlimited, February 13, 2003).

Through lines of credit at Chinese banks, China supports Zimbabwe's small and medium sized enterprises (SMEs). With this assistance, Zimbabwe's Ministry of Small and Medium Enterprises has set aside $12 billion for disbursement to SMEs. Industries receiving funds include textile, soap, tile and fiberglass manufacturers. Large state-owned firms, like the Zimbabwe Iron and Steel Company, which is presently being refurbished, also receive Chinese assistance.

China also fosters person-to-person contacts through "soft" economic approaches. In 2004, Beijing and Harare signed a tourism agreement that Zimbabwe hopes will boost Chinese tourists from 10,000 to 25,000. Conferences and talk shops, like the 6th Joint Committee on China-Zimbabwe Economy and Trade held in Beijing last September, also play a role in bolstering personal ties among elites and underscore Beijing's commitment to Harare.

Yet, perhaps most appealing to Beijing are Zimbabwe's vast mineral and precious metal deposits and its inability to unearth these assets due to the nation's vast poverty and estrangement from the West. Zimbabwe has the second largest deposits of platinum in the world, estimated at over $500 billion, but due to resource limitations that wealth remains untapped. In all, the country has deposits of more than 40 minerals including ferrochrome, gold, silver, and copper.

Nor have Zimbabwe's leaders hesitated to use natural resources as a lure. Witness the remark by the Reserve Bank of Zimbabwe's Governor, Dr. Gideon Gono, in a meeting with the Deputy Governor of the People's Bank of China: "I would like to unveil to the Chinese people the vast investment opportunities that ... abound in Zimbabwe, including our natural resource endowments" (The Herald [Harare], May 25, 2005). Beijing already has deals in place for coal and coke concessions in return for financing and mining equipment. In return for Harare's guarantees, China's National Aero-Technology Import and Export Corporation (CATIC) and China North Industries Corporation (NORINCO) have agreed to finance multi-billion dollar expansion projects by Zimbabwe Electricity

Supply Authority and Hwange Colliery Company, respectively (*Financial Gazette* [Harare], May 20, 2005). It is worth noting that the U.S. government sanctioned NORINCO on several occasions for proliferation related activities.

Diplomatic and Military Ties

As can be expected, China and Zimbabwe have supported each other's initiatives in international organizations. In 2004, the two nations collaborated at the UN Commission on Human Rights to block resolutions that would have seen both condemned for human rights abuses. Previously, at the second meeting of the Forum on China-Africa Cooperation (FOCAC) in December 2003, Mugabe said: "China's politics have always been pro-Africa, pro-third world, anti-imperial and anti-hegemonic" (*China Daily*, December 15, 2003).

China does not seek to encourage Zimbabwe's political reform or observance to human rights standards. Generally speaking, Beijing's only real condition on Harare has been its adherence to China's "One-China" principle. Zimbabwe's leaders have gladly obliged, regularly expressing their enthusiasm for Chinese "reunification."

Moreover, Chinese and Zimbabwean military ties are among the closest on the African continent. In April 2005, Zimbabwe's air force received six K8 jet aircraft to be used for training jet fighter pilots and for "low intensity" military operations, and the year before, a Chinese radar system was installed at Mugabe's $13 million mansion in the Harare suburbs. Most importantly, in June 2004, Zimbabwe's state-run press reported the purchase of military equipment from China, including 12 FC-1 fighter planes and 100 military vehicles, worth an estimated $240 million. This order, which had been kept secret, circumvented the state procurement board tasked with appropriating Zimbabwe's $136 million defense budget (Johannesberg Radio 702 [English], June 10, 2004).

Implications for Zimbabwe and the Region

As Zimbabwe has spiraled into chaos, its neighbors have not remained immune. In June 2005, Mozambique's President Armando Guebuza and European Commission President Jose Manuel Barroso met and discussed the harm cause by Zimbabwe to Mozambique's economy. The effects of thousands of displaced Zimbabwean refugees living on the Mozambique boarder has been destabilizing. In total, almost 3 million Zimbabweans desperate for work and food have fled to Mozambique and neighboring South Africa and Botswana.

Beijing's arms sales to Harare directly oppose South African Foreign Affairs Minister Nkosazana Dlamini-Zuma's request that China stop selling arms in sub-Saharan Africa. South Africa—Zimbabwe's most influential neighbor—has been roundly criticized for ignoring Zimbabwe's collapse. Thabo Mbeki, South Africa's president, is largely responsible for this failure. The EU in particular has led the charge with Baroso calling on the African Union and South Africa to confront Mugabe, and voicing his disappointment with the results. The *People's Daily* on June 26, 2006, reporting on Baroso's trip to Mozambique and South Africa, wrote: "Mbeki has been under increasing pressures in recent days for his 'diplomatic silence' on Zimbabwe's ongoing clean up campaign" (*People's Daily*, June 26, 2005).

Coincidentally, as Baroso and Mbeki argued in Pretoria, a CCP delegation arrived in Harare. Mugabe hailed Sino-Zimbabwe ties since the "liberation struggle," while the delegations leader Tan Jalin discussed the need to "exploit opportunities existing in one another's country to derive mutual benefits" (Xinhua, June 26, 2005). This coincidence, coupled with the absence of a statement by Baroso on China's support for Zimbabwe, highlights Beijing's ability to leverage its influence to avoid public criticism.

Looking Forward

It seems likely that Mugabe will become increasingly reliant on Beijing for economic and military support as Zimbabwe deteriorates. Thus, in the short-term Zimbabwe's chaotic condition may be an advantage for Beijing. This also means Beijing will continue to support Harare unconditionally while piling up various claims on Zimbabwe's natural resources and other commodities.

But cracks are beginning to emerge in the relationship. In May, Nyasha Chikwinya, the head of the Zanu PF women's league, called for police to crack down on Chinese "engaging in illegal foreign currency deals" (*Daily Mirror* [Zimbabwe], May 27, 2005). Zimbabwe's markets are flush with cheap Chinese goods and traders, catalyzing budding anti-Chinese sentiments. Yet, as long as Mugabe retains power it is unlikely these feelings will harm the broader relationship.

> *Without competition from Western firms, Zimbabwe will remain China's exclusive resource base as long as Mugabe is president*

Mugabe is 81 and the cult-of-personality by which he rules will almost certainly fail to provide a smooth leadership succession. The current fragile state of the country makes civil war the most likely outcome if the President dies in office. Beijing would do well to take note of Zimbabwe's land redistribution strategy. China's Zimbabwe investments, particularly in the agricultural and mining sectors, carry significant sovereign risk and Beijing is gambling it can manage relations to guarantee its claims in what will almost certainly be the chaotic transition period to come.

Originally published in *China Brief:* Volume 5 Issue 15 on July 5, 2005.

CONTRIBUTORS

Dr. Andrew McGregor is the Director of Aberfoyle International Security in Toronto, Canada.

Dr. Arthur Waldron is the Lauder Professor of International Relations in the Department of History at the University of Pennsylvania. Dr. Waldron is an Associate at the Fairbank Center for East Asian Research and the Olin Institute for Strategic Studies, both at Harvard University. His books include *The Great Wall of China: from History to Myth* (1992); *How the Peace Was Lost: The 1935 Memorandum* "Developments Affecting American Policy in the Far East" (1992); *From War to Nationalism: China's Turning Point 1924-1925* (1995). He has edited and contributed to several volumes, including *The Modernization of Inner Asia* (1991), *The People in Arms: Military Myth and National Mobilization since the French Revolution* (2003); The Chinese for the Blackwell series "The People of Asia," and *Mao's Road to Power: Evolutionary Writings, 1912-1949*, both forthcoming.

Chris Zambelis is an Associate with Helios Global, Inc., an international political and security risk analysis and management firm based in the Washington, DC area. He specializes in Middle East politics. He is a regular contributor to a number of publications, where he writes on Middle East politics, international terrorism, and related issues. He has extensive international experience, including living and working in the Middle East, East Europe and the former Yugoslavia, and Latin Americ. He is a graduate of New York University and holds an M.S. in Foreign Service from Georgetown University.

Christopher Thompson is the Research and Administrative Manager at the Brenthurst Foundation.

David Shinn served 37 years at the Department of State, in the capacity of Desk Officer for Somalia, Djibouti, and assistant for Ethiopia, State Department coordinator for Somalia during the U.S. intervention, Director of East and Horn of African Affairs, Deputy Chief of Mission at the U.S. Embassy in Sudan, and Ambassador to Ethiopia. He is now an adjunct professor in the Elliott School of International Affairs at George Washington University.

Drew Thompson is the Director of China Studies and Starr Senior Fellow at The Nixon Center in Washington, DC. He was formerly the National Director of the China-MSD HIV/AIDS Partnership in Beijing and the Assistant Director of the Freeman Chair in China Studies at the Center for Strategic and International Studies (CSIS).

Dr. Greg Mills heads the Brenthurst Foundation in Johannesburg, South Africa, and during 2008 is on secondment to Rwanda as the 'Strategic Adviser to the President.'

Dr. Ian Taylor is an Associate Professor in the School of International Relations, University of St. Andrews, Scotland, and a Visiting Professor at the University of Stellenbosch, South Africa.

Dr. John C.K. Daly is currently a Fellow in Eurasian Defense and Security Affairs for The Jamestown Foundation. He has also been a commentator on current events for CNN, the Hudson Institute, the Middle East Institute, Press TV, National Public Radio, White House Chronicle, Al-Arabiyya, and the *Christian Science Monitor*, along with being a contributing editor for *Vanity Fair* on terrorism. Dr. Daly has also addressed CIA, NSA and DIA audiences on terrorism.

Joshua Eisenman is the co-editor of *China and the Developing World: Beijing's Strategy for the 21st Century,* and author of the book's chapter on China's strategy towards Africa (M.E. Sharpe 2006).

Mauro De Lorenzo is a Resident Fellow at the American Enterprise Institute. He conducted research in Rwanda, Burundi, Uganda and Democratic Republic of the Congo for a number of years between 1998 and 2004, and revisited Kigali and Bujumbura in February 2007.

Ambassador Paul Hare is the Executive Director of the U.S.-Angola Chamber of Commerce. He served as the U.S. Ambassador to Zambia from 1985 to 1988 and as the U.S. Special Representative for the Angolan Peace Process from 1993-1998. From 1988-1989, he also served as the Principal Deputy Assistant Secretary of State in the Bureau of the Near East and South Asian Affairs of the Department of State.

Colonel Susan M. Puska (retired) is a former U.S. Army Attaché. She currently works for Defense Group, Inc., in Washington, D.C.

Dr. Wenran Jiang is the Director of the China Institute at the University of Alberta. He is currently President of the Chinese Canadian Professors Association, a Board Member of the East Asian Council of Canadian Asian Studies Association, a Board Member of the Canadian Consortium on Asia Pacific Security, twice a Japan Foundation Fellow, and visiting scholar to a number of universities in East Asia over the years.

Dr. Yitzhak Shichor is a Professor of East Asian Studies and Political Science at the University of Haifa, and Senior Fellow at the Harry S. Truman Research Institute for the Advancement of Peace, the Hebrew University of Jerusalem, Israel.

Dr. Christopher Alden is the Director of the China in Africa Project at SAIIA and author of the book, *China in Africa* (Zed 2007).

Table I: PRC's Transfer of Conventional Weapons to African Countries 1980-2007

Recipient/Licenser (L)	Year of Order/ License	Year of Delivery	No. Ordered	Weapon Designation	Weapon Description	Value expressed in US$ m. at constant (1990) prices.
Algeria						
	1988	1990	1	Mourafik	Support ship	45
	1989	1990-1991	7	Chui-E	Patrol craft	80
	1999	2000-2002	25	C-802/CSS-N-8/Saccade	Anti-ship missile	35
						Total: 160
Burkina Faso						
	1984	1985	4	Type-63 107mm	MRL	<.5
						Total: <.5
Congo						
	2005	2006	4	WZ-551	APC	1
						Total: 1
DR Congo (Zaire)						
	1981	1981	15	D-74 122mm	Towed gun	6
	1982	1982	8	Type-59-1 130mm	Towed gun	5
	1986	1987	2	Type-062/Shanghai	Patrol craft	20
						Total: 31
Egypt						
	1980	1980	30	F-7A	Fighter aircraft	270
	1980	1982	2	Romeo/Type-633	Submarine	1702
	1982	1982-1986	80	F-7A	Fighter aircraft	
	1981	1982-1983	50	F-6	Fighter aircraft	
	1982	1983	2	Hainan/Type-037	Patrol craft	
	1982	1984-1985	16	HY-1/SY-1/CSS-N-1	Anti-ship missile	
	1982	1984-1985	2	Jianghu/Type-510	Frigate	
	1982	1984	2	Romeo/Type-633	Submarine	

1983	1984	6	Hainan/Type-037	Patrol craft		
1983	1984	6	Hegu/Type-024	FAC(M)		
1983	1985	1	JLG-43	Height-finding radar		
1983	1985	1	JLP-40	Air surv radar		
1983	1984	4	Type-062/Shanghai	Patrol craft		
1984	1984	24	HY-2/SY-1A/CSS-N-2	Anti-ship missile		
1992	1993	1	JY-9	Air surv radar		
1985**	1986-1995	400	Type-59-1 130mm	Towed gun	242	
1999**	2001-2005	80	K-8 Karakorum-8	Trainer/combat ac	189	
					Total: 2403	

Eritrea

1994	1994	4	Y-12	Transport aircraft	4

Gabon

2004	2004	16	Type-63 107mm	MRL	
2004	2004	10	Type-63 130mm	MRL	5
2004	2004	4	Type-90 122mm	MRL	
2005	2006	6	WZ-551	APC	1
					Total: 6

Gambia

1989	1989	2	Type-062/Shanghai	Patrol craft	13
					Total: 13

Ghana

2006	2007	4	K-8 Karakorum-8	Trainer/combat ac	9
					Total: 9

Guinea Bissau

1983	1984	20	BTR-152	APC	1
					Total: 1

Kenya

1996	1997	6	Y-12	Transport aircraft	9
					Total: 9

Libya

	-1980	1980-1984	250	Type-63 107mm	MRL	15
						Total: 15

Mali

	1980	1981	18	Type-62	Light tank	16
	2000	2000	2	AS-365/AS-565 Panther	Helicopter	7
						Total: 23

Mauritania

	1994	1995-1996	2	Y-12	Transport aircraft	4
	1996	1997	1	Y-7	Transport aircraft	8
	2001	2002	1	Huangpu	Patrol craft	15
	2002	2003	2	AS-365/AS-565 Panther	Helicopter	7
						Total: 34

Namibia

	1997	1997	2	Y-12	Transport aircraft	3
	2000	2001	4	K-8 Karakorum-8	Trainer/combat ac	9
	2005	2006-2007	12	F-7MG	Fighter aircraft	132
						Total: 144

Niger

	2005	2006	6	Type-53 120mm	Mortar	<.5
						Total: <.5

Nigeria

	2005		15	F-7M Airguard	Fighter aircraft	
	2005		20	PL-9	SRAAM	
						Total: n/a

Sierra Leone

	1985	1987	2	Type-062/Shanghai	Patrol craft	20
	1997	1997	1	Haizhui/Type-062-1	Patrol craft	8
						Total: 28

Somalia

	1979	1980-1981	30	F-6	Fighter aircraft	168
	1982	1982	10	Type-59-1 130mm	Towed gun	2
						Total: 170

Sudan

	1980	1981	14	F-6	Fighter aircraft	
	1980	1981	20	M-1938/M-30 122mm	Towed gun	
	1980	1981	20	Type-59-1 130mm	Towed gun	107
	1981	1981	50	YW-531/Type-63	APC	
	1986	1987	12	F-7B	Fighter aircraft	114
	1988	1989	10	Type-59-1 130mm	Towed gun	7
	1991	1992	18	D-30 122mm	Towed gun	6
	1991	1991	2	Y-8	Transport aircraft	46
	1995	1997	6	F-7M Airguard	Fighter aircraft	66
	2001	2002-2003	10	Type-85-IIAP	Tank	
	2002	2003	3	A-5C Fantan	FGA aircraft	38
	2003	2004	10	WZ-551	APC	2
	2004	2006	12*	K-8 Karakorum-8	Trainer/combat ac	14
						Total: 400

Tanzania

	1980	1981	12	F-7B	Fighter aircraft	114
	1982	1982	20	M-1938/M-30 122mm	Towed gun	6
	1991	1992	2	Type-062/Shanghai	Patrol craft	20
	1994	1994	2	Y-12	Transport aircraft	3
	2002	2003	2	Y-8	Transport aircraft	46
	2005	2006	2	WZ-551	APC	<.5
						Total: 189

Tunisia

	1993	1994	3	Haizhui/Type-062-1	Patrol craft	23
						Total: 23

Zambia

	1983	1983	18	Type-59-1 130mm	Towed gun	12
	1994	1996	3	Y-12	Transport aircraft	5
	1998	2000	8	K-8 Karakorum-8	Trainer/combat ac	19
	2005	2006	2	MA-60	Transport aircraft	23
	2006	2006-2007	5	Y-12	Transport aircraft	

						Total: 59

Zimbabwe

1981	1982	30	YW-531/Type-63	APC	6	
1983	1983	4	D-74 122mm	Towed gun	2	
1984	1986	12	F-7M Airguard	Fighter aircraft		
1984	1986	2	FT-5	Trainer aircraft	159	
1984	1985-1986	22	WZ-120/Type-59	Tank		
1986	1987	10	WZ-121/Type-69	Tank	16	
1990	1991	2	F-7B	Fighter aircraft		
1991	1991	1	Y-12	Transport aircraft	21	
2005	2005	6	K-8 Karakorum-8	Trainer/combat ac	14	
2006	2006	6	K-8 Karakorum-8	Trainer/combat ac	14	
					Total: 232	

Source: Information adapted from the SIPRI Arms Transfers Database, URL
http://armstrade.sipri.org/
Notes: *Only six of the twelve units ordered were delivered
** Transfer of technology necessary for the production of military equipment by the recipient (licensed production)

Abbreviations Key:	APC- Armored personnel carrier/command post
	MRL- Multiple rocket launcher
	FGA- Fighter/ground attack
	FAC- Fast attack craft
	(M)- Missile-armed

Table II: PRC's Transfer of Small Arms and Light Weapons to African Countries in Trade Value

Export Receiving Country	Year	Trade Value	Export Receiving Country	Year	Trade Value
Algeria			**Djibouti**		
	1996	$1,001,129		1998	$129,249
	1997	$2,028,094		1999	$27,434
	1998	$11,294,435		2002	$7,839
	2004	$28,272		**Total:**	**$164,522**
	2005	$22,502			
	2006	$6,730	**Egypt**		
	Total:	**$14,381,162**		1996	$123,243
				1997	$293,235
Botswana				1998	$319,766
	2000	$2,578		1999	$230,783
	2002	$12,878		2000	$274,136
	2005	$18,785		2001	$295,621
	Total:	**$34,241**		2002	$230,421
				2003	$131,304
				2004	$85,943
Burundi				2005	$680
	2005	$1,500		2006	$29,837
	Total:	**$1,500**		**Total:**	**$2,014,969**
Cameroon			**Eritrea**		
	1996	$11,354		2003	$40
	2001	$10,280		**Total:**	**$40**
	2004	$11,335			
	2005	$52,962	**Ethiopia**		
	Total:	**$85,931**		1998	$7,797,688
				2002	$106,537
Congo				2004	$378
	2004	$4,276		**Total:**	**$7,904,603**
	2006	$303			
	Total:	**$4,579**	**Ghana**		
				2005	$332
Côte d'Ivoire				2006	$3,978
	2003	$240,000		**Total:**	**$4,310**
	Total:	**$240,000**			
			Gabon		
Dem. Rep. of the Congo				1996	$699
				2006	$168,950
	1998	$29,319,103		**Total:**	**$169,649**
	Total:	**$29,319,103**			

Export Receiving Country	Year	Trade Value
Kenya		
	2001	$66,915
	Total:	**$66,915**
Libya		
	2001	$46,493
	2002	$28,000
	2006	$1,119
	Total:	**$75,612**
Mali		
	2006	$3,386
	Total:	**$3,386**
Mauritania		
	2006	$2,028
	Total:	**$2,028**
Morocco		
	1998	$14,194,679
	2005	$33,271
	2006	$24,960
	Total:	**$14,252,910**
Mozambique		
	2002	$11,211
	2005	$3,352
	Total:	**$14,563**
Nigeria		
	1998	$38,953
	2002	$55,056
	2003	$166,386
	2004	$10,796
	2005	$9,488
	2006	$26,389
	Total:	**$307,068**
Rwanda		
	1998	$13,169
	Total:	**$13,169**
Senegal		
	2003	$783
	2005	$9,816
	Total:	**$10,599**

Export Receiving Country	Year	Trade Value
South Africa		
	2001	$8,781
	2002	$453,480
	2002	$43,248
	2003	$1,438,579
	2003	$8,760
	2004	1,408,121
	2005	$559,841
	2005	$1,060
	2006	$342,722
	2006	$805
	Total:	**$2,826,818**
Sudan		
	1998	$197,433
	2001	$10,951
	2002	$4
	2003	$420,438
	2004	$176,245
	2005	$447,605
	2006	$130,136
	Total:	**$1,382,812**
Tanzania		
	1998	$2,019,049
	2001	$355,557
	2006	$56,951
	Total:	**$2,431,557**
Togo		
	1996	$849
	Total:	**$849**
Tunisia		
	1999	$1,070
	2001	$1,500
	2005	$1,910
	Total:	**$4,480**

TABLE II: SMALL ARMS AND LIGHT WEAPONS

Export Receiving Country	Year	Trade Value
Uganda		
	1996	$30,880
	1998	$1,834,982
	2000	$7,554
	2001	$2,606
	2002	$14,580
	2004	$63,544
	Total:	**$1,954,146**
Zambia		
	2005	$1,285
	2006	$14,238
	Total:	**$15,523**
Zimbabwe		
	1996	$45,453
	1997	$90,012
	1998	$569,445
	1999	$166,671
	2000	$45,655
	2001	$45,655
	2005	$50
	Total:	**$962,941**

Source: Information Adapted from the United Nations Commodity Trade Statistics Database

Table III: PRC's Energy Investments in Africa

North Africa		
Algeria	2002	China Petroleum and Chemical Corporation (Sinopec) joins with Algeria's state-owned oil and gas company Sonatrach to invest $525 million in a project to develop the Zarzaitine oil field in the Sahara Desert.
	2003	China National Petroleum Corporation (CNPC) signs an exploration license and acquires a 75 percent equity in Blocks 112/102a and 350 onshore with Sonatrach. The blocks are located in the northern region of Algeria and covers 9,923 square kilometers.
		CNPC signs an agreement an exploration license for Block 350 (Oued Mya Basin) with Sonatrach. CNPC owns 75 percent equity of the block, which is located in northern Algeria near the Mediterranean Sea and covers an area of 8,666 square kilometers.
		CNPC wins the bid for the Adrar upstream and downstream integrated project. The contract, in which China agrees to invest $31 million, is set to last 23 years and made up of oilfield appraisal and development, the construction of a refinery and the eventual sale of the finished product. CNPC and Sonatrach have 70 percent and 30 percent holdings in the project respectively. The refinery was completed in 2007.
	2004	CNPC wins the bid for the exploration of Block 438B in the north of the Sahara, which spans an area of 4,354 square kilometers. CNPC enters into a production-sharing contract lasting for seven years of exploration and 25 years of production. According to the agreement the CNPC owns 100 percent equity in the project.
	2005	CNPC and Sonatrach sign a contract for the construction of the Sidka Gas Condensate Refinery at a value of $450 million (28 billion dinars).
Libya	2002	CNPC won the bid for the construction of a 1,050-km long pipeline in western Libya. The project is a joint venture with Libya's National Oil Corporation and Italy's Agip. The pipeline was completed and put into operation in 2004.
	2005	CNPC signs an exploration and production sharing agreement with Libya's National Oil Corporation for offshore Block 17-4 (Pelagian Basin) that spans an area of 2,566 square kilometers.
Tunisia	2004	CNPC acquired the rights to the NK exploration block and 50 percent equity in the SLK Oilfield. The two blocks together span an area of 3, 332 square kilometers.
West Africa		
Mauritania	2004	CNPC signs a contract with the Ministry of Industry and Mining of Mauritania for the exploration of and development of Blocks Ta13 and Ta21 (Taoudeni Basin) and Block 12 (a coastal basin). Under the contract the exploration period will last nine years and the development period 25 years.
		CNPC agreed to invest $1 million in an oil and gas exploration project in Mauritania.

		2005	CNPC became the operator of Block 20 in a coastal basin after signing a Farm-out Agreement with Brimax Petroleum Limited. In 2006, oil and gas shows were observed in the first exploration well Heron-1 in this block.
Niger		2003	CNPC signs an agreement with the Government of Niger on the exploration license for the 60,000 square kilometers Bilma Block and Tenere Block. Under the contract the CNPC is the operator of the two blocks, owning 100 percent and 80 percent holdings of the two blocks respectively.
		2008	CNPC signs a $5 billion contract with Niger that included provisions for exploration, drilling and the construction of additional oil possessing infrastructure in the Agadem Block. The Niger government estimates that the block contains 324 million barrels of oil. The refinery would have a capacity of 20,000 bpd.
Nigeria		2004	Sinopec and Nigerian Petroleum Development Company sign an agreement to develop Oil Mining Lease (OML) 64 and 66 located in the deep waters of the Niger Delta.
		2005	China National Offshore Oil Corporation (CNOOC) makes a $2.27 billion investment in the Nigerian oil industry, paying for 45 percent equity in the Akpo field offshore.
		2006	PetroChina signs an $800 million contract guaranteeing 30,000 bpd to China over a five year period.
			CNPC wins the tender for Oil Production Lease (OPL) 298, 471, 721 and 732. Two of the blocks are located in the Niger Delta and two are located in the inland Chad Basin, in exchange for a promised $4 billion to be spent on power stations and a railroad for Nigeria.
			CNOOC bought 45 percent equity in Oil Mining License (OML) 130 in for $2.268 billion.
		2008	CNPC, Sinopec and CNOOC agreed to build a refinery in the southern delta region.
			Sinopec and Canadian oil company Addax Petroleum reportedly will spend $73.8 million on prospecting in two blocks of the São Tomé and Príncipe/Nigeria Joint Development Zone located in the São Tomé archipelago. São Tomé and Príncipe and Nigeria hold 40 percent and 60 percent equity respectively in the Zone.
			China agrees to lend Nigeria $2.5 billion for infrastructure projects in a renewed attempt to win access to energy reserves and an oil industry dominated by Western groups such as Royal Dutch Shell and ExxonMobil. China has offered the loan in parallel with talks about gaining energy exploration rights, but no specific oil blocks were tied to the agreement.
			CNPC wins a $5 billion deal to develop oil reserves in the large Agadem block, eastern Niger. CNPC agreed to bring into production within three years, which has proven reserves so far of 324-million barrels.

East Africa		
Ethiopia	2006	Zhongyuan Petroleum Exploration Bureau (ZPEB), a subsidiary of Sinopec, subcontracted by Petronas, which was given Block G (Gambella region) concession in 2003, drills its first exploratory well in the Gambella Basin. Block G covers an area of 15,356 square kilometers within the Gambella Basin.
Kenya	2006	CNOOC signs an offshore exploration deal to explore in six blocks covering 115,343 sq km (44,500 sq miles) in the north and south of Kenya.
Somalia	2006	CNOOC and China International Oil and Gas Group (CIOG) sign a production-sharing contract with the interim government in May 2006. The contract gives the government 51 per cent of oil revenues.
	2007	CNOOC wins exploration rights in the north Mudug region, some 500km north-east of the capital.
Sudan	1996	CNPC acquires a 40 percent share in the Greater Nile Petroleum Operating Company (GNPOC), which is jointly owned by Petronas of Malaysia, ONGC of India and Sudapet of Sudan.
		CNPC acquires 100 percent equity in the Block 6 (Muglad Basin) project.
		CNPC wins the bid for a 40 percent holding in the Blocks 1, 2 & 4 (Muglad Basin).
	1998	CNPC and the Sudanese Ministry of Energy and Mining commence construction of the Khartoum Refinery. CNPC owns 50 percent of the refinery. It would become operational two years later with an annual processing capacity of 2.5 million tons of oil.
	1999	GNPOC completes a 1,506 kilometer long pipeline linking the Heglig Oilfield and Marsa al-Bashir (a terminal located near Port Sudan on the Red Sea). The pipeline has a daily output of 150,000 barrels per day.
	2000	CNPC wins the tender for Blocks 3 & 7 (Melut Basin) becoming the majority (41 percent) equityholder and operator of the blocks. Sinopec has 6 percent equity in Block 3 and 7.
	2001	CNPC discovers the Fula Oilfield in Block 6 (Muglad Basin) and was put into production in 2004 with an output of 10,600 bpd.
	2004	Harbin Power Engineering Company Limited builds the first phase of the El-Gaili Power Station, which is an oil-fired power station project located 50 km north of Khartoum. The project costs $149 million and is paid for by China's Central Bank. The second phase of the project was near completion in 2007.
	2005	CNPC as well as Petronas, Nigerian Express, Sudapet and the Hi-tech Group sign a production sharing contract with the Sudanese Government for exploration and development of Sudan's Block 15. The block is located in the Northeastern region of the country and spans an area of 24,377 square kilometers; the majority of which is in the Red Sea.

	2007	CNPC signs a production sharing contract with the Sudanese government, Pertamina, Sudapet, Sudan's state-owned oil company Dindir Petroleum International (DINDIR), Nigerian Express and AFRICAENERGY for exploration and development of Block 13 located in the northern coastal waters of the Red Sea. Block 13 covers an area of 38,200 square kilometers.
		CNPC signs a 20-year contract with Sudan for exploration of a shallow water bloc in the Red Sea, with CNPC having a majority share of 35-40 percent.
Madagascar	2006	CNPC concluded a joint venture with MPIL to explore the Mahajanga block—onshore and offshore—in the prospect of finding an estimated 15 billion barrels. The expected minimal production would be 10,000 bpd for the onshore exploitation and 50,000 bpd for the offshore.
		Sino Union Petroleum and Chemical International Limited (Sunpec), which owns a large equity in Malagasy oil venture, MEIL, is prospecting and developing Block 3113 (Sakarahain).
		Hong Kong based Credit Card DNA Security Systems (Holdings), which owns 10.5 percent equity in MPIL, announced plans that MPIL will partner with CNPC through its fully owned subsidiary Liaohe Petroleum Exploration Bureau to pursue development of onshore block 2104.
Uganda	2006	China and Uganda sign an agreement at that year's Forum on China-Africa Cooperation (FOCAC) meeting to allow the China National Oil and Gas Exploration and Development Corp (CNODC) and CNOOC to drill for oil in the Albertine Graben region and the western Rift Valley.
Central Africa		
Chad	2003	CNPC signs an agreement with the Swiss Cliveden Corporation to buy shares in the exploration of Block H, which is comprised of seven depositional basins: the Chad Lake, Madiago, Bongor, Doba, Doseo, Salamat and Erdis.
	2006	CNPC obtains all the equity of Block H.
	2007	CNPC and the Chadian Ministry of Petroleum sign an agreement on the construction of a joint-venture refinery north of N'Djamena.
Gabon	2004	Total Gabon signs a contract with Sinopec under which Gabonese crude oil will be sold to China for the first time.
		Sinopec signs a technical evaluation deal for three onshore oilfields for possible production-sharing contract: LT2000, is located approximately 120 miles southeast of Port Gentil. The other two blocks, DR200 and GT2000, are approximately 60 miles northeast of Port Gentil.
	2006	China secures a $3 billion contract to exclusively develop iron ore reserves in Belinga. China National Machinery and Equipment Import and Export Corporation (CMEC) acquires 85 percent equity in the joint-venture with the Gabonese government.
Equatorial Guinea	2006	CNPC signs a Simplified Purchase Agreement for Block M (Rio Muni basin) with the Fruitex Group. Block M spans an area of 2,703 square kilometers.

		CNPC has 70 percent equity in the project.
Republic of Congo	2005	China and the Congolese government signed two deals that authorize Sinopec to explore off-shore blocks designated as Marine XII and High Sea C for development and production.

Southern Africa

Angola	2004	Angola accepts China Exim Bank's offer of a $2 billion oil-backed loan, helping Sinopec to get concessions for further oil exploration. The loan was connected to the guaranteed delivery of 10,000 bpd.
		Angola's state-owned oil company Sonangol gives 50 percent equity-equity to Sinopec in offshore Block 18 (Lower Congo Basin).
	2006	Sinopec and Sonangol strike a $2.2 billion deal to develop Blocks 17 & 18 with estimated reserves of 4.5 million barrels.
		Sinopec formed a partnership with Sonangol to operate Block 3/05 (formerly Block 3/80), whose operation was transferred from Total to Sonangol: Sinopec has production rights for Block 3/05.
		CNPC acquires 50 percent equity in offshore Block 18 after Shell's withdrawal.
		Sonangol and Sinopec reportedly eyeing future concession rounds, particularly for 23 blocks in the Kwanza Basin onshore area and the relinquished parts of Blocks 15, 17, and 18, currently operated by Exxon, Total and BP.

110

INDEX